Corpus Anarchicum

HM
886
.D33
2012

Corpus Anarchicum

Political Protest, Suicidal Violence, and the Making of the Posthuman Body

Hamid Dabashi

Feb 2016

8 1504

CHICAGO THEOLOGICAL SEMINARY
LEARNING COMMONS
1407 East 60th Street
Chicago, Illinois 60637-1507

palgrave
macmillan

CORPUS ANARCHICUM

Copyright © Hamid Dabashi, 2012.

All rights reserved.

First published in 2012 by PALGRAVE MACMILLAN® in the United States—a division of St. Martin's Press LLC, 175 Fifth Avenue, New York, NY 10010.

Where this book is distributed in the UK, Europe and the rest of the world, this is by Palgrave Macmillan, a division of Macmillan Publishers Limited, registered in England, company number 785998, of Houndmills, Basingstoke, Hampshire RG21 6XS.

Palgrave Macmillan is the global academic imprint of the above companies and has companies and representatives throughout the world.

Palgrave® and Macmillan® are registered trademarks in the United States, the United Kingdom, Europe and other countries.

ISBN: 978-1-137-26411-4

Library of Congress Cataloging-in-Publication Data

Dabashi, Hamid, 1951–
Corpus anarchicum: political protest, suicidal violence, and the making of the posthuman body / Hamid Dabashi.
p. cm.
Includes bibliographical references and index.
ISBN 978-1-137-26411-4 (hbk.: alk. paper) — ISBN 978-1-137-26412-1 (pbk.: alk. paper)
1. Violence. 2. Suicide bombings—Social aspects. 3. Human body—Political aspects. 4. Political violence—Social aspects. 5. Terrorism—Religious aspects—Islam. I. Title.

HM886.D33 2012
303.6—dc23 2012013160

A catalogue record of the book is available from the British Library.

Design by Scribe Inc.

First edition: October 2012

10 9 8 7 6 5 4 3 2 1

Printed in the United States of America.

In Memoriam
Innocent victims of 9/11
on both sides of all borders

There is more wisdom in your body than in your deepest philosophy. And who knows for what purpose your body requires precisely your best philosophy?

—Friedrich Nietzsche, *Thus Spoke Zarathustra* (1885)

Contents

Acknowledgments

This book has been simmering in my mind for more than a decade. Since the events of 9/11 I have been thinking and writing about the matter of "suicidal violence." But it was not until the fateful events we call the Arab Spring a decade later that I knew my book was ready. It was the suicide of Mohamed Bouazizi (1984–2011), the young Tunisian street vendor who set himself on fire on December 17, 2010, in protest to police harassments, that dramatically concluded the whole notion of "suicidal violence" I was developing in this book and thus effectively completed my thoughts on the matter. Before that tragic event setting a massive transnational revolution in motion, it was the "suicidal violence" that targeted both the *self* and the *other* of the suicidal person that had triggered my study. After Mohamed Bouazizi's suicide, it was the solitary site of that violence, the body of the person, and the sparing of others from the site of his suicide that gave the whole topography of my thinking about the matter its closure.

Earlier versions of a number of the following chapters have appeared in various venues. A much shorter version of "Bodiless Faces" was published in *Visual Anthropology* (1998). My thanks go to Walter Armburst for his having first asked me to write on veiling. An earlier draft of "In the Absence of the Face" appeared in a special issue of *Social Research* (Spring 2000) devoted to *face*. I am grateful to Arien Mack for the opportunity to reflect on the Biblical/Qur'anic figure of Joseph's face in the essay that is now Chapter 2, "In the Absence of the Face." Thanks to Georgio Verzotti, an earlier version of "Bordercrossings" was the catalogue text of a major retrospective that he had organized on the work of Shirin Neshat at Castello di Rivoli in Turin. My thanks go to him and to Ida Gianelli for their invitation to write the text. I wrote the chapter on "Voice, Vision, and Veiling" when Francesco Bernardelli graciously invited me on behalf of the Castello di Rivoli to open a major retrospective on Iranian filmmakers in Turin in March 2002. My sincere gratitude goes to Sara Bershtel for her cherished friendship and the caring confidence with which she received me in the peace and serenity of her home in Vermont where the idea of this book finally came together. Finally, my sincere gratitude goes to Farideh Koohi-Kamali of Palgrave Macmillan for all her gracious encouragements to bring this book finally to fruition.

Introduction

In the middle of High Street was the Barclays Bank. The Barclay brothers, who started Barclays Bank, were slave-traders. That is how they made their money. When the English outlawed the slave trade, the Barclay brothers went into banking. It made them even richer. It's possible that when they saw how rich banking made them, they gave themselves a good beating for opposing an end to slave trading . . . People just a little older than I am can recite the name of and the day the first black person was hired as a cashier at this very same Barclays Bank in Antigua. Do you ever wonder why some people blow things up? I can imagine that if my life had taken a certain turn, there would be the Barclays Bank, and there I would be, both of us in ashes.

—Jamaica Kincaid, *A Small Place* (1988)

On September 11, 2001, a handful of young Arabs hijacked four American airplanes and crashed three of them into the World Trade Center in New York City and the Pentagon in Washington, DC, right before the fourth went down into the woods of Pennsylvania.

I remember that when I saw President George W. Bush on television a few days later, standing on the rubble of the World Trade Center, hugging a New York firefighter under the American flag, and declaring that those responsible for the act would be punished, I had a sinking sense of macabre emptiness about his words. How could they be punished? They were all dead—dead and done with, pulverized into smithereens right under his feet or hanging in suspended dust over his head. They were beyond all earthly punishments or revolutionary rewards. They had either joined some supernal bliss or else descended into a cavernous hell—in either case, beyond the reach of the US military might. They could hear nothing. They were beyond reproach. They were beyond.

I remember that when I went down to the vicinity of Ground Zero on that fateful September 11, I noticed the bizarre spectacle of a band of Japanese tourists collecting the ashes that were falling down on cars parked in the Soho areas. What were they doing? What strange conception of a souvenir was that? There, in that gathered dust the Japanese tourists were collecting, were the ashes of the World Trade Center and its inhabitants and assailants, all pounded into a grayish powder. The Persian poet in me was suddenly incorrigible—it was surely the ghostly sight of all those dead human beings turned into collected dust and now gently brushed into plastic bags by Japanese tourists that reminded me of—who else?—Omar Khayyam:

> Listen again. One evening at the Close
> Of Ramazan, ere the better Moon arose,
> In that old Potter's Shop I stood alone
> With the clay Population round in Row.

This I remembered from Edward FitzGerald's reading of Omar Khayyam. But I also remembered the gist of another quatrain—this one from my own mother's popular version—that included a suggestion to the effect that when you wipe dust from your forehead, be very gentle, because the dust you are disturbing could very well be the remains of a kind and tender human being. Nothing was delicate on that horrific Tuesday afternoon down on the corner of Houston and Hell, however. But Edward FitzGerald's Omar Khayyam would not let go:

> And, Strange to tell, among that Earthen Lot
> Some could articulate, while others not:
> And suddenly one more impatient cried:
> "Who is the Potter, pray, and who the Pot?"
> Then said another: "Surely not in vain
> My substance from the common Earth was ta'en,
> That He who subtly wrought me into Shape
> Should stamp me back to common Earth again."

There was dust everywhere, asbestos-infested air raining gray ashes on the city and its inhabitants. What were these ashes? Human beings, of course—inhabitants and assailants alike—falling down on us, a crowd of mismatched natives and immigrants, all of us bewildered, sad in a muted way, and more numb than scared:

> That ev'n my buried Ashes such a Snare
> Of perfume shall fling up into the Air,
> As not a True Believer passing by
> But shall be overtaken unaware.

They were all dead—assailants and inhabitants—turned into a powdery soft dust: No Muslims here, no Jews, no Christians—all agnostic particles of atomized ashes, beyond the pales of reason, outside the shades of sanity, collected in small plastic bags by Japanese tourists, piled in between huge pieces of cement blocks loaded on a caravan of ominous trucks speeding in front of me—standing deaf, dumb, but all eyes, right on MacDougal with my back to Bleeker—off to the West Side Highway, to where? Nowhere? No words could be spoken to them, but Omar Khayyam was still there—undaunted:

> Ah, make the most of what we yet may spend,
> Before we too into the Dust descend:
> Dust into dust, and under Dust, to lie,
> Sans Wine, sans Song, sans Singer, and—sans End![1]

It was Strangeness Incarnate. Hours ago these ashes were all wonder and woe, hatred and love, prejudice and poetry, oblivious to their pending fate, awaiting nothing. Hours ago they were shades of fear, signs of trembling, reasons for anger, and gestures of resignation, joyous hope, or ambiguous melancholy. What happened to the universe they inhabited, the people they loved, and the people who loved them back? These ashes still smelled of suspicion and suggested trust, tasted like sadness and appeared like bewilderment, felt like curiosity, and looked like ambition. What happened to them? These ashes were bones and muscles only a cup of coffee ago, tissues and blood vessels, high cholesterol levels and painful arthritis; tuition bills and laptop computers were on the minds and bodies of these ashes just about a nap or two doughnuts ago. How is one to understand such sudden decimation of physical existence and the restful falling down of human beings as ashes and dust?

SUICIDAL VIOLENCE

Suicidal violence—what does that mean, exactly? Whence the rage, wherefore the pain, the loss, the void?

The fact and phenomenon of suicidal violence are too visible to be seen, too close to be examined. How can a person just blow himself or herself up or crash himself or herself and a multitude of others into a building, blowing up everything around and about him or her? How is that possible? Madness, martyrdom, spontaneous insanity, prolonged heroism, murderous disposition, revolutionary sacrifice, political commitments, fanatical manipulation, ideological predilection, imaginative audacity—there are slews of dismissive designations that seek to clarify but in fact further conceal the force and fury of suicidal violence, its nature and disposition, its purpose and politics, its prevalence and frequency. Our received conceptions—psychological, sociological, or political—mean very little anymore. Are these acts of suicidal violence altruistic or egoistic, apathetic or anomic, deviant or normative, fatalistic or triumphalist? Are they cultural—Islamic, Judaic, Christian, Hindu, anarchic, atheist, agnostic—or are they acultural, on the borderline of a new configuration of sense and sensibilities? I am convinced that understanding suicidal violence requires a whole new language of inquiry, mode of thinking, and manner of reflection that altogether defy our received wisdom, disciplinary divisions, academic dispositions, theoretical proclivity, and customary cultures. Thinking about suicidal violence, we have to imagine the unimaginable.

The book you are about to read is the record of an attempt to understand suicidal violence in the immediate context of its most recent political upsurge:

the decade between 2001 and 2011, from the suicidal mission of Muhammad Atta and his band in the United States to the suicide of Mohamed Bouazizi in 2010 in Tunisia. After the former, a devastating military strike and the occupation of two Muslim countries commenced, and after the latter, a massive transnational democratic uprising ensued. The first act targeted thousands of innocent people in the vicinity of the suicidal attackers, and in the second not a single other human being was hurt. The first was a militant act of terrorizing desperation, inaugurating an even more terrorizing military act of vengeance, hatred, death, destruction, and conquest. The second was an act of economic desperation that set millions of human beings free from habitual complacency and sent them off on a historic course of liberation.

Suicidal violence is neither specific to Islam nor peculiar to our time. It has been manifested in practically all cultures and religions throughout human history. But the suicidal violence we witness today is of an entirely different disposition—that is my principal argument in this book—because the *bodies* on which it is perpetrated (both of the assailant and of the assailed) are no longer the *human bodies* of our belated Enlightenment assumption; we are witnessing, in fact, the contour of *posthuman bodies*. Through a succession of reflections on visual and performing arts in the immediate vicinity of Islamic cultures, I have gradually narrowed in on the subject of suicidal violence and its implications for an emerging conception of a *posthuman body*. The *posthuman body*, as I propose it here, is the body of a contingent and contextual being and as such an object of disposable knowledge, while the *human body* that it has superseded was corporeally integral, autonomous, rational, indispensible, and above all the site of a knowing subject.

I believe that the subject of my reflection—why and how is it that people just blow themselves up—is something rather crucial and yet beyond the disciplinary limits of our forms of knowledge production or the normative parameters of our cultural formations or ideological dispositions. So far as we condemn or condone suicidal violence, we disqualify ourselves to understand it. We cannot enter the site of suicidal violence as Muslims, Jews, Christians, or Hindus nor indeed as Arabs, Israelis, or Americans. We have to check all such tiresome tirades and assumptions at the door before we enter the site of suicidal violence and look at the charred and dismembered bodies of the *two* victims of the violence—both the assailant and the assailed—with equal and identical care and capacity. In the pages you are about to read, I have tried patiently to pace my way toward the site of the *posthuman body* with detailed attention to a crosscurrent of politics and aesthetics that has been the harbinger of its quintessential mutation from its immediate predecessor—the *human body* of the Enlightenment imagination—into the *posthuman body* of the globalized capital and its changing culture.

This book is a critical reading of the phenomenon of *suicidal violence* in its immediate *historical* context through a close examination of the changing conception of the *body* in visual and performing arts—photography, video installations, and cinema in particular. Of that *historical* context I have an entirely *dialogical* (and decidedly antiessentialist) conception, in which *Islam* as a medieval faith (and as a key signifier in this case) has perforce mutated into the site of political resistance to a globalized empire. This *Islam* is dialogical with *the West* that has imagined it and that it too has imagined back. The result of this detection of the *posthuman body* on the borderline between a globalizing empire and an Islamist resistance to it is that the *corpus particularis* I configure in this book has already mutated into a *corpus universalis* far beyond any cultural particularity. *Islam and the West* is a site of contestation, a battleground, fictive and ferocious at one and the same time—a fantasy that has deadly factual consequences, with suicidal violence as one (but not the only) critical register of this encounter. The *posthuman body* I describe in this book is neither Islamic nor non-Islamic, neither American nor anti-American. It is the singular achievement of the *globalized capital* in a cross-cultural manner that I wish to describe in some analytical detail and through the unsuspecting lenses of the most globally celebrated visual and performing arts. The self-exploded suicidal body is a sign, which I wish to read in the frame of a larger visual regime.

In his excellent study *On Suicide Bombing* (2007), Talal Asad has successfully taken to task the US-media-facilitated fabrication of an "Islamic culture" exclusively identified with suicidal violence. Beyond that, he has challenged the very religious disposition of this assumption that a bizarre concoction called "Islamic Jihadism" is responsible for this mode of violence. Asad's remains an exemplary critical study exposing the discursive formation of "Islamic terrorism" as the *modus operandi* of suicidal violence. My concern in this book, however, is different from Asad's. I completely identify with his project and concur with his conclusions, but I wish to move the question in an entirely different direction and take the exploded body of the suicide bomber as the first and final site of my investigation into the phenomenon of suicidal violence; I wonder what that exploded body ultimately means and signifies in a world no longer divisible into East and West—the indivisible world that has conditioned that suicide. To do so, I will have to take the exploded body of the suicide bomber as the *locus classicus* of my meditations. The Muslim identity of the perpetrators of 9/11, as a result, is one among many signs I need to decipher in the signature of suicidal violence. But the transmutation of the *human body* to a *posthuman body* is something upstream from being a Muslim (Muhammad Atta), a Jew (Baruch Goldstein), a Christian (Seung-Hui Cho), and so on. If I have thought through the phenomenon of the *posthuman body* in an Islamic context, it does not mean I am after an "Islamic explanation" of suicidal violence. In my reading of it, suicidal violence of any sort, by Muslims or otherwise, has no "explanation." I am after a historic location to see the transformation of the *human* into the *posthuman body*—a transmutation I believe to be upstream from any religious affiliation and embedded in the current condition of the globalized capital. No investigation into the religious identity of suicidal violence will reduce it to any culture-specific contexts, for the investigation has to come to terms with the formation of the *posthuman body* from the ground up.

By positing the *posthuman body* as a semiological sign of the event, and in order to conjecture it in an Islamic provenance, I trace the troubling absence of the *face* in the Qur'an through a close reading of some crucial passages, the chapter on Joseph in particular. I carefully detect the site of the *absent face* in the Qur'an while having a running conversation with the dual conceptions of sign/signifier in continental philosophy in order to show that in reading *body* we habitually fall into a semiological mode doctrinally alien to the Islamic semiotics, which I will thus try to retrieve and theorize. From there I move to the creative reconfiguration of the *posthuman body* in contemporary visual arts. The cinematic output of some of the most globally celebrated filmmakers, photographers, and video installation artists are the subjects of my detailed analysis demonstrating the radically reconfigured conception of *the body*. I will then pay particular attention to a number of filmmakers and through their work examine the historical absence and the recent rise of the feminine gaze in the course of Islamic encounter with colonial modernity. The continental divide between the Qur'an, as the site of the Islamic collective consciousness, and contemporary visual and performing arts, as the site of a post-Islamic imaginary, is bridged, I propose, by the aggressive mutation of Islam from its *ideological* phase in the nineteenth and twentieth centuries into an *iconic* and *spectral* phase in the twenty-first century.

A combination of *aterritorial* colonial conquest and local tyranny, I will demonstrate, has resulted in the figurative formation of an *amorphous body*, and that in turn has paved the way toward the shaping of an *anarchic body*, a *disposable body* that defies the politics of power by denying it its singular site of violence by a violence that ends all violence to it. My proposal here—in conversation with Max Weber and Michel Foucault, among others—is that *nationalized territory* is no longer the site of ([il]legitimate) violence historically at the disposal of the state apparatus. I argue that the globalized states can no longer sustain any claim to sovereignty over an identifiable territorial boundary and that in the absence of such physical territory the human body has emerged as the solitary site of ([il]legitimate) state violence. Suicidal violence, I conclude, is the ultimate denial of the state its singular and final site of legitimacy.

My conclusion is that the globalized capital has made the national state apparatus entirely aterritorial and contingent on the equally globalized practice of the political, which no longer corresponds to territorial sovereignty and has had to narrow in on the *human body* as its singular site of self-legitimizing violence. Meanwhile, the same amorphous capital has transfigured the Enlightenment integrity of the *human body* and pushed its anarchic defiance of state violence to the formative edges of a *posthuman disposable body*. On the globalized sites of the aterritorial capital, the *posthuman body* and its suicidal violence now best represent this metamorphosis of land into body as the first and final site of self-legitimizing state violence.

THE MAKING OF A POSTHUMAN BODY

My way toward a clear conception of the *posthuman body* has been paced with a deliberate and sustained reflection on its semantics and semiology. It was not until the very last chapter of this book, "*Corpus Anarchicum*," that I realized what I had been grappling with in all the preceding chapters was an articulation of the site and sight of an emerging conception of body in conversation with the parameters of globalized capital and its corresponding state. In Chapter 1, "Body Doubles," I set out to mark the point when, as early as the Algerian Revolution, Frantz Fanon had (rather inadvertently) stumbled on the normative mutation of the *feminine body* into a site of colonial contestation. Yet by the time I was writing the concluding chapter, I realized that my reflections on aspects of Palestinian cinema in Chapter 1 had implications beyond what I had articulated. The same circular reinforcement of my argument sustained the dialectic of my narrative throughout the rest of the book; the conclusion of each chapter pushed me toward the conclusive evidence of my final argument. In Chapter 2, "In the Absence of the Face," I explore how, in the inaugural moment of a revelation, defiant signs resist their doctrinal legislation into the semiology of a religion. I opted to work my way through Qur'anic passages that emphasize the primacy of the word against the principality of vision and how the Qur'anic *repressed* in fact returns narratively to haunt the text—thus do I propose that I have by serendipity detected the central tension that animates the Islamic sacred text. Only in looking back from the last chapter did I recognize that both in face and in body even the revelatory language of a faith cannot successfully legislate their uncontrollable signation and that both body and face evade the tyranny of their state-sponsored regimentation by any means necessary, including their own eradication.

In the Chapter 3, "Bodiless Faces," I am primarily concerned with the mischievous ways in which faces betray the memory of their respective bodies, even though state-mandated coverage of those bodies—in this case, an Islamic Republic forcing its women citizens to wear veils top to toe contrary to their will—may attempt to prevent them from doing so. But again it was toward the end of the book that I realized that *bodily memories* are creative and anarchic and that they can entirely outmaneuver the state in ways that it cannot anticipate or control. When I concentrated exclusively on the work of Shirin Neshat in Chapter 4, "Bordercrossings," I wanted to show how, in the creative imagination of an artist and the erotic register of its politics, bodily memories are provoked in order to have them work against their inherited inhibitions. By the time I finished delivering my argument, however, I noticed that what might appear as the *corpus particularis* of a definable culture is in fact constitutional to a more universal remodulation of the body. The global reception and celebration of Shirin Neshat's work had suggested that to me when I was writing this chapter, but it was only later that I recognized that this reception and celebration demanded a critical attention to the *corpus universalis* that now embraces all possible cultural variations.

In Chapter 5, "Voice, Vision, and Veiling," I am principally concerned with testing a reversal of the direction of the gaze. Here I want to show, through a reading of a number of female filmmakers and poets, how being allowed to see was the occasion of being seen, of placing the observer visibly in the world, and that this imagining of one in the world was integral to a form of subjection and agency beyond the forced aversion and prevention of the gaze. It took the writing of my last chapter, however, to articulate how once a bodily memory thus imagines itself in public it is endowed with an uncontrollable energy to defy its entrapment in and by political power. As late as Chapter 6, "*Corpus Amorphous*," I thought I was simply documenting the varieties of ways in which bodies mutate in both compliance and defiance of the amorphous texture of the globalized capital. Now I think that my blind spot in that argument was in fact the very perspective that had made it possible—namely, my conscious decision to place my camera, as it were, on the colonial site and watch things from that angle. But that perspective both made my vision possible and blinded me to the fact that the *corpus particularis* I had outlined was the very silhouette of the *corpus universalis* I delineate in Chapter 7, "*Corpus Anarchicum.*" Why is it that an Islamic, Arab, or Palestinian body is the site of this *corpus universalis* I discuss in some analytical detail that implicates the colonial consequences of the globalized capital and the amorphous empire that now seeks to serve and sustain it—and precisely by virtue of that point of contact between the colonial site and the amorphous empire does that *corpus particularis* become the template of a *corpus universalis.*

In what you are about to read, I propose the contested site of the human body and the navigated sight of the human face as the territorial loci of cultures and their claim to sustained legitimacy. I have opted to narrow in on the body as the evidence of an interface between politics and aesthetics—between the violently repressive measures of a culture we code-name its *politics* and its creative defiance by the works of art domestic to its predicament, too hastily dismissed as its *aesthetics*. The location of my investigation is the claim, clime, and constitution of a colonially mutated *Islam* on the body, and the site of my defiant aesthetics is where that mutation meets the world and is thus globalized. What I put forward are the analytical outlines of an emerging *posthuman body*—particular in my detection, universal in its implications. I mean and suggest that particularity as the template of a more universal moment in our critical need to reimagine the continental claim of the body and the islandish surface of the face. My documentation is on the basis of this *corpus particularis.* By the last chapter, however, I have cautiously ventured out toward the *corpus universalis* that it implicates. The site of the shattered body of the suicidal bomber, the ground zero of his or her self-explosion and his or her final denial of the state authority, is where I collect the evidence of my *corpus universalis.* By then I have something serious to say about the globalized empire into which the United States has now aggressively mutated. I suggest that the amorphous polity of that globalized empire corresponds to the amorphous texture of the capital it seeks to serve and has as a result given birth to an amorphous body to match it. The amorphous empire has inevitably met its final resistance in a *corpus anarchicum* that denies its final site of violence by self-exploding by a violence equal in its vacuity and intensity.

My principal proposition in this book is very simple: Bodies are signs, and signs are not signifiers. Suicidal violence is the final, irretrievable register of the defiant sign of the body resisting legislation into a semantics of obedience to the globalized signature of the state. I have worked my way toward that argument very deliberately. In Chapter 1, "Body Doubles," I trace the mutation of the feminine body into a site of colonial contestation to Fanon's reflections on veiling and violence during the Algerian revolution. I do so because I believe Fanon had accidentally stumbled on a momentous occasion when body had already retrieved its troubling sensations as a sign that yields to no transcendental signifier. I then take my critique of Fanon and read it through a crucial component of the most recent Palestinian cinema before concluding on an equally important short film by Mohsen Makhmalbaf about the phenomenon of veiling among young Afghan women. In Chapter 2, "In the Absence of the Face," I demonstrate how the unruly sign of the body, before it is forcefully legislated into a language (code-named *metaphysics*) and made to speak a body language (code-named *revelation*), solicits an entirely different mode of command and control from the systematic tyranny that represses its constitutional defiance. By the end of these two chapters I will have established the *sign* as the defiant fact of our ontic existence and designated all acts of *signification* as tyrannical regimes forcing the repressive obedience of those signs against their will and toward the legislation of an orderly life—with body as its evidence.

In Chapter 3, "Bodiless Faces," I give specific examples of clandestine correspondences between faces and their bodies when, under the oppressive measures of a theocracy, they must resort to subterranean and subversive measures. The dialogical negotiations between faces and the respective bodies they mount and manifest embrace the anamnesis of every cultural formation. The bodily memories invested in the faces they sustain are constitutional to the vernacular languages a body can speak in defiance of the Latinized tyranny of their presiding culture. When under dire circumstances, such as an Islamic Republic, bodies are denied visibility and their memories repressed; faces act as their archival repositories, telling their forbidden tales. Chapter 4, "Bordercrossings," is my longest sustained reflection on the works of Shirin Neshat, in my judgment the most perceptive contemporary artist who dares the elements of her globalized audience and restores to the body its originary entropy. In "Voice, Vision, and Veiling," Chapter 5, I dwell on the paradoxical moment of veiling as the occasion of not-seeing (blindness) and *not* of not-being-seen (invisibility). That paradoxical moment is critical to our understanding of the dynamic tension between the physical body and the symbolic body politic. By the conclusion of the fifth chapter, I will have demonstrated the dialectic of reveiling (as revealing) by which creative works of art tease out the emancipatory *signs* from the depth of their incarceration in legislated and enforced *signification*.

Chapter 6, "*Corpus Amorphous*," is my negotiated way into an understanding of the body in its *posthuman* reconfiguration. I believe that we have all been sent on a wild-goose chase of trying to restore agency to the subject in the advent of technological modernity, while globalized capital is running amuck in an entirely different, markedly *posthuman* direction, where European humanism is too busy being *secular* to be of any help in sustaining the physical boundaries of the body and the body politic. In Chapter 7, "*Corpus Anarchicum*," I will finally concentrate on the self-explosive body of the suicide bomber, who eradicates the site of political violence by a violence equal in its intensity, once and for all denying the state its site of legitimacy. I consider the exploded body of the suicide bomber the excavated territory of the state where it has been categorically rendered obsolete. By the conclusion of this book, I will have outlined my argument that the *posthuman body* has self-exploded in the face of the illegitimate state by denying it its first and final site of repression and has thus liberated the sign of the body from the legislated semantics of its incarceration in the politically tyrannical and constitutionally illegitimate state. That argument, I propose, is quintessential in our understanding of the miasmatic mutation of the state in unforeseen directions, now marked by an open-ended war on *terrorism*. As one singular state, the United States, is mutating itself in a vaporous global reconfiguration of an empire in order to emulate the etherized capital, the *posthuman* body is equally inflected, making it impossible for the globalized state to abuse it as the site of its constitutional violence.

In the chapters preceding the last, I have sought to document and define the *politics* of constituting the body as the primary site of state-sponsored violence and the *aesthetic* resistances launched to face and defuse that violence. In the final chapter, I wish to trace the parameters of that *particular* to the contours of a more *universal* reconstitution of the body, because I am convinced that the *corpus particularis* I have outlined is the microcosmic reflection of a *corpus universalis* operative beyond all its variations. In the final chapter, I will look at the self-exploded body of the suicide bomber as the last will and testament, the self-excavated site, of that more universal mutation. My principal objective in that concluding chapter is to show how body as *sign* is making its final exit from the site of its *significant* mutation into the territorial claim of state legitimacy. Body, I will argue in this final chapter, not geographical expansion, is the principal site of the violence that states will have to perpetrate in order to constitute and demonstrate their legitimacy. The phenomenon that I will outline as *corpus anarchicum* is no longer limited to its modes of operation in an *Islamic* manner of resistance to a globalized empire. The rampant proliferation of suicidal violence over the last decade has now globally disseminated the *amorphous* body in *anarchic* directions. Thus, in addition to this primary objective, I also wish to challenge and dismantle the customary bifurcation made between the so-called *metropole* and all its peripheries. There is neither now nor has there ever been either a *center* or any *periphery* to the global operation of capital. While the Enlightenment modernity is principally responsible for this disfiguring and power-basing distinction, the entire project of so-called *postcolonial studies* is now chiefly in charge of propagating it. The colonial site of the capital is integral to its operation, in both its economic foregrounding and its cultural consequences. The condition now code-named *globalization* has once and for all lifted the smoke screen of the distinction customarily made between colonialism in the immediate subaltern vicinity of the capital and colonialism geographically distanced from it. But the ideological assumption of a *metropole* and a *periphery* to the operation of the capital was an entirely colonial construct designed to divide the world and thus to conquer it better. Tehran, Bombay, Tokyo, Cairo, Johannesburg, Rio, and Mexico City are as much the *metropoli* of the global operation of the capital as New York, London, or Paris. The constitution of the *corpus particularis* I have carefully outlined is integral to the *corpus universalis* that has now self-exploded in the figure of the suicidal assailant. The site of that violent self-explosion is the provenance of reading that sign against all its enforced legislations in the bodily self-justification of any state and its exclusive claim to legitimate violence, as Max Weber defined it. Thus body denies the globalized state the first and foremost site of its constitutional violence by a violence that ends all violence.

Clouds of Ashes

For weeks and months after September 11, 2001, health officials responsible for our safety in New York were deeply concerned about the asbestos-infested air and clouds of grayish ashes that kept descending on our bodies and dusting our sight. The velocities of winds and directions of their habitual movements were measured and monitored—in Uptown, Midtown, Downtown, East River, West River, Soho, Tribeca, Chelsea, and then Queens, Bronx, Brooklyn, Staten Island, Long Island. Dust was in the air and dust was everywhere. "Dust into Dust, and under Dust" we were. Frightened by the prospect of yet another dust of death and destruction descending on other innocent human beings halfway around the globe, I began to put together a bootleg video screening of Mohsen Makhmalbaf's *Kandahar* (2001) at Columbia University, where I teach. To this event I invited, among others, Marisa Berenson, UNICEF ambassador of goodwill. Marisa Berenson is an actress and a model who divides her time between New York and Europe. She has acted in such classics as Luchino Visconti's *Death in Venice* (1971), Bob Fossey's *Cabaret* (1972; for which she was nominated for a Golden Globe Award for Best Supporting Actress), Stanley Kubrick's *Barry Lyndon* (1975), Blake Edwards's *S.O.B.* (1981), and Clint Eastwood's *White Hunter, Black Heart* (1990). After September 11, 2001, UNESCO had nominated her *Artist for Peace*. Marissa Berenson is also the sister of Berry Berenson Perkins. Berry Berenson Perkins was born Berinthia Berenson in New York in 1948. She was the granddaughter of Paris fashion designer Elsa Schiaparelli. She pursued a career in modeling and acting, and she appeared in such films as *Remember My Name* (1978), *Winter Kills* (1979), and *Cat People* (1982). In 1973, she met and subsequently married Anthony Perkins, the famous actor who immortalized the troubled Norman Bates in Alfred Hitchcock's masterpiece *Psycho* (1960). Berry Berenson Perkins pursued a successful career as a photographer while mothering two sons, Osgood and Elvis, with her husband. She became a widow when her husband died of HIV-related complications in 1992. Berinthia Berenson Perkins was 53 years old when she boarded an airplane in Boston, Massachusetts, bound for Los Angeles, California.

American Airlines Flight 11, BOS-LAX, crashed into the North Tower of the World Trade Center at approximately 8:45 a.m. on Tuesday, September 11, 2001, carrying 93 people: 82 passengers (including 5 hijackers), 9 flight attendants, and 2 pilots.

Chapter 1

Body Doubles

"It is a remarkable piece of apparatus," said the officer to the explorer and surveyed with a certain air of admiration the apparatus which was after all quite familiar to him.

—Franz Kafka, *In the Penal Colony* (1914)

Suicidal violence submits the site of the otherwise coded and condemned body as the singular citation of a defiance against the politics of power and all its claims to (legitimate) violence—of and by commandants, officers, soldiers, and chains. In their flesh and blood, bodies are signs, and signs are not signifiers. Resisting their citation as obedient signifiers, bodies deny their state-sponsored mutations into colonial subjects, obedient nationals, law-abiding citizens, innocent civilians, native inhabitants, condemned criminals, or any other pacifying displacement. Suicidal violence, as a result, is the final, irretrievable register of the defiant sign of the body resisting legislation into a semantics of obedience to any conception of (the now globalized) state. The transmutation of the Enlightenment body into a site of violence—for and against state—is now squarely located in the colonial consequences of modernity. In what follows I will pick one particularly troubling moment in colonial history and trace the mutation of the (feminine) body into a site of colonial contestation to Fanon's reflections on *veiling* during the Algerian revolution. Fanon was a witness to a critical moment in colonial history when in his own defiant opposition to colonialism he in fact contributed critically in that aggressive transmorphing of the human body—the feminine body in particular—into a political proposition. Quite unbeknownst to himself—and thus the power of his observations—Fanon had by accident stumbled on a momentous occasion when the colonial body had already retrieved its troubling sensations as a sign that yields to no transcendental signifier. Yet, by insisting on its *veiling* as a sign of resisting colonialism, Fanon marked the moment when the body was no longer a mere biological proposition and had radically metamorphosed into a site of colonial contestation between the colonizer and the colonized. In reading Fanon on veiling, we will tap into a particularly significant archeological layer when body had already morphed into a political simulacrum of the *national territory* as the principal site of violence for the state—native or colonial, reactionary or revolutionary—to claim, assert, and exact its legitimacy. Once we sight the mutated colonial body on the site of that critical transformation, there is not much of a distance between the *metamorphic body* and the *metaphoric body* and then between the *metaphoric body* and the *disposable body*—the body that blows itself up for a particular political purpose.

VEILING AS COUNTERVAILING THE COLONIAL

In his famous 1959 essay "Algeria Unveiled," Fanon noticed the significance of veiling in countervailing a colonial context.[1] Availing against colonialism, veiling for Fanon became a mode of anticolonial fortification. The body of the veiled Algerian woman represented a *terra incognita*, a *territory* that French colonialism could neither know nor conquer. As such, the body of the Algerian woman became the haven where Algerian revolutionaries would gather to mobilize against the colonial occupation of their homeland. "Every rejected veil," Fanon asserted emphatically and with solid revolutionary conviction, "disclosed to the eyes of the colonialists horizons until then forbidden, and revealed to them, piece by piece, *the flesh of Algeria* laid bare."[2] Nothing reveals more accurately than the phrase *the flesh of Algeria* his almost unconscious identification of the Algerian land with the feminine body—to the point that *veiling* that flesh seems to be tantamount to keeping the French at the Mediterranean bay.[3] This conception of veiling as contravallation against colonialism, as a defensive fortification set up to protect the besieged revolutionaries, assumes an increasingly more ominous, and less metaphoric, tone: "The occupier's aggressiveness, and hence his hopes, multiplied ten-fold each time a new face was uncovered." Fanon's identification of the Algerian feminine body with a site of contestation becomes increasingly more militant: "Every new Algerian woman unveiled announced to the occupier an Algerian society whose system of defense were in the process of dislocation, open and breached." The metaphor begins to unfold almost by the force of its own logic, but Fanon gives it full throttle—ultimately identifying the colonial occupation of Algeria with the colonial officer's raping of the Algerian woman. The moment is frightful: "Every veil that fell, every body that became liberated from the traditional embrace of the *haïk*, every face that offered itself to the bold and impatient glance of the occupier, was a negative expression of the fact that Algeria was beginning to deny herself and was accepting the rape of the colonizer."

What is astonishing about these passages and the entire essay is that Fanon has almost inadvertently given a record of the historical moment when the feminine body has become the site of contestation between *two*—not just one—modes of bodily domination: the colonial and the anticolonial. Fanon's essentialist assumptions about "Algerian women" and their clothing habits are of course entirely false and shockingly simplistic—to the point that he does not see how aggressively he is in fact contributing to the mutation of the human (feminine) body into a political battlefield between two claims on its symbolic significance: those of the French colonial officers and the Algerian revolutionary movement. The driving force of all the essays collected in this volume of Fanon—on veiling, radio, family, and medicine—is his argument that from the soil of Algerian revolution "a new society has come to birth," and that "onto the national soil" has emerged "a new humanity."[4] The problem with that laudatory assumption is Fanon's own captured imagination and tortured arguments that the Algerian *man* ought to make a gut-wrenching choice between either appearing as backward and misogynist or else "admitting defeat . . . [and] prostituting his wife."[5] Why it is that if an Algerian woman opts to dress in a manner Fanon or his colonial interlocutor would consider "un-traditional" her husband has prostituted her never crosses Fanon's mind, not so much because his own revolutionary politics is so frightfully masculinist but because he is in fact a witness to a critical historical moment when he is radically contributing to the mutation of the human body into the site of physical violence by both the colonial and the anticolonial movements. In this essay, Fanon is not just a witness to the historic moment when body has *metamorphosed* into a *metaphor* (and from there soon to become *disposable*); he is in fact significantly contributing to it.

Some six years after Fanon published his "Algeria Unveiled" (1959), Gillo Pontecorvo's masterpiece of revolutionary uprising *The Battle of Algiers* (1965) was made and set in 1957—two years before the publication of Fanon's essay. It is exceptionally instructive to compare Pontecorvo's far superior and infinitely more intelligent conception of Algerian veiling with Fanon's. Shot in 1965, released in 1967, set in the Algeria of 1957, and banned for many years in France, Gillo Pontecorvo's *The Battle of Algiers* is an apocalyptic vision of colonial and revolutionary violence that corresponds perfectly with Fanon's essay on veiling in Algeria—and yet what a difference in perception and precision! There are two critical moments in *The Battle of Algiers* when women have a central role to play. One is at the very beginning of the film when under the cover of the winding alleys and veiled women the rookie revolutionary Ali is being tested by his superiors in a fake assassination attempt. Here we see Algerian women in their habitual veiling, which they use with perfect decorum and felicity to smuggle the gun to Ali to assassinate the French officer. Halfway through the film, when the French have set up a barricade around the European section of Algiers to prevent Algerian revolutionaries from crossing over and wreaking havoc on them, a group of Algerian women dress themselves as Europeans so successfully and effortlessly that the French soldiers not only let them through the barricades but in fact on occasions even flirt with them—having no clue that the women are carrying explosives in their hand bags and very shortly will blow the soldiers up in a number of public spaces. The moral of the story is that the so-called European clothing, of which Fanon was so mysteriously afraid and convinced that it will open up the Algerian society to colonial domination, is in fact used precisely in reverse order and as a kind of veiling to disguise the Algerian women and fool the French officers into letting them and the explosives they are carrying into their quarters. The only earth-shattering thing that happens after the Algerian women take off their veiling and assume European clothing, as it were, is the ground under the feet of the white colonial settlers shattering in massive explosions that blow the French colonizers to smithereens.

Fanon's problem in "Algeria Unveiled" is rooted in his assumptions about what he calls "clothing traditions" in the Maghrib in general and Algeria in particular—assumptions he makes without the slightest attention to history, geography, climate, or class. For one of the most perceptive and radical minds of his generation, Fanon could not be any more touristic in his observations about Algerian veiling: "In the Arab Maghrib, the veil belongs to the clothing traditions of the Tunisian, Algerian, Moroccan and Libyan national societies . . . In the case of the Algerian man . . . regional modifications can be noted: the fez in urban centers, turbans and djellabas in the countryside. The masculine garb allows a certain margin of choice, a modicum of heterogeneity. The woman seen in her white veil unifies the perception that one has of Algerian feminine society. Obviously what we have here is a uniform which tolerates no modification, no variant."[6] This is an astonishingly simplistic, essentialist, and ahistorical assessment—and simply not true. Fanon himself catches the implausibility of his own assertion and in an immediate footnote to this passage seeks to modify his generic assertion by pointing out that "we do not here consider rural areas where the woman is often unveiled. Nor do we take into account the Kabyle woman who, except in large cities, never uses a veil." But why not? Why should the rural and tribal women not be considered? Would that inclusion not give a fuller and more comprehensive picture of the question of veiling or not veiling in a Muslim or any other society? Fanon's categorical dismissal of alternative sites of veiling or unveiling Algerian women leads him to conclude the very same footnote meant to modify his generic statement with yet another false assertion about "absolutely original clothing traditions."

Veiling in Algeria or in any other part of the Muslim world is the "absolutely original" aspect of absolutely nothing—except cultural practices that have been formed (and are periodically reformed) under the working conditions of women. The rural and tribal contexts that Fanon notes but disregards in the bottom of a footnote allow no room for veiling because in such contexts women *have to work*, and for that very simple reason they need their two free hands totally exposed. Throughout the Muslim world, the Maghrib included, veiling is an urban phenomenon (and urbanism a very limited aspect of the society at large), where major family labor migrations have produced a surplus working force and thus gendered the working class and forced women into veiling. The sort of veiling Fanon describes is an entirely transitional phase when rural and tribal women have left their habitual working environments (in which they are not veiled) for the cities and yet have not entered the ranks of the urban proletariat full fledge. This has absolutely nothing to do with the figment of imagination that Fanon calls "absolutely original clothing traditions." It is quite puzzling how Fanon could have entirely disregarded this critical component of the working class in both colonial and precolonial contexts and attributed transhistorical significance to an item of clothing, calling it "traditional Algerian garb." Fanon was and remained a dedicated revolutionary, but at the end of the day he was a traveling tourist to Algeria.

What Fanon does thrive at in this essay is his detailed outlining of the sociopathology of the French colonial administration and how they sought to turn the Algerian women into their native agents of domination—"let's win over the women and the rest will follow."[7] But in order to demonstrate that, Fanon need not have resorted to such assumptions as the officials of the French administration in Algeria being "committed to destroying the people's originality." There is no *originality* to any people except the unfolding dialectic of their moral and material being, and even if there were, the French would not have minded safeguarding it if it served their colonial purpose, as the British did not mind manipulating the South Asian caste system (though there was not anything categorical about its social operation except when it served their colonial interests).[8] But what Fanon far more importantly, and yet entirely unbeknownst to himself, ends up describing in "Algeria Unveiled" is the systematic mutation of the site of the feminine body into the battlefield between the colonial domination and anticolonial resistance, without the Algerian women themselves (in their plurality) having a say in the matter. Two—not just one—masculine conceptions of their bodies, one as the site of conquering Algeria and the other as the location of resistance to that conquest, came to conflicting claims and thus constituted either an *originality* or else a *freedom* for it. What remained constant was the transformation of a *metamorphic body* into a *metaphoric body* soon to be turned into a *posthuman, disposable body*—not just the women's bodies, but bodies as such. Thus the question of forced veiling or forced unveiling of women and suicidal violence at large are deeply connected.

Many of Fanon's psychological observations about the challenge that the Algerian man faces when, for example, invited by a French colleague for dinner are so preoccupied with racial relations of power that he completely disregards the gendering of that very power relation. The result is the systematic accumulation of a raw *masculine rage*, articulated and accented in precisely such terms that would put the French and Algerian men face to face—on the site of the Algerian woman's body. Even at moments when Fanon sees the bizarre battle between what he calls "Islam and Western culture" over the Algerian, he still cannot see beyond what he believes to be "a distinct identity" of the native subjects. This is particularly disappointing because in his introductory remarks to *A Dying Colonialism*, Fanon insists repeatedly that he in fact is giving a report from the trenches of a "new humanity." But there is something very old—ancient, in fact—about this *new humanity* that even at the moment of its revolutionary emancipation still cannot see through the colonial mutation of the human body into a site of resistance to power. This is all the more disappointing because Fanon was on the verge of articulating a *new humanity* that is shaped and formed in a state of permanent change and constant revolution, when both foreign and domestic terms of domination are to be faced simultaneously. What Fanon ends up doing, however, is strengthening the domestic terms of domination by way of blindly positing a site of resistance to colonialism that ipso facto is in need of no metaphysical decentralization. Fanon did not live to see it. But Ali Shari'ati, a prominent Iranian revolutionary who was fascinated by his ideas and in fact corresponded with him from Paris, became instrumental in the ideological articulation of a revolution that would decades later succeed not only in toppling a colonial monarchy but, in effect, turning the Iranian woman's body into the site of one of the most brutal executions of precisely those "people's "originality."

Marking the Colonial Body

What Fanon had marked and mapped on the colonized Algerian body in the course of the Algerian revolution against French colonialism in the late 1950s was fully blown up in the course of the Palestinian resistance to the colonial occupation of their homeland since the 1950s—with the obvious distinction that the French colonialists failed while the European Zionists succeeded; the Algerian revolutionaries triumphed while the Palestinian nation is yet to achieve its liberation. Fanon's demarcation of the feminine body as the site of political contestation between the colonizer and the colonized is contrapuntally verified by Gillo Pontecorvo's entirely intuitive rejection of that assumption in his classic *The Battle of Algiers*, in which revolutionary participation of Algerian women in the liberation of their homeland is entirely irrelevant to what form of clothing they opt to wear. Fanon thus both marked and massively contributed to the critical moment of the transmutation of the human body into the territorial simulacrum of the space at the disposal of the state violence.

The rise of suicidal violence in Palestine during the *Second Intifada* ushered the world into the twenty-first century by marking a radically advanced stage in the mutation of human body into the site of political contestation of power—far beyond what Fanon had marked and noted. The reasons and circumstances for this radical mutation of the human body into an instrumental weapon of deadly destruction will have to be detected in the transformation of classical colonialism into the aggressive formation of a predatory empire and the obvious catalytic impacts it has had on global geopolitics. What we are witnessing in Palestine are the deadly signs of the effective mutation of Zionism as an initially colonial project into an instrumental mediation for US empire-building designs. For this reason, the Palestinian case of suicidal violence has normative implications in the global production of the *posthuman body* far beyond its immediate political and ideological contexts (as soon became evident in Afghanistan and Iraq after the US-led invasions of October 2001 and March 2003, respectively).

Because of the incessant demonization of *the Palestinian, the Arab, and the Muslim* in the aftermath of 9/11, it is critically important to see the *corpus particularis* of the Palestinian suicidal bomber as the normative template of a *corpus universalis* that is far more global in its diagnosis of what has happened to the *posthuman body*. Blind to that insight, today anthropologists are once again at the forefront of trying to read suicidal violence with tired old clichés presumed domestic to what they call a *culture*. The alarming rise of suicidal violence throughout the world requires a manner of reading it that can no longer remain culture specific. The implication of Islamic cultures, societies, and doctrines in the rise of suicidal violence will have to be read as integral to a global context in which Islam, as all other religions and cultures, is geographically located and historically implicated. One can scarce find a more suicidal replication of the Massada Complex by trying to establish a colonial Jewish settlement in the heart of the Arab and Muslim world. The problem with the rampant regurgitations of historical cases of suicidal violence in Islamic (or Jewish, Christian, Buddhist, etc.) contexts by way of explaining 9/11 is that they may make for some entertaining reading, but they reveal absolutely nothing about the *specificity* of its rise at the threshold of the twenty-first century—in terms domestic to the global reconfiguration of power and the polities it posits, the global capital and the economies it necessitates, and the global hegemony and the cultures it engenders.[9] The tedious tribalization of global events, of which anthropologists have made a cumbersome career, tends to localize critically important contemporary phenomena whose provenance is far more universal and pervasive than imagined in the constitutionally racist discipline of anthropology. The choice is not between an antisuicidal violence interpretation and a prosuicidal violence interpretation. No sane person can believe in any act of violence—genocidal, homicidal, or suicidal—in that (not just alphabetical) or any other order. The task is to detect the *thematic specificity* of the deadly phenomenon and then locate it in the global configuration of power that it implicates. Just to drop a paragraph at the beginning of a study to the effect that suicidal violence is not specific to Islam and that we witness it in other cultures—for example, among the Tamil Tigers—and then proceed to give historical examples of suicidal violence in an Islamic setting does nothing to address the peculiar nature of violence in the time of the globalized capital and predatory empire-building except further exoticize and demonize Muslims as a breed apart from the fold of humanity.

There *is* something Islamic about the rise of suicidal violence in our time. But the *specificity* of that *something* will have to be read with Muslims placed in the contemporaneity of their globalized culture, in the fold of humanity at large, and in what has happened to that humanity, and not by yet another tiresome repetition of historical cases of suicidal violence that can be found in any number of religions and cultures (all the way back to Samson and Masada). No archival succession of their cases amounts to an insight into its present nature and function. All the historical examples that are offered (by not so subtle sublation of old-fashioned Orientalism into a sleek anthropological language) as antecedents of contemporary manifestations of suicidal violence are no such things and contain significant differences. The Isma'ili *assassins*, so called by such adventurers as Marco Polo and Orientalists such as Bernard Lewis, *were not* suicidal. Militant Isma'ilis may have believed in some sort of paradisial compensation or justification for their acts of political violence, but they did not deliberately commit suicide the way a young Palestinian, a Japanese kamikaze pilot, an Iraqi resisting the US-led occupation of his homeland, a Tamil Tiger, or the two students at Columbine High School in Colorado killed themselves and those around them at one and the same time. Giving the case of the third Shi'i Imam's battle at Karbala in 680 as an example of suicidal violence is a singular note of historical illiteracy. Hussein ibn Ali was not suicidal. He may have politically miscalculated the help that his Kufan supporters promised him in his fight against Mu'awiyyah and the Umayyads. But that does not mean that he was suicidal. There are in fact historical indications that he was an exceptionally ambitious and worldly contender to power. The anthropologizing subtext of studies that enumerate such cases as the antecedents of contemporary suicidal violence leading to and following 9/11 remains astonishingly dumb and mute on the causes and circumstances of suicidal violence and speaks of it in terms of *casting*, *script* and *action*—of *ideologies*, *desires*, and *symbolic constructs*—rather than in terms of the moral and material indignities suffered by real human beings driven to desperate measures by a predatory operation of imperial power that has left no luxurious room for religious (Islamic or otherwise) authenticity. The assumption that "the suicide bomber's thumb pressing the detonator simultaneously clocks him into paradise" is simply obscene, not only in the obvious objection of how did the anthropologist exactly collect that piece of data from the native, but in the more immediate analytical paralysis of not seeing that exploded body in the earthly hell of its immediate texture and context.[10]

Take the case of Palestinian suicidal violence, not to justify, explain, or understand it, but to *place* it in the more global context of its reverberations, resonances, and tremors. The history of the Palestinian resistance to the colonial occupation of their homeland is the chronicle of a complete and irretrievable mutation of their physical body into the principal site of contestation between the Zionist state and the Palestinian territory. It is as if when Palestinians lost their homeland to the Zionists they turned their own bodies into the functional equivalent—metamorphic representation, metaphoric suggestion—of their land, which by possessing they could deny their colonial settlers recognition and legitimacy. What has happened in Palestine, though, is only the tip of the iceberg of a much larger and more universal development in the rest of the world colonially globalized by the predatory capital. The *corpus particularis* of the Palestinian body is now the template of a *corpus universalis* that has metamorphosed into a metaphoric site of resistance to the globalized (United) State(s) that can no longer have any claim to legitimate violence to sustain itself. The relationship between the Zionist state and the *corpus particularis* of the Palestinian body is the genetic alphabet of the more planetary relationship between the globalized (United) State(s) and the *corpus universalis* of the globalized subject citizen. The close and critical intimacy between the United States and Israel bespeaks and betrays this affinity.

The gradual mutation of Israel from a European colonial settlement into one of the deadliest military machineries in human history is no longer even true to the original design of pioneering Zionists that dreamt of a Jewish state. As a military camp completely given to the imperial designs of the United States, Israel has become one piece of indispensable hardware in the US military organism set on a course of complete and unilateral planetary (and of course extraterrestrial) control. With the end of World War II (1939–1945), the declining power of the French and British colonialism in particular, and the emergence of the Soviet Union as a nuclear superpower, the zenith of European colonialism subsided and gave rise to the dawn of two imperial designs on the world—those of the United States and the USSR. Created by British colonialism and sustained by US imperialism, the state of Israel is the only colonial settlement that links the declining ebb of one form of world domination to the rising flow of another, and this it has achieved on the broken back of another nation. Thus what we are witnessing in the streets and back alleys of Palestine today has far-reaching implications beyond the destruction of the World Trade Center or the Pentagon.

The explosion of the Palestinian body in the face of Israeli colonialism—now extended into similar acts of bodily mutiny in Afghanistan, Pakistan, Iraq, Turkey, Chechnya, Saudi Arabia, Malaysia, Morocco, Yemen, the United States, and elsewhere—is the harbinger of an anarchic incongruity between the illegitimate state and its militant objectors and by extension between the globalizing (United) State(s) and its rebel citizens, the predatory empire and its insurgent subjects. That proposition makes the critical case of Palestinian *suicidal* violence—in the wake of *genocidal* and *homicidal* violence perpetrated against them by the Israelis—globally consequential. With a grave and irreparable injustice at the center of its paradoxical existence, at the core of the Palestinian experience stands the overwhelming *presence of an absence* the world may want to forget but is destined violently to keep in mind. A nation denied its nation-state, a people robbed of their ancestral homeland, the state of being a Palestinian is one of paradoxical affirmation and affirmative negation: there by virtue of not being there, an empty space at the center of an emotive universe. Their land stolen right from under their feet in the broad daylight of history, the Palestinians became Palestinian at the very moment of their denominational denial; they were born at the instance of their death, dead at the moment of their birth, stillborn into history, denied as the world confirmed them in their loss. That *defiant denial* has become the negative space at the heart of the Palestinian experience, a vacant memory, given to them by history at the very moment of their birth—when they were stillborn.

With their land lost and their nation-state denied, their body and soul mutated into their body and soil and then substituted for the site and psyche of their collective identity as Palestinians. Their bodies scattered all over the world—the *Wandering Jews* having replaced their historical suffering for another body, giving it to the Palestinians to carry it for them around the world—the Palestinian creative psyche has been the sole source of their collective memory. Unable to fight their battle where it had to be fought, the

Zionists had picked up a fight somewhere else where they could win: in Palestine, with a people weaker than themselves, already ravaged at the throws of Ottoman sultanism and European colonialism. Dispersed around the world by a criminal act of outright thievery that robbed them of their homeland, the Palestinian body has become a *corpus cavitas*, a hollowed body, vacated by the soul of its homeland. That *corpus cavitas* sounds an emptied occupation of space, a hollowed affirmation of identity, translucent and void in the siteless space that it emphatically occupies. As the Enlightenment project of the nation-state gave birth to the very idea of a Palestinian nation in the post-Ottoman rise of nationalism, the Zionist occupation of the space that would have been Palestine negated that idea at the very time that it confirmed it by stealing it. A Palestinian thus becomes a Palestinian by not being allowed to be a Palestinian, a contradiction in terms, a promise not kept, a message not delivered, a space at once hollowed and hallowed.

The presence of this absence at the peripheral center of Palestine as an idea makes the *corpus cavitas* of its inhabitants amorphous with the land that has been denied it. Nowhere else is the evidence of this bodily mutation more evident than in the rising significance of Palestinian cinema. Abdel Salam Shehada's gut-wrenching film *Debris* (2002) is an example *par excellence* of the active mutation of *body and soil* (replacing the *body and soul*) in the Palestinian psyche. "Every time I saw a tree being uprooted," says the young Palestinian boy to the camera as he remembers the scene of Israeli bulldozers razing his parents' olive grove, "I felt a part of my body was being ripped out." This entire short film is a visual mutation of the elders of a family and their children and grandchildren with and into their ancestral land, as they all persist in cultivating it while the Israeli bulldozers, covered by their tanks, persist in razing it. The elders of the family walk through their olive trees as the embodiment of the memory that sustains this land and marks it *Palestinian*. The elders claim the land with their memory, as their children and their olive trees grow on it. Populating the land with living Palestinians becomes the key element in preventing the *question* of Palestine to remain a *question*, a mere *metaphor*, and lose its claim on being a *reality*. "Palestine is an issue," interjects Mahmoud Darwish at one point in the course of a conversation with Edward Said in Charles Bruce's *In Search of Palestine* (1998), "not an essence." But how do a *people* prevent themselves from becoming just a *metaphor*? Palestine today is the scar of a lasting shame on the face of modern history, a fact of metaphoric proportion that resists collapsing into a mere metaphor. Palestine is not a metaphor nor are Palestinians metaphoric, insists Darwish by virtue of his own poetic presence. Palestinians insist on remaining a reality, kept right at the gate of a metaphor, by planting trees for every child that is born in the land that would be Palestine and carving the names of the children on their trunks, as Shehada does pointedly in *Debris* precisely at a moment when they are being cut down, as if the shot down children of the *Intifada*. As the *Palestinian soul* becomes the *Palestinian soil*, the mutation of *body and soil* into each other sublates into the site of *corpus cavitas* laying its claim on its denied history.

What is suicidal violence other than the explosion of the Palestinian *corpus cavitas* in the face of a colonial occupation that commences with the armed robbery of a nation of its ancestral land and concludes with the denial of the very identity of the people thus wronged by this shameless act of thievery? From the very commencement of the state of Israel, the Palestinians have endured *genocidal* and *homicidal* violence and are now left to respond by *suicidal* violence, the explosion of their vacated bodies, which are now an occupied territory robbed of their *national soul* and metamorphosed into their *territorial soil*. By no means is suicidal violence the sole mode of resistance to domination and annihilation. In fact, nonviolent civil disobedience is the most prevalent mode of Palestinian resistance. Palestinians also resist by critical and creative writing, in art and scholarship, poetry and photography—at once sustaining and enriching their collective memory. It is in that context that Palestinian suicidal violence is to be located. Suicidal violence is the extreme identification of *the body with soil* and then the sudden explosion of that *soil* by way of denying it to the colonial state as the sole site of its failed legitimacy. Suicidal self-explosion is the absolutely final denying of the colonial state its measures of power, its site of violence, and its pretension to legitimacy. It is the *coup de grâce*, the very last nail in the coffin, of summarizing the ancestral homeland of a people in the physical bodies of its fragile youth and then blowing them up to deny the colonial power its last site of aggression. As the last and supreme example of a colonial state (a relic of its sort because the emerging US Empire has superseded classical colonialism and now has no use for Israel except as a major geopolitical piece of hardware in the arsenal of its military machinery), Israel is already built on the broken back of Palestinians; that broken back is now exploding itself and whoever and whatever is standing on it. Having forcefully occupied a land that does not belong to it, Israel's principal site of the violence that it perpetrates in order to legitimize its otherwise illegitimate state is targeted perforce toward the physical body of the native inhabitants of that land, by either physically eliminating them by having them mass murdered at Deir Yasin or Sabra and Shatila, expelling them from historical Palestine by incarcerating them in the West Bank and the Gaza Strip (now reducing them to enclaves and ghettos), or else subjecting them to second-rate citizenship in their own homeland and—just to add insult to injury—calling them "Israeli Arabs." The only "Israelis," as it were, who legitimately belong there are *Palestinian Jews*, and *Palestinian Jews* cannot call Palestinian Christians, Palestinian Muslims, and the whole spectrum of Palestinians at large "Israeli Arabs"—*that* is the supreme obscenity of the Zionist project that is now exploding in the face of the very proposition called "Israel." Illegitimate if it were left to its own devices, the state of "Israel" has no claim to any territorial integrity. In the absence of that territorial integrity, the physical bodies of the dispossessed Palestinians are the only site of violence on which the illegitimate state seeks to legitimize itself. Suicidal violence of the Palestinian youth is the denial of the illegitimate state its only site of self-legitimizing violence by once and for all eliminating the solitary site of that violence.

The aesthetic reflection of this politics of dispossession has nowhere been more visually evident than in the Palestinian cinema, in which we see an imperceptible mutation of human *body* into *the memorial site* of a stolen landscape. From their childhood to their old age, the portrayal of Palestinians in their own cinema is persistently metamorphic, almost categorically metaphoric, and inextricably referential—the body as a pronoun or a proverb for the land. The proverbial body, thus imagined and constituted, is always already something else, somewhere else, anecdotal in its references, and suggestive in its remembrances, not in its own flesh and blood, but the indexical expression of an all-but-forgotten homeland that is made of valleys and hills, rivers and lakes, horizons and landscapes, playgrounds and cemeteries—and not of broken bones and fractured skeletons, torn flesh and splashed-out blood, shattered nerves and ruptured dreams. It is as if when a Palestinian holds a camera in his or her hand and looks through the visor, human bodies appear as the protruded extensions of the landscape, mobile memories of its hidden histories, tangible results of its intangible fact, possessive pronouns of its dispossessed title deeds.

There is an almost obsessive fixation in Palestinian cinema with children—and for perfectly understandable reasons—that marks the turbulent map of Palestine on young bodies. Hicham Kayed's *Childhood in the Midst of Mines* (2002), for example, is a piercing short documentary on the fate of children playing in landmines left by Israelis in Southern Lebanon after they were defeated by the Lebanese liberation forces and expelled from the country. The paralyzing spot between children not playing at all or risking crippling injuries for life is where Kayed places his camera in order to capture the frozen moment of their wasted lives. Mai Masri's *Children of Fire* (1990) is an equally compelling account of the children of the Palestinian town of Nablus and the new generation of young Palestinians who risk their lives daily to sustain their youthful conception of a national trauma. The liberation of Palestine now seems inerasable from the body of the Palestinian youth. Masri's other great documentary, *Children of Shatila* (1998), traces the horrors of the Sabra-Shatila massacre that took place in Lebanon soon after the Israeli invasion in 1982. Located in what is known as *Beirut's belt of misery*, the Shatila refugee camp is home to some 15,000 poor and desolate Palestinians and Lebanese. What is paramount in Masri's documentary is the reflection of the idea of Palestine on the minds and souls of children born and bred on the site of a refugee camp only *proverbially* related to their homeland. Farah and Issa become the ears and eyes of Masri as she tries to trace the sight and sound of their imaginative geography—spread right in front of their eyes, mapped out deep and wide on their fragile bodies.

Nizar Hassan's *Cut* (2000) is an account of the director's attempts to make a short film about Mohamed al-Dorra, the young Palestinian boy murdered by Israeli soldiers. The impossibility of telling this story turns out to be the most telling example of the crisis of representation the Palestinian cinema faces at large. But what is paramount in this film is how the fragile image of the young Mohammad al-Dorra is in fact palimpsestically drawn on the impossibility of telling his story. There is an invisible link between Hassan's *Cut* and Elia Suleiman's *Cyber Palestine* (2000), the story of a couple modeled on Joseph and Mary, living in Gaza, who try to reach Bethlehem on the eve of the millennium with no less miraculous expectations to get there. In Suleiman's short film, the Biblical story assumes the status of an exegetical gloss on current Palestinian predicament. Whether or not the child of this Joseph and Mary is born to safety is now a matter integral to the collective fear of Palestinians for their future in their homeland. The fate of the newborn baby is now entirely contingent on a turbulent map of Palestine on which he has been miraculously conceived. The frightened face and scooped up body of Muhammad al-Dorra curling behind his petrified father seconds before his fragile figure is shot and murdered by an Israeli soldier is the resurrected image of a film that Hassan could not make and Suleiman would not picture. Their respective films, as a result, are figurative reflections of an absented body reflected onto a camera obscura that has the decency and intelligence of knowing when to close its eyes and shut its diaphragm in order to take a perfectly precise picture.

The youth are not faring any better than children do in Palestinian cinema. In his *Canticle of Stones* (1990), Michel Khleifi opts for a tortured love story between two Palestinians whose fate is radically changed when the man's acts of resistance to the colonial occupation of his homeland lands him in Israeli jail for life and the woman is forced to leave Palestine and choose a life in exile. They are brought back together decades later during the Palestinian Intifada—he having just been released from jail, she researching the meaning of sacrifice in his occupied homeland. The arrested love affair between these two Palestinians and the children that they could have raised maps out the barren landscape of a tormented topography of emotions. In the fragmented and pulled-apart bodies of these two young and beautiful Palestinians, in their arrested erotics and repressed sensuality, is evident the postponed promises of a future now contingent on a denied past, serendipitous to an impossible present. How full of children are this couple, how emptied of hope—as if the entire landscape of Palestine is populated by their unborn, aborted, unconceived, forbidden, prenatal, preempted, metaphorically murdered children.

Wise, wondrous, playful, frivolity the soul of its wit, Elia Suleiman's beautifully conceived and brilliantly executed *Chronicle of a Disappearance* (1996) teases the symbiotic ampelopsis of suggesting a climbing vine around the idea of being a Palestinian in a colonized modernity that has run abusively ahead of itself. In this chronicle of his own disappearance as a Palestinian national, Suleiman posits himself for what he is, or purports to be—a Palestinian filmmaker who has just returned from New York to his homeland: the Palestine of his childhood and early upbringing in Nazareth in the 1960s. Where are his roots? Is man a tree, a shrub, a bush, or a vine winding up toward an idea, plunging deep into a soil? Suleiman is uncanny in his ability to give a visual summation of his own disappearance as a Palestinian. He appears in his own films but only as the fragmented evidence of his own disappearance. The chronicle that he purports cannot and does not have a lasting claim on any chronic longevity; it is spontaneous, momentary, fragmented, with no telos to its ethos, no mythos to its ethnos. The chronicle of this disappearance is thus neither chronic nor apparent. It is the contradiction of its own terms, the return of its own repressed, the evidence of its own fiction, the body of its own soul, the presence of its own absence. The result is the visual simulacrum of a body that is translucent on the face of its historical refutation, charting itself transparently on the map of its denials, imagining itself on the site of its colonial erasure. No Musad agent can catch this body as it smuggles itself into the virtual imaginary of its homeland; no Israeli Defense Force can kill this resurrected body of Mohammad al-Dorra. He has slipped by the border guards, passed through checkpoints, fooled the custom officers, cheated his own benighted history, and lied to tell the truth.

The appearance of Elia Suleiman's disappearing body becomes more of a visible viability when one compares it with the agonizing body of Esam, a young Palestinian who makes a living in Tel Aviv as a male prostitute in Tawfik Abu Wael's *Diary of a Male Whore* (2001). His own sexual fantasies, while catering to those of his Israeli homosexual customers, navigate the borderlines of pain and pleasure as the memories of his mother being raped by Israeli soldiers haunt his tormented moments of orgasmic climax. Esam's haunted memories map out his arrested erotics, which is neither homosexual nor heterosexual, neither masculinist nor feminist—a mere matter of detained gesticulations and circumspect responses, vacated of all sense and sensibility, bodily pleasures and emotive joy. Esam's asexual disposition and laden demeanor are counterintuitive to his profession as a male whore, and thus his sexual encounters posit his body more as the occupied territory of tormented memories than the physical evidence of his pleasures. What contradicts that evidence is the absence of any sustained narrative in this diary of a male whore, which in the incongruity of its time and tale is almost identical with the chronicle presumed in Suleiman's disappearance—yet drastically different from its spirit of freedom and frivolity. What is remarkable about these two films is their identical insistence on a *chronicle* or a *diary* when there is no evidence of either. It is as if the vacated body, filled and occupied by territorial allusions, has overcompensated for its bodily absence by an emptied insistence on duration and longevity.

Perhaps the most powerful aspect of Palestinian cinema is the portrayal of the elderly Palestinians reminiscing about their lost homeland. When in *Blanche's Homeland* (2001) Maryse Gargour traces an elderly Palestinian woman who was born in Jaffa in Palestine and from which she was exiled in 1948, we can visibly see the traces of her exilic memories on the topography of her aging face—traveling from Palestine to Lebanon and then to Europe and the United States. The most important driving energy of Blanche is her single-minded determination to resist forgetfulness, and thus the refined atlas of her fading memory suggests and sustains the map of a perpetual Palestine. As a wondering Palestinian woman, Blanche is the exterior of the interior that Michel Khleifi's pioneering film *Fertile Memory* (1980) portrays in Farah Hatoum, a widow living with her children and grandchildren in Nazareth after the formation of the Israeli state in 1948, and in Sahar Khalifé, a novelist from Nablus. The way Khleifi portrays Farah, she is the physical landscape of Palestine incarnate. "The sequences of her at work," in Edward Said's precise reading of this seminal film, "show a combination of very close detail and highly concentrated repetition, especially in household chores of the sort normally taken for granted by other family members. The impression one gets of this almost frighteningly concrete expenditure of energy is that it sustains life in ways that are just below the threshold of consciousness."[11] That subconscious level is precisely where Khleifi's long shots and at times utterly motionless camera work register the visual identification of elderly Palestinian women with their land.

The relationship between Farah Hatoum and the Palestinian territory becomes even more metamorphic when her children begin to insist that she sell her already expropriated land to its current illegal tenant. "She'll have none of it," Edward Said explains her response, "A large, jowly woman, she sits rocklike at the kitchen table, unmoved by the logic of financial well-being and peace of mind being offered her. No, no, no, she says. I want to keep the land. But you don't actually have it, is the rejoinder which makes those of us living in exile quietly feel even more sympathy for her, since she at least continues to assert the value of some, any, connection with the land."[12] But the relationship between Farah and her land is no longer *possessive*; it is *metamorphic*—she no longer has possession of her land (the Israelis have expropriated it); she *is* the land. "I don't have the land now," says Farah, "but who knows what will happen? We were here first, then the Jews came, and others will come after them. I own the land. I will die. But it will stay here, despite all the comings and goings." The metamorphic moment dwells precisely in the metaphoric sublation of "I own the land. I will die. But it will stay here." That "But *it* will stay here," might as well be (and is) "But *I* will stay here." That is what she is telling her children. This is not "a logic that defies understanding," as Said observes, if we hear it coming from the transmuted bodies of the eloquent Farah and her silent land. Said captures with astonishing precision, beauty, and eloquence the very soul and purpose of this bodily incarnation when he watches Farah taken to her land and remembers his own dispossessed mother:

> Somehow, Khleifi has managed in his film to record Farah's first visit to her land. We see her step tentatively onto a field; then she turns around slowly with arms outstretched. A look of puzzled serenity comes over her face. There is little hint on it of pride in ownership [remember Said's adjective for Farah Hatoum, "rocklike"—rocks are not proud; we take pride in standing on them]. The film unobtrusively registers the fact that she is there on her land, which is also there; as for the circumstances intervening between these two facts, we remember the useless title deed and Israeli possession, neither of which is actually visible. Immediately then we realize that what we see on the screen, or in any picture representing the solidity of Palestinians in the interior, is only that, a utopian image making possible a connection between Palestinian individuals and Palestinian land. Farah's connection with her land, merely formal though it is, called up, and even calmed, the painful memory of my mother and the identity

taken from her in 1932. An aesthetic experience a generation later, partially healing the wound.[13]

The second Palestinian woman that Michel Khleifi opts to portray in *Fertile Memory*, Sahar Khalifé, is a single divorced woman who is an accomplished novelist. Throughout his brilliant cinematic career, Khleifi has had a knack for capturing the arrested erotics of the young Palestinians. Whereas Farah has many children and grandchildren, Sahar has none, and thus the fertility of her memories has transmuted into her writing Palestine rather than breeding it. In his reading of the lives of these two women in Khleifi's *Fertile Memory*, Edward Said marks his own exilic separation from such experiences within the 1948 borders of Palestine appropriated by the colonial state: "Yet because I am separated from those experiences by time, by gender, by distance—they are, after all, experiences of an interior I cannot inhabit—I am reconfirmed in my outsider's role. This in turn leads me, defensively perhaps, to protect the integrity of exile by noting the compromise of life in the Palestinian interior—the forgetfulness and carelessness that have historically characterized the losing battle with Zionism, the too close perspective that allows thoughts to be unthought, sights unrecorded, persons unmemorialized, and time thrown away."[14] What Said's own reflections on exile mark are the constitutional separation between the Palestinian *interiorized body* and the Palestinian *exteriorized memory* when a body is no longer in possession of its own creative memorial remembrances nor are the memories thus engendered bodily anchored. So when the prominent Palestinian poet Mahmoud Darwish writes a book of poetry and calls it *Memory for Forgetfulness*, the poem is memorably manufactured abroad (Beirut in this case) and then mailed inside, because Darwish himself (like Edward Said and Michel Khleifi) has no bodily capacity to hold it, while the *territorial body* left in Palestine—with "too close a perspective" on its own territoriality—cannot manufacture a freedom to imagine and remember for itself.[15] Pulled apart like the two Palestinian lovers in Khleifi's other masterpiece, *Canticle of Stones* (1990), the body and its memorial remembrances of itself fall apart—with the *fertility* of the soil a memorial gift that only its exilic children can bring home to it. Rashid Masharawi's *Curfew* (1994) is the best example of the desolation that the infertility of that land—were it to be left to its own barren devices, just like Sahar Khalifé—causes and casts on the Palestinian urban landscape. The sight of Palestinian urban settings is the vacated ghost towns of perpetual curfews, internalized darkness, extended silence, a state of unending siege—all culminating in a condition of cancerous despair, ossified desolation, and contagious melancholy. Roaming through these desolate streets are ghosts that have lost and buried their bodies in the soil of Palestine.

BODIES VEILED, BODIES UNVEILED

The transmutation of the Palestinian body over the last half a century and on into a *proverbial* reference to their colonially expropriated homeland occurred somewhere between Frantz Fanon telling the Algerian women in the 1950s that their bodies were colonially under attack—and that veiling them would ward off French colonialism—and Mohsen Makhmalbaf visualizing the unveiling of the Afghan women in the early 2000s as quintessential to opposing Islamic despotism. While Fanon wanted *to veil* the women of Algeria to protect their homeland against colonial occupation, at the threshold of the US invasion of Afghanistan in October 2001 Makhmalbaf sought visually *to unveil* the young Afghan women to save their homeland from domestic tyranny. Whether the target is colonial occupation or domestic oppression, the site of contestation remains the human body (the feminine in particular). But in the case of Makhmalbaf's cinema, we notice a critical occasion when the body starts *doubling* itself, splitting and replicating itself into a *substantive body* and a *substitutional body*, transmuting irretrievably from a *metamorphic* into a *metaphoric* state—there always to mean something beyond its flesh, bone, and blood.

But the *metaphoric body* can, and does, *crossmetaphorize*. The self-exploding body is not just denying the illegitimate state its very last possible site of violence by a violence that ends all violence; it also defies its involuntary mutation from an anarchic *sign* into a law-abiding *signifier*. As body is forced to become a *signifier* of the land it represents, the exploded body of the suicidal bomber is the site of a defiance against that forced signification—a last, desperate, attempt to restore to itself the *sign* of its undecidability. The function of art is to negotiate between the *unruly sign* and the *trapped signifier*.

Soon after its initial premier at the Cannes Film Festival in May 2001, and just when it was about to become a spectacular international success, Mohsen Makhmalbaf's *Kandahar* (2001) received a much less noticed but far more consequential award in Paris. The Federico Fellini Award that *Kandahar* received from UNESCO in October 2001, weeks after 9/11, ushered in a succession of more recognitions that brought Makhmalbaf, among other things, a request from UNESCO officials to make a short documentary on the predicament of Afghan children inside their own country or in various refugee camps in Iran and Pakistan. Soon after his return to Tehran from Paris, Makhmalbaf traveled to Zabol and Zahedan, two Iranian border towns near Afghanistan, and shot a short film, *The Afghan Alphabet* (2001), commissioned by UNESCO with the specific purpose of raising both the global consciousness and the necessary funds to attend to the immediate needs of millions of Afghan children. His shooting on the location of a couple of Afghan refugee camps done, Makhmalbaf began a sustained project of raising funds to educate the Afghan children in and outside their country. This project, for which Makhmalbaf effectively abandoned his own cinematic career, was predicated on his conviction that whatever calamity has befallen countries like Afghanistan is rooted in the absence of public (religiously neutral) education—for women in particular.

By the time Makhmalbaf had opted to relocate his camera from Iran to Afghanistan, the epistemic template of a metamorphic doubling had already been thematically formed and politically postured; Afghanistan was now going to stand in for Iran and Iran for Afghanistan. He could now tell about

Afghanistan what he could not about Iran. The two states substituted and replaced each other, moved into each other's spaces, reminiscent of their precolonial history when in fact they were one and the same. Because of his own experiences under the brutalities of an Islamic Republic, and partially in penance for having once served it well, Makhmalbaf had become convinced that retrograde movements such as the Taliban in Afghanistan (standing metaphorically for the Hezbollah in Iran) would not be as readily possible were the Afghan children to achieve their moral and intellectual freedom through a public (religiously atonal) education. During his frequent trips to Afghanistan, Makhmalbaf had witnessed firsthand the dire circumstances under which Afghan parents had to entrust their children to Taliban schooling first in Pakistan and then in Afghanistan, where the children had been turned into zealot soldiers at the service of some fictitious Islam that was instrumental to the Pakistani ties to the US imperial interests in the region. Afghanistan under Taliban, as a result, became a proxy space—a territorial double, a proverbial shadow—for the Iran that begat Makhmalbaf's own religious zealotry and militant political activism as a young teenager. But Makhmalbaf the globally celebrated filmmaker was now a social activist increasingly drawn to the post-Khatami environment of hope and despair in Iranian domestic politics. As a result, when Makhmalbaf looked at the face of a young Afghan child he saw in him his own liberated future, just as when he looked at the face of an old Taliban fighter he saw his own youthful zealotry. Iran and Afghanistan, as two sovereign nation-states, had started reflecting and crossmetaphorizing each other. They were now in each other's spaces, not where they were physically, but where they were pointing metaphysically. The mere fact of Makhmalbaf physically moving with his family and camera crew from Iran to Afghanistan and shooting a film on a transgressive border between the two states rendered both states instantly metamorphic, metaphorically standing for each other, their territoriality made permanently circular, substitutional, interchangeable, vacant of their substantive body, and filled with their substitutional evidence.

A bipolar alterity was thus formed in the space between Iran and Afghanistan, with the old Makhmalbaf/young Afghan child on its positive bar and the young Makhmalbaf/old Afghan Taliban on its negative side. Predicated on this bipolarity, Makhmalbaf the filmmaker wanted to intervene providentially, creatively, and divinely in the transgressive space between two polities—Iran and Afghanistan—and prevent the young Afghan child (promising the old Makhmalbaf) from becoming the old Afghan Taliban fighter (reminiscent of the young fanatic Makhmalbaf). There was a *temporal double take* on the reverse when Makhmalbaf the old Iranian filmmaker looked at the faces of the young Afghan children and saw their distant reflections in the faces of the aging Taliban terrorizing their nation. The temporal space, generated and sustained in Makhmalbaf's cinema, was a cinematic presence in which Makhmalbaf wanted to reenact his own youth and prevent the young Makhmalbaf (writ large on the faces of the Afghan children) from becoming the guerrilla fighter (writ large on the face of the Afghan Taliban). Not only was the *space* in between Iran and Afghanistan being metamorphosed, but the *time* in between the young and the old Makhmalbaf, and the young and the old Afghans, was being transmuted as well. The presence of Makhmalbaf in Afghanistan was metaphorically circular, open-endedly crossreferential: he was always somewhere else.

An immediate antecedent of this sort of cinematic *body doubling* goes back at least to Makhmalbaf's *A Moment of Innocence* (1996), in which he narratively splits his own body into a teenage urban guerilla and a mature filmmaker making a film about him while splitting the body of his would-be victim into a young police officer and a mature would-be actor. The strategy worked astonishingly well and resulted in one of Makhmalbaf's best films. The mirroring effect of his lenses and the visual suggestions of spatial and chronic doubling were thus integral to his creative imagination when he set on himself the task of operating on a transgressive space between Iran and Afghanistan, using each as the metaphor of the other. In *A Moment of Innocence*, bodies are split; in *The Afghan Alphabet*, territories are split. In both, bodies and territories stand for each other. *"Cho Iran nabashad tan-e man mabad!"* reads a hemistich from a famous line in Ferdowsi's *Shahnameh*: "Were *Iran* not to be, may my *body* not to be!" There cannot be any more direct link between body and the homeland. Splitting them into two crossreferential sites crossmetaphorizes both—each standing for the other.

Because of this spatial and temporal double bind between the old Iranian Makhmalbaf and the young Afghan children (and the young Makhmalbaf and the old Taliban), on many occasions Makhmalbaf went overboard in his severe criticism of religious sentiments and began to demonize the entirety of a culture; an overcompensation for his own youthful indiscretions thus resulted in a zealotry of a different sort, where *public education* and *universal suffrage* became the panacea of all ills and predicaments. For precisely the same set of crosscultural, double-bodied reasons, Makhmalbaf became an overzealous advocate of "secular education" and Enlightenment modernity—oblivious to the paradoxes of its domestic European origins that culminated in the horrors of the Holocaust and the perils of its colonial consequences that continue to wreak havoc on what it calls and condemns as "the rest of the world." Located in the transgressive and yet binding space between Iran and Afghanistan, Makhmalbaf convinced himself that a modern, secular education was the answer to all the problems hecategorically attributed to what he invariably called *Traditional*, *Eastern*, or *Islamic* cultures. As a result, he became as uncompromising in his condemnation of the Afghan culture as he was committed to raising funds, establishing schools, and feeding, nursing, and educating Afghan children. This resulted in yet another massive ossification of the dialectic antagonism—a double-bodied summersault—presumed and operative between *secularism* and *religion*, *modernity* and *tradition*, by far the most catastrophic construction in the history of all colonial encounters with European Enlightenment modernity.

None of these pendulum swings into the pending promises of colonial modernity and binary suppositions between *the secular* and *the religious* came at the expense of Makhmalbaf's critical acumen, however. He never lost sight of the grand scheme of the US imperial designs in the region, and he was always first and foremost critical of the global conditions that had not just allowed but in fact necessitated the creation of the Taliban by Pakistani intelligence forces in order to serve the US interests in the region, both during and after the Soviet occupation of Afghanistan. Nevertheless, his criticism of the US imperialism in the region was colored by his unexamined fixation with what he categorically called *modern secular education* posited against what he dismissed as *traditional eastern fanaticism*. He was thus politically trapped inside a binary opposition between a *tradition* and a *modernity* whose invented provenance he could neither see nor trespass. But the same binary enabled him to raise substantial funds, effect changes in Iranian legislation, and educate Afghan children—at the same time that it prevented him from seeing that he had become an instrument of an imperialism of a different sort than the one he was criticizing. He failed to see that imperialism came in more shapes and shades than just F-16's and Tomahawk missiles; it could take the form, for example, of invented binaries that carried within them the slanted power relation presumed between a *secular center* in the operation of capital and a *traditional periphery* in its colonial consequences.

Art prevails where politics fails: by disposition, Makhmalbaf is as much a theoretician of social action as a practitioner of visual speculation. His repeated travels to Afghanistan and the ravages that global operations of the empire and its local consequences had visited on the Afghans in human misery and material tolls had made him wary of too much speculative hesitation. He wanted to do something and do something quickly, even though it may be on shaky moral and intellectual grounds. Altogether, when one looks at the balance of Makhmalbaf's work, he has done much more good than harm for Afghan children by intuitively moving away from a politics of despair and toward an aesthetics of emancipation, where the epistemic template of *metamorphic doubling* breaks through its debilitating political posture and reaches out toward a *parabolics of freedom*. Here is where a revolutionary aesthetics defies its own debilitating politics. The truism that no author is in total control of his or her own text has a hidden truth to it that Makhmalbaf scarcely noted: no politics is in total control of the aesthetics it implicates. That is a much more rambunctious Pandora's box than the one the dead author leaves behind in his living text. Within the same token that politics is the monopoly of physical violence (resisted by any means possible), the aesthetics of resisting its power is borne out of a no less violent defiance of the prose of its history.

Makhmalbaf shot *The Afghan Alphabet* in about two weeks on digital video, returned to Tehran for editing and mixing, and within a couple more weeks had it ready for screening. As with most of his other films, he soon forgot about *The Afghan Alphabet* itself and went about his business of attending to what he thought were the urgent needs of Afghan children. Most important, he began to cash in on his own revolutionary credentials and lobbied heavily in the Iranian parliament and with President Khatami to make necessary legislative changes to allocate sufficient funds to educate the Afghan children in refugee camps inside Iran, effectively linking them to the mandatory literacy programs applied to Iranian children. Consider the irony here that Makhmalbaf himself allowed (if not encouraged) his own children to drop out of school the minute they said so and opted for their homeschooling—under his own tutorial supervision—while he fought tooth and nail to get Afghan children to school. This irony posits yet another set of *metamorphic doubling* where factual and fictive children we either father or fathom begin to mutate into each other. For a father who has opted for homeschooling (both for himself and for his children), Makhmalbaf protests too much about public schooling. But the paradox is already a prolepsis: an anticipation of the *fictive* in the *factual*. Makhmalbaf wants to get Afghan children out of the Taliban schools much more than he wants to get them into Iranian schools, and planting the Afghan children inside the schools of the Islamic Republic (not known exactly for the liberality of their pedagogy) is as much to destabilize the rampant racism against the Afghans in Iran as to save the Afghan children from Taliban schooling. This *strategic doubling* works very effectively when the Afghan children's education away from the Taliban schooling in Afghanistan and Pakistan posits itself as an antidote against rampant Talibanism in the Islamic Republic of Iran itself. Makhmalbaf was severely criticized in and outside of his country for having abandoned the cause of his own nation and opted to attend to the predicament of Afghanistan. In that rampant racism, the "religious right" and the "secular left"—the custodians of the sacred terror inside and of the expatriate bourgeoisie outside—were identical.

The concerted effort to educate the Afghan children inside Iran was in conjunction with Makhmalbaf's other major campaign to prevent the forced expulsion of about two million Afghans from the country. He used his status as a major public figure to moderate, if not completely reverse, the rather nasty racist sentiments of Iranians against the Afghans and helped keep the majority of them in Iran, changing the Iranian laws in such a way that would allow for the inclusion of Afghan children in the Iranian literacy programs. There was much more that needed to be done. Makhmalbaf began to travel to Europe, to places as far and far-fetched as the royal palace of Luxemburg, fundraising for the construction of a school system near Kabul in Afghanistan. On many of these trips, the lead actress and the inspiration behind *Kandahar*, Nelofer Pazira, accompanied him, and the two of them were moderately successful in their efforts. Makhmalbaf categorically boycotted the United States, however, after his last trip there in March 2001 when he and his wife, along with all other Iranians who come to United States, were treated like suspected criminals. The UNESCO officials in New York, however, were eager to join this fundraising project, but an unexpected problem emerged when they saw *The Afghan Alphabet* and found a major problem with it.

The objection of the UNESCO officials in New York had to do with a critical scene in which Makhmalbaf asks a reluctant Afghan girl to reveal her name. She refuses. He insists. Finally, the Afghan girl reveals her name. The UNESCO officials objected that according to their regulations no child should be forced to reveal his or her identity on camera, and that this scene prevents them from screening it under their auspices. Makhmalbaf was furious when he heard this objection.[16] The UNESCO officials were extremely polite and accommodating, wondering if there might be a way for Makhmalbaf to reedit the film and just excise that scene. Makhmalbaf refused, and they parted ways. *The Afghan Alphabet* had modest success in the United States after Tribeca Film Festival picked it up for its inaugural edition in May 2002. A few other minor festivals also screened it here and there. But no wide distribution of the film ensued.

The fate of *The Afghan Alphabet* might in fact shed some light on the critical character of cultural intervention in the lives of millions of Afghans and by extension all Muslim women on the question of veiling their bodies. The first instance of the *metaphoric doubling* occurs between the name and the named, between *the signifier* and *the signified*: "I won't tell you my name," objects the young Afghan girl, "because you will show me on television." The body of the Afghan girl and her name become interchangeable, and revealing one meant revealing the other. But what the UNESCO people had failed to notice is that when the young girl in *The Afghan Alphabet* says her name is *Samira*, she is playing with Makhmalbaf because *Samira* is not her name—*Samira* is Makhmalbaf's own daughter's name. Another Afghan student introduces herself as *Marziyeh*, the name of Makhmalbaf's wife. Neither of the two names that the two Afghan girls give (one voluntarily and the other involuntarily) are theirs—they are Makhmalbaf's daughter's and wife's names. The operation of the *pronominal mirroring* does not stop here, because Samira is not the real name of Samira Makhmalbaf either; Samira Makhmalbaf's real name is Zeynab—a habitual practice in Iran where children are given both a religious and a common name. All Makhmalbaf's children have these double names: Samira is Zeynab, Meysam is Ayyub, and Hana is Khatereh.

The identification of the name and the named, the signifier and the signified, the person and the personified, radically compromises the body and implicates its shadows. The *proverbial shadow* of the body thus moves from its *pronominal mirroring* toward a mutation of the *personal* into the *professional*, the *factual* into the *fictional*, and thus radically complicates the very conception of *documentary* filmmaking. *The Afghan Alphabet* is not a *documentary* in an ordinary understanding of the term. The very foundation of the best that has happened in Iranian cinema is this radical complication of the document that we are supposed to find evident in reality, a development deeply rooted in the creative crisis of mimetic representation in all colonial aesthetics. *The Afghan Alphabet* borrows its visual vocabulary and narrative design directly from Forough Farrokhzad's groundbreaking *The House Is Black* (1962), a film about a leprosy colony that to this day has remained at the very creative center of the contemporary Iranian cinema, where fact and fantasy conspire to tell the truth.[17]

Upon telling Makhmalbaf that her name is Samira but refusing to unveil and wash her face, the girl is dismissed by her teacher from class. She goes out followed by her friend Marziyeh, and the two of them start a dialogue—Marziyeh insisting and Samira resisting to unveil and wash her face in front of the camera. The privilege of Makhmalbaf as an artist is that the emancipatory power of his aesthetics defies the paralysis of his politics. But how exactly does that work? As said earlier, within the same token that politics is the monopoly of physical violence (resisted by any means possible), the aesthetics of resisting its power is borne out of a no less violent defiance of the prose of its history. The fictitious violence of naming is necessary for the factual emancipation to take place. What we are watching here is not a dialogue between *two* characters but a monologue within *one* character having given herself two fictitious names, one of Makhmalbaf's own daughter and the other of his own wife. The aesthetic emancipation occurs via *body doubling* that operates through an interior monologue that on the screen appears like an exterior dialogue. This shadow talk, this whispery echoing of one's own voice in the eardrums of one's internalized other, appears on the screen like two girls who are none other than one person split and personified into two. *Samira*, as it were, is not having a whispery conversation with someone else. That girl is *Samira* herself, talking to herself, split into two and projected onto the screen for the whole world to be able to see her better. That is all. The liberation is manufactured from within, via an interior monologue (modulated into an exterior dialogue for the whole world to see). This shadow talk, this whispery echo from within, will have had to be forced out by a violent revelation of a fictive name in order to make the factual evidence of that freedom real.

When the young Afghan girl refuses to reveal her real name and gives Makhmalbaf a reel name, her body in effect refuses to be signified and thus retrieves the inarticulate defiance of its sign while concealing it under the veil of anonymity. For all we know the final face that unveils and washes for the camera to see and marvel may or may not be that of the young Afghan girl who refused to give her name or reveal her face and thus declined to put a name to her body, sustaining not the anonymity of her character but the unanimity of her name and body.

The Material and the Metaphoric Bodies

On the location of Makhmalbaf's making of *The Afghan Alphabet* we witness the active mutation of the feminine body, in correspondence to and with the land she represents, into two complementary citations—one substantive and the other substitutional, one material and the other metaphoric, but both standing in lieu of each other. This body-doubling thus expands the territorial boundaries of the *corpus politicus* and cites it as the site of contestation between two claims to political control—one colonial and the other anticolonial, one imperial and the other nativist resistance to the imperial. What we were witnessing in the wake of 9/11, when suicidal violence was flown into the heart of the empire and thus initiated the project of ending states by the globalized (United) State(s) through an open-ended war on terrorism (a terrorism that will end all terrorism), were the iconic registrations of an event well under way prior to its inaugural US appearance. The cataclysmic rise of suicidal violence at the turn of the millennium corresponds to the official announcement of the agenda of a predatory empire, marking the apocalyptic mutation of human bodies, not only in their explosive shattering into charred fragments, but also into their own duplicates and triplicates and thus the multiplicities of themselves.

Let me take the case of two conjoined twins who became famous in the news in the summer of 2003 and read their material body through its metaphoric suggestion of the oddly coupled configuration of an Islamic Republic—by way of yet another example of the metamorphic identification of the human body with the body politic. The extraordinary global attention suddenly paid to a set of adult Iranian twins, Laleh and Ladan Bijani, who early in December 2002 burst into international news when they decided to undergo a major operation intended to separate their conjoined heads, demands an attention beyond their personal and well into their public perceptions. Physicians in Singapore accepted the challenge of separating the pair of 28-year-old twin sisters who had been joined at the head since birth. The twins underwent intense physical and psychological tests before their operation, and then by May 2003 they were ready for their dangerous operation. The global attention drawn to the event made the conjoined twins send a message of thanks to their well-wishers on July 6, 2003:

> Dear Friends,
>
> Thank you for all your good wishes and kind thoughts. We are touched by all the cards and emails pouring in every day from people all over the world. Your kind gestures have brought much comfort to us as we anxiously wait for surgery next week. We have been praying every day for our operation. We are excited about it as we've waited 28 years for it![18]

Ladan and Laleh Bijani had been told that they had a 50 percent chance of survival, but they said they were willing to risk their lives for the chance of leading separate lives. The operation at the Raffles hospital involved an international team of 28 doctors and 100 medical assistants and was expected to last for 48 hours. On July 8, 2003, doctors in Singapore began the unprecedented surgery to separate the twin sisters, but the twins died in the course of the operation. Neurosurgeons discovered that the brains of Ladan and Laleh Bijani had become tightly fused over the past 28 years.

Both in Iran and throughout the world, an unprecedented amount of attention was paid to this case. In Iran itself, the story of the twin sisters and their operation soon became a matter of *national metaphor*, their *substantive* bodies *substitutional* for further claims on history, hope, politics, and triumph over despair. Moving editorials were written, and many paid tribute to the twins' courage and bid them an "eternal farewell." President Khatami's office suggested that the twins' birthday be celebrated as a national "Day of Hope." "Laleh and Ladan belong to all Iranians," read some newspaper headlines.

"Laleh and Ladan will go to sleep in the arms of the earth," mourned another paper. "Their memory will bring to mind their spirit of perseverance and tirelessness, which will remain alive forever," said another editorial. Editorials were pouring the national sentiments into their resurrected bodies, as their dead bodies were being buried in the Iranian soil—there to keep alive for perpetuity the hopes of the nation and its perseverance against adversities. It was mostly the reformist, and beleaguered, national papers that were aggressively appropriating the twins for their progressive (antiestablishment) projects. The dead twins had become a national metaphor. There were discussions of awarding an annual *statue of bravery* and a *medal of hope* on every anniversary of their tragic death. On July 12, 2003, thousands of Iranians gathered for the funeral and burial of the separated but dead twins. The press was very particular in noting how they were interred in two separate graves—their wishes, in effect, fulfilled in a tangible and visible afterlife. In the southwestern village of Lohrasb, where the separated twins were buried, the villagers placed their pictures on lampposts and placards, honoring their memory, and claiming their perseverance and posthumous victory. Stories began to surface in the Iranian media about the life of the twins and how they were separated from their biological parents when they were young because they were too poor, and that they were adopted by another set of parents in Tehran from whom they had been estranged later in their lives. Laleh and Ladan became the heroic figures of a collective legend, a moving myth, that Iranian national newspapers were telling to the nation on a daily and nightly basis—a very recent story, told in very ancient terms.

One of the most poignant political commentaries on this event was written by Ramin Ahmadi, an Iranian physician and expatriate political activist who wrote a piece in Persian and pointed out that Laden and Laleh represented yet another mismatched set of twins: the one between the two incongruent ideas of *Islam* and *republic*. He observed that the late Ayatollah Khomeini did not allow separating early in their lives, and it had now become too late to divide *Islam* and *republic* without a similar mortal danger.[19] What the comparison sustained and suggested was the physical evidence of a conjoined set of twins risking to die separately rather than opting to live together, as the *corporeal predicament* of a mismatched Islamic Republic opting to live an awkward life rather than risking a noble death. Ramin Ahmadi's figure of speech echoed Mohsen Makhmalbaf's configuration of an interior monologue in *The Afghan Alphabet* as an exterior dialogue between two Afghan girls whom are given two fictitious names. What we were witnessing here is a thematic link between the creative mind of Makhmalbaf and the critical intelligence of Ramin Ahmadi, figuratively identifying both the *fictive* and *factual* bodies of two young girls as the *landed metaphors* of the nations they represent—their *substantive* evidence the *substitutional* signs of their nations at large.

TEHRAN IN THE MIRROR OF PARIS

The mandatory *veiling* of women in Iran and Afghanistan is now matched and mirrored by their mandatory *unveiling* in France—with similar sentiments now rampant in the rest of Europe. What is common between the tyrannical policies of the Islamic Republic and the racist policies of France is the violent citation of the women's bodies (not what they wear but what they expose and hide) as the principal site of state legitimacy. Mandatory *unveiling* in France is the functional equivalent of mandatory *veiling* in Iran, both aggressively denying women autonomous agency and beyond that asserting state power over the bodies of its (alien) citizens. The exposing of the women's bodies in France is meant to publicly cite those premises as the site of the state's operation and legitimacy. The covering of the selfsame bodies in Iran is to prevent the accumulation (and thus denying) of *memorial agency*. In this respect, the *Islamic* Republic of Iran and the so-called *secular* republic of France are two sides of the same coin: the prevention and denial of *memorial agency* on one side and the complete occupation on the other. The Islamic Republic wants to prevent women from accumulating bodily memory for the same reason that France wants to occupy that vacated space with a totalitarian gaze that wishes to leave no room for a (Nietzschean) *defiant reason* that challenges the legitimacy of its (Kantian) *public reason*. Opposing mandatory veiling in Iran and mandatory unveiling in France harbors not a logical fallacy but a dialectical logic. By denying women their freedom of choice (to unveil in Iran if so they choose and veil in France if they so choose), both France and Iran are exposing their tyrannical mutation of the feminine body into a site of political contestation between the legislated semantics of state policies and the defiant semiotics of bodily memory. The complementary correlation between Iran and France, by a bizarre historical coincidence, repeats the complementary logic of Fanon insisting that the Algerian women should veil to be revolutionary, while the French colonial administration wished them unveiled in lieu of becoming collaborators in the occupation of their own homeland. It did not occur to either Fanon or the French colonial administrators that Algerian women could both unveil and rise against the colonial occupation of their homeland. What both Fanon and the French colonial administrators (and now the French government and the Islamic Republic) document and sustain is the systematic mutation of the (feminine) body into a site of state violence and political legitimacy. The inclusion of the Jewish yarmulke and the Christian cross along with the Muslim scarf in the French edict is the real giveaway in this respect, because in a supercilious attempt to be ecumenical in its racism the French policy reveals that it is not so much what people *wear* (scarf, yarmulke, cross) that matters as what they *cover* (parts of their body) that is particularly anxiety provoking to the state.

The systematic mutation of the human body into a site of political contestation marks its palimpsestic inscription by a *postterritorial polity* that links the anticolonial struggles of African nations like Algeria to those of Arab nations like Palestine as it equally links the revolutionary movements of

Muslim countries like Iran to the imperial designs on Central Asian nations like Afghanistan. While the Algerians faced the French colonial domination of Africa and the Palestinians have suffered and resisted the colonial conquest of their land by Zionism, the cases of Iran and Afghanistan mark the specific transition of European colonialism into the (now outdated) Soviet and the (now updated) US Empires. While Iran and Afghanistan are now trapped in the grip of a notorious nexus of domestic despotism and globalized empire, Palestine is at the brink of total annihilation under the rapacious metamorphosis of Israel from a merely racist colonial outpost into a critical component of the US imperial machinery. The self-exploded body of the Palestinian suicidal bomber is the excavated (*excavatus—ex* + *cavare* = out + hollow: to make hollow) site of a categorical denial of the illegitimate state its very last location of violence. The spectacular destruction of the World Trade Center by the transcontinental extension of suicidal violence in 9/11 became the globalized citation of that localized template writ large.

But the self-exploded body of the suicidal bomber has also liberated the *sign* of the body from the legislated semantics of its inscription in the contentious nexus that holds the empire and all its acts of resistance together. The living body self-explodes against its will to live, and that encrypted codification of the flesh is the most brutal mark of a politics of dispossession cauterized on a possessed body. As the body explodes to steal itself from the state and thus deny the state its last site of legitimacy, it equally steals itself from the brutal game of political inscription between the colonizer and the colonized. As *defiant sign*, the body resents them both; as *reluctant signifier*, it is the football field of a murderous sport. But the double indemnity of this dual task crossmetaphorizes and saves the body at the very moment of its destruction, liberates it at the moment of destroying it. The same body that explodes in the face of the predatory empire to deny it its last possible territorial legitimacy ipso facto emancipates the *physical sign* of the body from its incarcerated (self-incriminating) implication between power and resistance, between the empire and the revolutions that resist it, between politics and the polities it inadvertently implicates. Suicidal violence is an *aesthetic* act of resistance against the *political* incrimination of the body in a politics of dispossession that posits it as a metaphor for something that can no longer exist. The exploded body is a metaphor with no referent, excavated and vacated of the very significance it ascribes to itself at the exact moment of its self-evacuation.

In return, by declaring war on the amorphous terror, the globalized (United) State(s)—which is and is not the United States of America—is trying to hide, but is in effect betraying, its permanent loss of legitimacy. The United States of America were anticolonially created and constitutionally crafted, as all other modern nation-states, to define and defend *their territorial integrity*. That *territorial integrity* is no more. Pennsylvania, Massachusetts, and New York have now given way to Qatar, Tajikistan, and the Indian Ocean. The United States has now completely vacated its historical referents to the operation of a *national* economy, polity, territory, and culture, and it has assumed the imperial apparatus of a global economy and its corresponding polity and culture (with the posthuman body its solitary site of violence). The US declaration of the *ending of states* and an open-ended *war on terrorism* is a two-edged sword: it is the harbinger of its own historical demise. The project commenced in Philadelphia on July 4, 1776, concluded on the ruins of the World Trade Center on September 11, 2001.

To demonstrate that fact, I know of no other scene in world cinema better than the very last sequence of Akira Kurosawa's *The Throne of Blood* (1961), a retelling of Shakespeare's *Macbeth.* Taketori Washizu (Toshiro Mifune—Macbeth) has murdered Kuniharu Tsuzuki (Takamaru Sasaki—Duncan), expelled Yoshiaki Miki (Minoru Chiaki—Banquo), and as his own wife and coconspirator, Lady Asaji (Isuzu Yamada—Lady Macbeth), has gone completely mad, the treacherous knight has gone back to the Spider Web Woods and received the news from the ghostly apparitions that his kingdom will collapse only when and if the trees of the jungle were to move. He is ecstatic with the news, because he is sure that these trees will never move. He comes back to his fortress and assures his assembled army there is nothing to fear. He laughs uproariously as he tells his army of the spirits' news, scoffing at the suggestion that trees could move—little does he know that he has just been the herald of his own demise, the instrument of his own undoing, because the very next day the trees of the Spider Web Woods do in fact start moving, as Yoshiaki Miki's army has disguised itself in shrubs and branches of the very same trees. The tower watch and gradually the rest of the army sees *the moving jungle* and is frightened out of their wits, because the prophecy that their own general had told them would mean the end of his murderous tyranny has come to pass. None other than Taketori Washizu has foretold to them his own demise. Had he not told them the prophecy, his soldiers and generals would have probably discovered the trick and handled it appropriately. But caught in the self-destructive premonition of Taketori Washizu himself, they conspire and murder him in one of the most spectacular scenes of an army mutiny in world cinema. The *war on terrorism* is no less a treacherous terrain than Kurosawa's *Spider Web Woods.* The figure of George W. Bush standing on the rubble of the World Trade Center and proclaiming that he will *avenge that crime* cuts an uncanny resemblance to Taketori Washizu assuring his army that his kingdom will last until hell (read *global warming*) freezes over.

THE SOLITARY SITE OF STATE VIOLENCE

From Algeria to Palestine; then from Saudi Arabia to the United States; next from Somalia to Iraq; and then from Afghanistan to Iran; from there to Turkey, Russia, Malaysia, Indonesia, and Singapore; then back to India, Pakistan, and Kenya; then to Morocco, the Philippines, Yemen, and Argentina—the suicidal body has now completely metastasized. As the amorphous capital has necessitated and generated a globalized (United) State(s), so has the globalized state narrowed in on the fragile *posthuman body* as the solitary site of its violence. And as the *posthuman body* has revolted against the globalized state, so has its suicidal urges metastasized beyond nations and boundaries, cultures and civilizations, religions and creeds. Thus has the *homo hierarchicus* yielded at large to a *corpus anarchicum*.

The metastasized body of suicidal violence coincided with a cinematic moment when the genocide of millions of Armenians who perished in Anatolia in the early twentieth century was memorialized by a singular act of creative genius in Atom Egoyan's *Ararat* (2002).

What, whence, and where is *Ararat*? As suicidal violence exacerbates the *corpus anarchicum* of a defiant body, the most successful cinematic remembrance of an ethnic genocide identifies itself with a dislocated *mountain* that is not *in* Armenia but *is* Armenia. The postnational body is located where the *corpus anarchicum*, remembering its own mass destruction, refuses to forget and go back to Armenia and prefers to continue to remember its own annihilation in diaspora despite the fact that the state of Armenia (mountains and rivers, valleys and lakes) exists. Armenia as a *territorial reality* seems to be entirely irrelevant to the fact and phenomenon of being Armenian, as the mourning body insists on forgetting about Armenia and instead dwelling on and remembering its own annihilation in diaspora. The Armenian identity, oddly, seems to prefer to register and assert itself on the brink of its own genocidal extinction. This is far different from the Zionist abuse of the Jewish holocaust, the production of a holocaust industry on the ashes of millions of innocent people perished in the Nazi Germany (that culminated in the mendacity of Steven Spielberg's *Schindler's List* [1993] smack in the middle of the Serbian genocide of Bosnian Muslims and then collapsed in the banality of Roman Polanski's *The Pianist* [2002] in the wake of the Israeli massacre of Palestinians in Jenin), simply to cash in on a legitimate European guilt in order to generate and sustain an illegitimate colonial state.[20] Armenians are after no colonial state; they are not abusing the memory of their perished ancestors to claim an illegitimate colony. They have opted to freeze the time on April 1915 and, on the perished bones of their innocent ancestors, remember and register themselves at the moment of their almost total annihilation. By making their forgetfulness contingent on an impossibility—that the contemporary Turks will admit guilt—they have sought, in effect, to remain on the brink of that destruction permanently.

By far the most daunting task that artists throughout ages and cultures have faced is the impossibility of representing the enormity of a catastrophe that has crossed the limits of imagination by being collectively mutated into a historical trauma at the core of a nation. Filmmakers in particular have had their greatest challenge in finding ways to sustain a corresponding measure between the depth of a catastrophe that haunts their national psyche and manners and modes of *representing* that catastrophe in a viable cinematic narrative that does not violate the sanctity of that memory. The nuclear holocaust caused by the US dropping of the atomic bomb on Japanese civilians during World War II remained at the heart of Akira Kurosawa's cinema until the end of his life and into his very last films, *Dream* (1990) and *Madadayo*

(1992). Gillo Pontecorvo's *Kapo* (1964) remains to this day by far the most successful attempt to convey the depth of the despair at the heart of the Jewish holocaust in Nazi Germany. Elem Klimov's *Come and See* (1985) opted for an elegiac, nightmarish, and confounding camerawork to tell the Russian side of the same atrocity. Ingmar Bergman's *Shame* (1968) and Terrence Malick's *The Thin Red Line* (1999) altogether lifted the horrors and bestiality at the core of such traumas to a miasmatic reflection beyond time and space, while today a succession of young Palestinian filmmakers—Michel Khleifi, Elia Suleiman, Hany Abu Assad, Rashid Masharawi, Mai Masri, and Mohammad Bakri—have been hard at work trying to come to terms with how to tell of the enormity of the injustice and terror visited on them by their being robbed of their ancestral homeland in the broad daylight of history.

The question and challenge will always remain: how does one actually convey the sheer magnitude of a horror visited on a nation, especially when the people historically responsible for that nightmare refuse to acknowledge or else seek to justify, excuse, whitewash, or dismiss it? What the Armenian population of Anatolia collectively, the Japanese civilians at large, and the German (and European) Jewry in particular have endured historically is today the daily reality of Palestinians, as it was for the Rwandans and Bosnians just about a blink of an eye ago. The challenge that an artist faces is not limited to how to represent a historical atrocity but how to do so responsibly in the context of contemporary atrocities. In such colossal catastrophes, the principal problem of *representation* rests on the fact that the reality itself surpasses all the narrative manners and mimetic modes at the disposal of an artist that can possibly convey it with full satisfaction. Visionary filmmakers have, each in their own way, sought and found ways of telling their national trauma in manners and modes at once ingeniously creative and yet traumatically palpitated with invisible cries and inaudible whispers. In his *Ararat*, Atom Egoyan follows in the footsteps of a succession of great filmmakers who have sought at one time or another to throw down their gauntlet, meet the almost impossible task, and tell the horrors of their national trauma.

The principal distinction of Egoyan's manner of telling the story of the Armenian genocide is a narrative device that works through a succession of *enframing*. A straight-forward epic narrative seems oddly to have commenced Egoyan's project and yet gradually mutated into a courageously inventive, worldly wise, deeply moving, and ingeniously crafted and controlled *displacing* of that epic inside the contemporaneity of Egoyan's own time and space in Toronto—with he behind the camera, his wife Arsine Khanjian in the lead role in front, and their son Arshile Gorky, the namesake of the central character of the film, having a cameo appearance as well. The *displacing* of the factual genocide of Armenians in Anatolia into the fictive story of a group of European and North American Armenians in search of a therapeutic reconciliation with their traumatized memory works through not one or two but in fact three simultaneous *enframings* from which a succession of others follow. All the successive and simultaneous *enframings* are ordered in a cumulative triumvirate, a variation on a thematic ménage-a-trois, a Christological trinity writ large.

The first and foremost troika that immediately frames the story of the genocide is the one formed between Ani, her son Raffi, and her stepdaughter Celia. Celia is the daughter of a man to whom Ani once married but betrayed by falling in love with another man who became the father of Raffi. That makes Raffi and Celia stepbrother and stepsister, and thus their love affair the first sign of an incestuous taboo that is injected into this ménage-a-trois. The second sign is when Ani enters her son's bedroom and Egoyan's mis-en-scene, camera movements, lighting, and directorial touch leaves no doubt as to an equally erotic, suggestively incestuous tension between the handsome, mature son and his attractive, young mother. Two visual and narrative suggestions of incestuous eroticism thus collide and give the first and most important *enframing* of the story its most immediately *dangerous liaison* on the porous borderlines of fact and fantasy.

The second *enframing*, equally consequential to the telling of *Ararat*, is among Rouben, a Hollywood scriptwriter; Edward Soroyan, a transnational film director; and Ani, an art historian: the first with a blatantly financial, the second an overtly emotional, and the third a devotedly scholarly stake in the manner in which the story is to be told. There are two crucial sequences: one is when Ani brings to the attention of Rouben and Edward that, from the village of Van, Mount Ararat is not visible, and the other is when Ani marches onto the set as Edward is shooting a particularly moving scene with the US Christian evangelical missionary Clarence Ussher pleading for the life of a young Armenian in a double-tongue, both in and out of character.

While the first *enframing* among Ani, Raffi, and Celia gives *Ararat* its charged emotive and erotic energy, the second *enframing* among Rouben, Edward, and Ani gives it its raw kitschy and prosaic disposition.

The third *enframing* that simultaneously braces Egoyan's narrative is among David, his son Phillip, and Phillip's homosexual Turkish-Canadian partner, Ali. David is a bitter and angry man, not only because his son Phillip has abandoned his married life and opted for a homosexual relationship, but even more palpably because Phillip's choice is a young Turkish Oriental who confirms all his racist and homophobic terrors. During the opening scene when we see David asking his grandchild to say grace before they start their meal, it is not so much the silence of Phillip sitting to David's right as the Muslim infidel sitting to his left that is particularly troubling to him, a fact accentuated by an advisedly cut and discarded scene in which David tells his grandson the Biblical story of Noah's Ark. This particular *enframing* characterizes and locates David as the principal interlocutor of *Ararat* and its primary narrative device: the non-Armenian, white, North American custom's officer to whom the Armenians of the film—not just Edward and Raffi as Egoyan's alter egos but Egoyan himself—tell their story.

From these three simultaneous *enframings* of the story, a number of other triumvirates follow. The young Arshile Gorky (or Vosdanig Adoian [1904–1948] to be exact), his mother, and the young son of the photographer constitute another triumvirate, as do Edward, Raffi, and Egoyan himself as the modular maneuvering of three filmmakers in one. Ani, her husband who committed suicide, and her lover who was killed while trying to assassinate a Turkish diplomat constitute yet another, as indeed do the dates 1915, 1934, and the present of Egoyan's Toronto. The theme is *three* and the variations many. But what is the function of these successive and simultaneous *enframings* of the story and history that is the Armenian genocide? How do they help or hinder the telling of the actual atrocity that factually happened? The cumulative function of these ingeniously crafted *enframings* is an entirely unprecedented and brilliantly successful *manner* of telling the *truth* of the Armenian genocide in a narrative mode that is first and foremost a monumental artistic testimony to its historical occurrence in an aesthetically liberating, morally forgiving, and politically disarming way.

The *narrative* function of the succession of *enframings* that brace the historical account of the Armenian genocide stylizes the manner in which its *truth is to be told*—especially a *truth* that is *denied*, a *denial* that is so categorically debilitating, paralyzing, and arresting. By placing his own syncretistic narrative in between Edward's highly stylized and kitschy vision of the genocide and Raffi's pathologically mutated documentary fixation, Egoyan both postulates his self-defeating options and yet holds them at bay—in other words, he does in fact manage creatively to have his cake and eat it too. In telling the truth of the Armenian genocide, Egoyan could have either opted for Edward's kitschy and vindictive vision or else been paralyzed by Raffi's mimetic paralysis—brilliantly suggested by a stack of exposed negative tin boxes that could contain either the rushes of a great film about the genocide or else heroin or perhaps both, suggesting the psychedelic corruption of an art that can be liberating and emancipatory into a hallucinogenic psychotomimeticism.

Instead of denying or suppressing these two very attractive and yet repellent options, Egoyan opts to admit, exorcise, interpolate, and incorporate them into his own transparently syncretistic narrative. This is by far the most consequential narrative triumvirate in *Ararat* because by both positing and appropriating Edward and Raffi as his own shadow filmmakers, Egoyan sustains the most definitive mode of his manner of truth telling. Edward's manner is kitschy and memorial, while Raffi's is documentary and paralyzingly *yet-to-be-told*. In between, Egoyan inserts his own *Ararat*: embracing, catholic, capacious, testimonial, and yet forgiving. It is critical to keep in mind that there is a stylistic seepage of the kitschy Edward and documentary Raffi in Egoyan's own *presentist* narrative, when the timing of the interlocution between David the customs agent and Raffi the assistant filmmaker is radically stylized. In his own commentary on *Ararat*, Egoyan goes into much unnecessary trouble trying to argue that the duration of this interview is not unrealistic because he has done his research and a customs officer can in fact hold a passenger for up to 24 hours. This fact or fantasy has absolutely nothing to do with the *stylistically elongated* duration of the timing in which Raffi tells the customs officer the truth of the Armenian genocide.

Multiplied narratives and altered characters come together in Egoyan's *Ararat* to tell—and then disperse in order not to tell—the truth of the Armenian genocide. The uncanny ability of telling the truth of a much denied genocide is achieved by an equally uncanny act of memorial remembrance in which the physical bodies of Armenians scattered throughout the world replace and become the territorial terrain of *Armenia itself*, no longer in need of the whole 29,800 square kilometers of the Armenian Republic. By naming the movie about the Armenian genocide *Ararat*, Egoyan places the referent of the Armenian always somewhere else, where Armenia is not, and where Armenians opt to forget about their homeland and instead remember themselves in the brutal atrocities of genocide perpetrated on their collective body.

As defiant sign and as reluctant signifier, the *body* has thus completely taken over the site and the citation that *territory* used to provide for any monopoly of physical violence that still calls itself a *state*. And as we saw at the commencement of the Arab Spring, it is precisely from this very site, the self-immolated body of Mohamed Bouazizi, that the revolt against the state takes place.

Chapter 2

In the Absence of the Face

"This Apparatus," he [the Officer] said . . . "was invented by our former Commandant. I assisted at the very earliest experiments and had a share in all the work until its completion. But the credit of inventing it belongs to him alone. Have you ever heard of our former Commandant? No? Well, it isn't saying too much if I tell you that the organization of the whole penal colony is his work. We who are his friends knew even before he died that the organization of the colony was so perfect that his successor, even a thousand new schemes in his head, would find it impossible to alter anything, at least for many years to come. And our prophecy has come true; the new Commandant has had to acknowledge its truth."

—Franz Kafka, *In the Penal Colony* (1914)

My principal concern during the last chapter was to mark the substantive evidence of the transmutation of the body into a substitutional representation of the territorial polity it is forced to represent. I have insisted on this forced mutation of *the defiant sign* of the body into *the reluctant signifier* of something that it quintessentially is not—the strapping of its bones and banalities to the machinery of some purposeful meaning—in order to suggest and sustain the dialectical force that keeps the suicidal body on the porous borderlines between its *material undecidability* and its *mimetic metamorphosis* into something else. In the following chapter, I dwell on an inaugural moment of the Qur'anic revelation when, I propose, the defiant *signs* put up an active resistance to their doctrinal legislation into a revelatory language and then a world religion. I have opted to work through Qur'anic passages that emphasize the primacy of *the word* against the principality of *the vision* in order to investigate how the Qur'anic repressed in effect returns narratively to haunt its own text. I believe that by doing so I have by serendipity detected the central tension that animates the revelatory resonances of the Islamic sacred text.

From the sight of the exploded corpus of the *suicidal body*, I move to the site of the Unseen author of the authority invested in the living flesh by way of restoring to the body its originary signature—arguing that body is a sign, and that sign is no signifier. Not in the politics of its despair but in the aesthetics of its will to resist power does the suicidal body posit itself as a defiant sign of its age. As a sign, the Muslim body—the *corpus particularis* that now stands for a *corpus universalis* beyond its cultural confinements—is located between a pre- and a post-Eternity. "We belong to God and to God we shall return," is a common prayer offered at the funeral of Muslims—martyred, murdered, self-exploded, sacrificed, or just plain dead. To that prayer returns the origin and the destination of the Muslim body, from the first instance when *Adhan* is whispered in the ear of the infant to the moment when ritual prayers are said at his or her bodily burial. In that span of time dwells the immemorial moment of a Muslim body: the sanctity of its composition reminiscent of the paradisial pause when God looked into a mirror, saw His Face, and called it *Insan* (the human).

His Face, presented in absentia—a vision of the Invisible.

SAVE HIS FACE

There is no God save Him.
Everything will perish save His Face.

—Surah al-Qisas[1]

Because Utterance is not like Visual Observation: . . . So that when the Prophet described the blessings of Paradise and the torments of Hell he would be able to say, "I Saw it," and not just "I heard it." Because that is logically more persuasive, it convinces more effectively and powerfully.

—Abu al-Fadl Rashid al-Din al-Maybudi[2]

Calling them [the idols] gods is not but a meaningless name. The reason is that the Name is not the Named. Because if the Name were the Named, then by virtue of calling them god they would be god and it would be proper to worship them, and they would have been god by attributes, and yet that is impossible.

—Shaykh Abu al-Futuh al-Razi[3]

I will speak. I will inevitably speak, as I will have to write: in the *absence* of the Sign and of the *absence* of the Face, all in the *presence* of the Unseen and thus in the Name of the Unseen.

The Unseen Face of the Unseen speaks and is spoken to: "In the Name of Allah, the Beneficent, the Merciful."[4] Presuming and resuming the Biblical, the Qur'anic narrative begins in the "Name," absenting the Face, which cannot be there.

It is impossible to commence in the "Face." The Face is forbidden, concealed, absent, and thus absented. In the absence of the Face of the Invisible, the Unseen, the Qur'an begins in the Name. In the absence of the Face, the Name casts a long and enduring shadow on the literariness of the Faith, on the concealing of the Face, on the substitution of a collection of Sacred Signatures for a constellation of Signs, on the collapsing of the Sign into the Signifier, so that it can point, ipso facto, to a Signified and thus implicate One Final Transcendental Signified, the Hermeneutic Center *and* Circle that hold the universe of Qur'anic imagination together. The word *Qur'an*, from *qr'*, means "to recite," the *Citation* presumed, the *Sightation* denied, and the Sign suppressed—closing the eyes, opening the ears.

I will thus write, inevitably, of an absence: the absence of the Face, and having to face up to the absence of the Face, where the Faith will have to begin.

Where the Face is de-Faced, the Sacred Signature sealed, the Sign mutated, the Signifier born, the Signified suggested, and the Transcendental Signified implicated: There is a story, in a Signed Language, waiting, inevitably, to be told.

The inaugural moment of the absence of the Face is in the inaugural Text of the Faith, the Sacred Constitution, and the aggressive repression of the absence of and in the word *ghayb* (the Unseen, the Absent): "Alif. Lam. Mim. This is the Scripture whereof there is no doubt, a guidance unto those who ward off (evil). Who believe in the Unseen, and establish worship, and spend of that which We have bestowed upon them; And who believe in that which is revealed unto thee (Muhammad) and that which was revealed before thee, and are certain of the Hereafter."[5] "Who believe in the Unseen"—who believes in the Unseen? Do you believe in the Unseen? The Birth of a Faceless Faith? Remembering a Faith-less Face?

The Inaugural Moment. The Ground Zero. The Primal Pause. The Unmoved Mover. In the absence of the Face is the commencement of the Faith. The Name cannot be seen. It is the Unseen. In the absence of the Face, we have to begin the Faith.

The inaugural moment of the Qur'an, of *Re-Citation*, is *alphabetical*. Audible, inarticulate, visible, meaning held at bay, and *alphabetical*: "Alif. Lam. Mim" means nothing. They are Signatures: letters coagulating to no word, Pseudo-Signs announcing themselves, Signifiers signifying nothing beyond their visuality, Signifiers feigning the Sign. "Alif. Lam. Mim" are the optical illusions of Signs precisely at the moment when they are about to suppress the visible absence of the Sign and mutate that absence, and thus that (in)ability, into the instrumentality of the Signifier, the Sacred, the *alphabetical* ordering of access to Truth Manifest. The Truth is about to be manifested right here where it cannot be Manifest and it *must* hide its (in)ability to be Manifest. Signatures of the Unseen—"Alif. Lam. Mim" are neither Signs nor Signifiers. They are both Signs and Signifiers. In that disabling contradiction is the enabling configuration that makes the Sacred—the aggressive substitution of a suggested Signification for the suppressed Sign, of the meaning of the Name for the shape of the Face, of the Hermeneutics of postponement for the Semiotics of the present, of the Metaphysics of fear for the Aesthetic of pleasure—possible.

"This is the Scripture" (*Dhalik al-Kitabu*) delivers the promise of that visible substitution of the invisible Sign by determinedly collapsing it into a pregnant Signifier. "The Scripture" is actually "the Book," or even more accurately "that which is written," or a collection thereof, and this framing has a meaning, the coagulation of a word, "The Word." In this inaugural moment of the Faith, in two strategic moves, is hidden the supreme anxiety of the Faith, in the absence of the Face, of the Supreme Transcendental Signified, actively implicated, plotted, by the mutation of the absent Sign into the present Signifier. The Book is one colossal Signifier, having just successfully concealed its otherwise paralyzing anxiety of lacking a Face, pointing to a Transcendental Signified. Faith is thus "having no doubt" (*la rayba fihi*), "whereof there is no doubt" that the Book is "a guidance unto those who ward off (evil)." In two moves, in the first two verses of the inaugurating moment of the Faith, the opening gambit of the optical illusion of *alphabetical* Signifiers masquerading as Signs while not relenting their Signifying claims, delivers the Faithful to the Book, the Written, the Transcendental Signifier, delivering the Truth Manifest at the very throne of the Transcendental Signified, the Truth Manifest, decidedly unmanifestable, the condition of having Faith in the un-Face, the very *condito sine qua non* of *Revelation*, revealing what cannot be seen, what is un-see-able.

"This is the Scripture" (*Dhalik al-Kitabu*) can also be read, and has also been read by some early commentators, as predicated on the subject of "Alif. Lam. Mim," which carries the visual inarticulate right to the doorstep of the written articulate, the Sign handing in, delivering, itself to the Signifier.[6] But even more emphatically, the substitution of the Transcendental Signifier for the absence of the Sign is implanted in the interlink "guidance" (*hudan*). *Hudan*, from *hdy*, is "to guide," "to point to," or "to lead" from one thing to another, as from a Signifier to a Signified. *Dhalik al-Kitabu la rayba fihi hudan li al-muttaqyn* is cataclysmic in its categorical pronouncement, its no-time-to-waste conclusion, that the Book, the Written, the promissory notation of the *Alphabetical*, is undoubtedly the guidance, the linking passage from here to there, for those who thus believe and so are Faithful and are therefore guided from (the absence of) the Sign to (the site of) the Signature to (the domain of) the Signifier, right to (the Presence) of the Transcendental Signified, implicated by and in a game far removed from its Sacred Claims.

What cannot be seen, the Face of the Unseen, is the defining moment of the Faithful and the Faith. "Who believe in the Unseen" (*alladhina yu'minuna bi al-ghayb*) is now confident in its doctrinal announcement its categorical imperative, of who has and who lacks Faith in the absence of the Face. In the twelfth century, Shaykh Abu al-Futuh al-Razi—summing up and summoning the authority of all his predecessors all the way back to the very father of Qur'anic hermeneutics, Ibn Abbas (d. c. 687), a cousin to the Prophet himself—is emphatic as to what the Unseen refers to: "As for *ghayb*, it refers to whatever is hidden from the eyes and yet visible in the heart."[7] What is it that is Most Hidden from the eye and Most Necessary in the heart? Not just any unseen, it is the Unseen. Delegated to the heart, itself an organ unseen, the Unseen cannot be seen by the eyes in the face. Because the Unseen cannot be seen by the eyes in our face, and because It is Faceless, we are de-Faced. The Faithful are thus those who believe in the Unseen, in That which cannot be seen. The Faithful are those who believe in the Faceless. "Establishing worship" (*wa yuqimuna al-salat*), "and spend of that which We have bestowed upon them" (*wa mimma razqnahum yunfiqun*) are now the qualifying attributes of those who have already moved from the absence of the Face into the Sacred site of the Signature and from there to the domain of the Transcendental Signifier to be carried forward to the Presence of the Transcendental Signified. The transaction is complete. The Faith is sealed. The Face is hidden. Its absence *aufgehoben*, sublated.

The cycle is not complete though. The repressed momentarily returns in the promissory notation of *Revelation*. What is *Revelation*? *Revelation* is the return of the repressed in check. "And who believe in that which is revealed unto thee (Muhammad) and that which was revealed before thee" (*wa alladhina yu'minuna bi-ma unzila ilayka wa ma unzila min qablika*) reconstitutes the visible *Alphabetical* ordering of the *Revelation*, or *bi-ma unzila* ("that which comes down"), as the Sign Itself, thus self-asserts itself by assigning the authority of who is actually in charge, and the *Alphabetical* Signifier replaces the (absence of) the Sign. Though *Alphabetical*, *Revelation* is now the "Sign," only analytically and postscripturally in quotation marks. And it is through *Revelation*—the *Alphabetically* manufactured "Sign"—that the Faithful, in the full absence of the Face, "are certain of the Hereafter" (*wa bi al-'akhirati hum yuqinun*). *Revelation* is thus in effect Concealment, a cover-up, of a Face that cannot be seen and the fact that it is Unseen because It is Invisible. *Revelation* promises to cover up the Face of a Faceless Unseen by Speaking on its behalf: Sound for Sight, Voice for Vision, an Ear for an Eye. *Revelation* promises an unmasking by delivering a *Re-Citation*, the Qur'an. It promises the vision by delivering the voice. *Revelation speaks* on behalf of an Invisible Face by reassuring that It is covering up a Face. *Revelation* pulls the screen of speech down over a Face that is not there. *Revelation* is a sound barrier shielding a nonexistent Face: a Sonic simulacrum of the Sign. *Revelation* is the Faith in the Unseen as *Revelation*. That is the monumental achievement of the Written, of the Book, all in the absence of the Face.

The Qur'an *conceals* what it cannot show, what cannot be seen, and in broad daylight calls the unshowable the *Unseen*, and yet it calls that act of concealment *Revelation*.

In *Revelation*, the return of the repressed is repressed.

Thus at the very commencement of the Faith we move from the absence of the Sign of the Face to the presence of the Name of the Unseen, toward the Sacred site of the Signature—the articulation of the Signifier "In the Name"—and we begin: "In the Name of Allah, the Beneficent, the Merciful." The Qur'an begins with a *fait accompli*, "In the Name," then moves to deliver. In that act of delivery dwells the inhibition of Seeing, because the Sign is absent, and the Name, as Signifier, has replaced it. Since the Qur'anic Unseen, on Whom the entire Sacred certitude is predicated, cannot be seen, the whole act of seeing is deprecated. But since the most markedly identifiable site of seeing is the Face, the very act of Faith is predicated on the constitutional impossibility of seeing, or showing, the Face of the Unseen. We cannot *show* because It, the Unseen, cannot be *seen*. We are not allowed to *see* because the Unseen cannot be *shown*. From the surface (sur-Face) site of the Absent Face we are then hermeneutically diverted toward the *meaning* of the Names. The conclusion is foregone: since the Face of the Unseen cannot be seen, no figural representation is possible precisely because no Face can be represented. Since we cannot see the Unseen, the seeing of no Face is permitted. The very act of *seeing* is suspect because every time we see a face we are reminded of *the* Face that cannot be seen. In order to forget that the Unseen, the promissory *Citation* of the *Re-Citation*, cannot ever be seen, we are not to be reminded of seeing.

Qur'anic *Re-Citation* is one massive act of hermeneutically pregnant amnesia.

The amnesia is made possible not by political *imposition* but by biological *implication*. We are *implicated* in a collective act of amnesia because the absence of the Face of the Unseen is *replicated* in our own inability to see our own Faces—mirrors notwithstanding.[8] The thing in the mirror is not the Face. It is always-already a Signifier, mutated by the *identity* of the person we recognize, and never the sign we behold. Because *we* cannot *see* our own Faces, we are *implicated* in the violent mutation of the meaningless Sign into the meaningful Signifier. We quell the anxiety of not being able to *see* our own Faces as Sign by aiding and abetting the colossal mutation of all Signs into Signifiers—in "believing in the Unseen."

The result is simple: In the absence of the Face of the Unseen, the Sign is collapsed, significantly mutated, into the Signifier, so that the Signifier can point to the Signified, and the whole gambit can implicate a Transcendental Signified that can in turn hold the whole game together. And that is the origin of the Qur'anic, and with that the Islamic, hermeneutics. The Islamic hermeneutics is categorically predicated on a constitutional mistrust of the Face value, of the sur-Face meaning, and the reverse trust in the promises of the Hidden in the Unseen, in that which is to be discovered, unveiled. That is the origin of the very idea of hermeneutics—extracting the Hidden meaning: the Signifier pointing to so many potentially Hidden Signifieds that it successfully represses its own permutation of the Sign, of having itself been significantly mutated from a Face Unseen, a Sign stolen. The hermeneutic wild-goose chase successfully conceals the verbal mutation of the word *goose* from the fat (unnameable) bird itself.

The Qur'anic, Re-Cited, Transcendental Signified is soon wedded to a borrowed Aristotelian metaphysics and results in an Islamic theo-ontology that represses and sublimates the Semiotics of the absented Sign into a Metaphysics of the implicated Transcendental Signified and calls it the *Wajib al-Wujud*, the Necessary Being, the hermeneutic *condito sine qua non* of Islamic theo-ontology. In other words, because Face as the site of Identity is denied the sight of the Unseen (since the Unseen cannot be seen), the Face is juridically forbidden and hermeneutically mistrusted. Because the Face is the singular site of recognition, identification, distinction, and acknowledgment of existence, the hermeneutic apparatus that is built to conceal the absence of the Face always-already begins from behind the Face, under the skin, going in the opposite direction of the sur-Face. Because the Face is forbidden, what we see on the sur-Face of the text is considered flawed, diminished, and spasmodic. In a hermeneutics that is predicated on the assumption of a *Revelation*, Face—as the site of vision and yet the Sight Unseen—is de-Faced. Because the Faithful cannot see the Face, the sur-Face is condemned and its opposite, Depth, is celebrated. Celebration of Depth is the occasion of the hermeneutics of *Revelation*. The hermeneutics of *Revelation* is the Qur'anic condition of celebrating the Hidden, the Deep, the Veiled, the Concealed. The active, inevitable glorification of Depth is predicated on the narrative postponement of the evidence of the sur-Face for the promise of the Depth, delegating the authority of the sur-Face to the principality of the Hidden. The Qur'an, in its *Revelatory* language, is thus a hermeneutics of postponement—from the evidence of the sur-Face to the promise of the Depth, from the Sign to the Signifier to the Invisible—and all because the Unseen cannot be seen and the Unseen is the narrative cornerstone of the whole act of *Revelation*. Because the Unseen cannot be seen, seeing is prohibited. The Qur'an *must* begin "In the Name" because it cannot begin "In the Face," and thus there is a categorical denial of the Sign, a strategic mutation of the Sign into the Signifier, an active implication of The Transcendental Signified, and a universal disposition toward a hermeneutics of postponement: from the Sign (mutated) to the Signature (sighted) to the Signifier (celebrated) to the Signified (implicated) to the Transcendental Signified (necessitated).

Due to the absence of the Face, the Qur'anic Semiology, which informs the Islamic theo-ontology, goes exactly the opposite direction of Christian Semiology in its mode of signification. In the Qur'an, there is not a physical manifestation of the Unseen in a figure like the Christ. In fact, in the Qur'anic Christology, the figure of Christ is just one prophet among many others.[9] The Qur'an is emphatic that "the likeness of Jesus with Allah is as likeness of Adam. He created him of dust, then He said unto him: Be! and he is."[10] But far more clearly stated is this passage: "O People of the Scripture! Do not exaggerate in your religion nor utter aught concerning Allah save the truth. The Messiah, Jesus son of Mary, was only a messenger of Allah, and His word which He conveyed unto Mary, and a spirit from Him. So believe in Allah and His messengers, and say not 'Three'—Cease! (it is) better for you!—Allah is only One God. Far is it removed from His Transcendent Majesty that He should have a son. He is all that is in the heavens and all that is in the earth. And Allah is sufficient as Defender."[11] This difference between the Christian and the Islamic Christology points to a major blind spot in the Christian unconscious of the European philosophy. Kevin Hart is correct in asserting that "because it regards God as a presence who, after the Fall, represents Himself and is represented by signs, Christian theology is always a study of signs. If we picture God according to His attributes—as omnipotent, omniscient and omnipresent—we are plainly imaging Him as a plenitude of presence, both ontologically and epistemologically. By dint of Adam's sin, though, God is for us an absent presence, and so any theology, whatever else it is, must also be a semiology."[12] The Qur'anic semiology, however, and obviously the theology it has engendered, emphatically denies the possibility of that physical Sign and in its categorical Monotheism sublimates Allah from any anthropomorphic affiliation into a theogeneric signification. Thus abstracted into the Unseen that is central to the Qur'anic narrative, the Facial absence of the Unseen demands an active mutation of the Sign into the Signifier of His Name. This is markedly different from the Christian theo-ontology where the Sign has *appeared* as Christ. It is precisely that *apparition* that leads Kevin Hart to remark that "[l]ike other signs, Christ is both signifier and signified, body and soul."[13] This, however, by virtue of the conversation that Hart has with a whole hermeneutic history, is over-Christianizing the world into a universal semiology. Hart has enough problems on his hands even with Christ alone: "But Christ is also unlike other signs, for here the signified—God—is perfectly expressed in the signifier. He is at once inside and outside the sign system, since Christ is God, what He signifies is signified in and of itself: He is what Derrida calls a 'transcendental signified.' Yet Christ is also a transcendental signifier. Miraculously formed, His body is uncontaminated by the very Fall which required the proliferation of signs and the distinction between presence and the sign of a presence."[14] Hart's problem as a semiotician, predicated on that of his predecessors, originates in the quintessentially Christian collapsing of the Sign and the Signifier that thus bypasses a whole generation of logocentric transmutations.

The immediate result of the hermeneutic deferral of the Sign in its Qur'anic context is that Islam, as a *Revelatory* language, is constitutionally a literal Faith, doctrinally predisposed to an excision of the Sign, wherein the absence of the Sign must be, and is, repressed with the primacy of the Signifier. For this reason, Islam must, and does, begin with a Book: "This is the Scripture (*al-Kitab*) whereof there is no doubt."[15] The Qur'an, as *Re-Citation*, swears by the pen and what it writes: "By the pen and that which they write [therewith]."[16] It commands the messenger to read in the Name of a God Whom it glorifies for having taught Man by the pen: "Read: In the name of thy Lord Who createth, Createth man from a clot. Read: And thy Lord is the Most Bounteous, Who teacheth by the pen."[17] The Qur'an must deprecate the Face, in the Name of the Faith, and opt for a literary move, precisely because in its literariness it represses and overcompensates for the absence of the Sign and its mutation into the primacy of the Signifier that lies at the center of its *Revelatory* language, at the gravitational commencement of its cosmogony, for which it cannot produce a visible testimony. The greatest achievement of Islamic hermeneutics, from its rational jurisprudence to its speculative theology to its polyvocal philosophical disposition, emerges from this self-conscious moment of its visual contingency on a postponed promise: the presence of an absence.

In reading these Qur'anic passages, we must make a fundamental distinction between the Sign and the Signifier. Identification of the *Sign* with the visible, the meaningless, and the Face, and conversely the *Signifier* with the Name and thus the meaningful and the Unseen, is precisely to underline the active mutation of the Sign into the Signifier as the first step away from a semiotics of sensibilities toward a hermeneutics—or metaphysics, as Jacques Derrida calls it—of positive presences. In the Qur'an, we see clearly the absence of the Sign and the mutation of that absence into the presence of the Signifier. Kevin Hart's application of Derrida's reading of the Sign categorically collapses the Sign and the Signifier into one. This is due to the immediately Christian nature of Hart's semiology, which is rooted in Derrida's (and before him Husserl's and Hegel's) equally Christian conceptions of the Sign (Derrida and Husserl's ancestral faith notwithstanding). Predicated on a Christian conception of the Fall, Hart correctly maintains that "[f] rom God's presence we pass to His absence; from immediacy to mediation; *from the perfect congruence of sign and referent* to the gap between word and object."[18] In the Qur'anic version the process is precisely the opposite. Although the Edenic account in the Qur'an is equally Biblical, the articulation of the Name of the Signifier, in such a way as to implicate a Transcendental Signified, begins with the Absence of the Face of the Unseen and works its way toward the Presence of the Name of the Unseen. It is true, as Derrida has noted, that "logocentricism and the metaphysics of presence . . . [is] the exigent, powerful, systematic, and irrepressible desire for such a [transcendental] signified."[19] But the assertion that "[f]rom the moment that there is meaning there are nothing but signs" or that "[w]e *think only in signs*" in effect de-Faces the Sign of "the absoluteness of its right" by categorically collapsing it into a fully functional Signifier.[20] The Sign, contrary to the over-Christianized Hegelian-Husserlian premise on which Derrida builds his deconstructive move, does not signify. It signates, or signals, or does anything but signify. Only Signifiers, already in the domain of the metaphysics of presence, signify—not Signs, which are ipso facto insignificant and meaningless.

The implications of the Islamic hermeneutic concealment of the Face in the realm of aesthetics are quite evident. Painting is forbidden because every time we see something (on its sur-Face) we are reminded that the Re-Cited Unseen cannot be seen, that the Unseen is constitutionally denied visibility and thus the ultimate testimonial of Existence. Visuality is denied the Unseen: The Re-Cited can force or feign forgetting but can never forget it. In the Islamic aesthetics, then, it is not so much the *painting* that is prohibited as *seeing* that is veiled and the *seen* that is preempted. The *seen* points to the sur-Face and the sur-Face to the Face, and because we cannot see the Face of the Unseen, the defining occasion of the Re-Cited as *Revelation*, we should not then look at any Face, because the mere visibility of every face reminds us of the absence of the One Face—the First and Final Face of the Unseen, the only Face that will not perish—that we cannot see. Every Face is reminiscent of what the Re-Cited must forget. And we, Face-less to ourselves, are complicit.

The story of Qur'anic *Revelation* as *Re-Citation*, predicated on the Biblical that it assumes and resumes, is one elaborate account of a *movement* from the Semiotics of the evident sur-Face to the hermeneutics of the promised Hidden, from the aesthetics of the Seen to the metaphysics of the Unseen.

The Unseen Cannot Be Seen

The Return of the Repressed—repressed.

Because the Unseen cannot be seen, it has a particular penchant for being seen: "Unto Allah belong the East and the West, and whithersoever ye turn, there is Allah's Countenance. Lo! Allah is All-Embracing, All-Knowing."[21] "[A]nd whithersoever ye turn, there is Allah's Countenance" (*fa-aynama Tuvallu fa-thamma wajhu Allah*) places the Face (*Wajh*) of the Unseen on everything, East and West, the geographical expansion of being, and this by way of de-Facing everything by sur-Facing the Unseen on everything. The Face of the Unseen de-Faces everything in order to see and show itself on the sur-Face of everything. Now that we cannot see the Unseen, the Unseen proclaims Itself as visible everywhere by de-Facing everything. But even this "seeing" of the Face of the Unseen is not an always-already *fait accompli*. It cannot be seen *ex nihilio*: "And whatsoever good thing ye spend, it is for yourself, when ye spend not save in search of Allah's Countenance."[22] And there is the rub, where the Face of things actually seen is effectively de-Signed back and away from the Named and onto the presumption of a Sign, a pseudo-Sign. The emerging Sign Language is circular, no longer unidirectional from the Sign to the Signifier and on to the Transcendental Signified. If everywhere we turn and everything we do is to see the Face of the Unseen, then the knowability of the named Signifieds—door, river, pencil, justice—is reverted back to the unnameable Sign, the pseudo-Sign, concealing the fact that the Unseen can really not be seen by arguing that everything we do see is Its Face. When the Face of things actually seen is effectively de-Signed, a pseudo-Sign is generated that now in turn lends legitimacy to the implicated Transcendental Signified that the originary mutation of the visible Sign into the Signifier had occasioned. The *Re-Citation* thus comes at the Sign from two directions: once by mutating it into a Signifier on the Site of the Sacred Signature and again by sur-Facing the Transcendental Signified that this signature generates on the sur-Face of all Signs, de-Signing them, and thus attributing the status of a Sign (a pseudo-Sign) to the Transcendental Signified. The actual Sign, the Face of the pagan idol observed, is metaphysically cornered.

The effect of this double negation, intended to result in a positive positing of a Face for the Unseen, is an extraordinarily self-conscious anxiety on part of the Re-Cited narrative. The supreme anxiety of the Faith in the Unseen, in the absence of Its Face, returns persistently throughout the Qur'an, most vividly in 28:88: "And cry not unto any other god along with Allah. There is no God save Him. Everything will perish save His Countenance. His is the command, and unto Him ye will be brought back."[23] "Everything will perish save His Countenance" (*kullu shay'in halikun illa wajhahu*) notes the promise of that which the Unseen exactly lacks—namely, a Face, a site of recognition, or a sight of identity—by not only attributing a Face to It but in fact identifying Its Face as the only thing that survives. This is an overcompensation for a pseudo-Sign that knows that It is not there.

It is this anxiety, the anxiety of Its Face not being visible, of not being there, that informs the Qur'anic reversal of "Everything will perish save His Countenance" (*kullu shay'in halikun illa wajhahu*). The greatest source of anxiety for the *Revelatory* language of the Faith, as for all other inaugurating moments of believing in the Unseen and replacing the Site of the Signature for the Sight of the Sign, is precisely this Presence of the Absence at the Center of its gravity. The Metaphysics of Presence is an architectonic replacement for a Visual Absence. Everything in the text is predicated on this central moment of an Absence (*ghaybah*) and thus the necessity of faith in the Absent, in the Unseen, and in effect in the unseeable. Architecturally, this Presence of the Absence, the effacement of the Face, is immediately identifiable by the void, the emptied space, that defines the center of *Islamic* sites from public squares to mosques. There is never an object that locates and defines the center of a public square or a mosque. The site is always defined by the surrounding walls that embrace an emptiness, tangential references that point to the Presence of an Absence, and yet thus locate and sanctify that absence. The *presence* of a pool at the center of the court, in a mosque or even a square, makes it impossible for anything even to *cross* the Absence of that Presence, let alone *stand* there.[24]

Believing in the Unseen, the cornerstone of Re-Citing the Qur'anic Truth, thus replaces the Site of the Sacred Signature for the Sight of the Visible Sign. The Metaphysics of Presence that results is there to conceal (but cannot but nervously reveal) the Visual Absence of any Sign at the center of one of the most fateful acts of Signification in written history.

In Re-Citing the Facial Absence, the overcompensation of the Qur'an for the persistent Presence of the Absence at the center of its narrative claims on a Metaphysics of Presence, an attempted retrieval of the Sign of the Face only to repress it even further, finds one of its most creative moments in the chapter on Joseph. This chapter is one of those few occasions in which the Qur'an begins with the staccatos of literal letters with no apparent meaning, at once announcing them as Signs and yet proclaiming them as entrants into the realm of the Sacred Signature, Signifiers about to happen: "Alif. Lam. Ra. These are verses of the Scripture that maketh plain."[25] Here the inarticulate Signifiers-to-be standing for Signs are emphatically proclaimed as "the verses of the Scripture that maketh plain." The strategic move of Sign-as-Signifier becomes even more specific in the next verse: "Lo! We have revealed it, a Lecture in Arabic, that ye may understand."[26] The "Lecture" (*Qur'an*) is actually the word with which the Text in its entirety is identified. The semi-Signs, "Alif. Lam. Ra," are here delivered as potential Signifiers in the specific domain of Arabic as a Sign Language, so that Muhammad—as the recipient of the *Revelation* and thus as human Signatory—and his audience may comprehend the message. The rhetorical implication is that had it not been for this practical purpose, the Sign and with it the Sacred Signature of the Face would have been possible and possibly visible. The stage is thus set for the Sign to mutate into Signifier. God the Unseen, the Qur'anic Narrator, thus addresses His chosen messenger and announces that He is about to tell a story by way of an admonition: "We narrate unto thee (Muhammad) the best of narratives in that We have inspired in thee this Qur'an, though aforetime thou wast of the heedless."[27] The "heedless" (*ghafiliyn*) are the generic doubters who irresistibly pull the upward mobility of the Signifier toward the Transcendental Signified back to the mutated Sign, always promised, never delivered.

The Qur'an is extraordinarily conscious of the presence of the absence of the Sign and equally aware of its deliberate moves away from the Sign and toward the Signifier, gestures that hold its narrative claims together. Because the "heedless" among the Qur'anic addressees always insist on the Sign, retarding the move toward the Signifier, the Unseen calls them blind and insists even more emphatically that He, the Unseen, has caused their blindness: "Hast thou seen him who maketh his desire his god, and Allah sendeth him astray purposely, and sealeth up his hearing and his heart, and setteth on his sight a covering? Then who will lead him after Allah (hath condemned him)? Will ye not then heed?"[28] We have from the Qur'an itself an account of what it is exactly that the "heedless" say and object: "And they say; There is naught but our life of the world; we die and we live, and naught destroyeth us save time, when they have no knowledge whatsoever of (all) that; they do but guess."[29]

The story that the Qur'an is about to tell is there to reclaim and de-Face, once and for all, the necessity of that Sign by subjecting it to a superior "Sign," the "Sign" in quotation marks, the one that one sees in dream with eyes wide shut, as it were. The story of Joseph begins with a dream. Joseph informs his father Jacob that he has just had a dream in which he has seen, with his eyes wide shut, 11 planets and the sun and the moon prostrating themselves to him. Jacob warns Joseph against informing his brothers of this dream lest they harm him. Joseph is thus singled out for the singularity of his vision. Not only are his wicked brothers incapable of "seeing" like Joseph does, with his eyes wide shut, but so is his father. The seeing is delegated to the realm of the dream and thus made more authoritative, then symbolized and made even more pregnant with possibilities of interpretation. Jacob's warning is in effect there to underline the significance of the dream, and of seeing while the eyes are closed, as a Sign of divine preference. Joseph sees with his eyes closed what others cannot see with their eyes open.

Jacob confirms for Joseph the significance of the dream, of seeing things with eyes wide shut, as an indication of God having chosen Joseph to be taught the interpretations of events as a Sign of perfecting His grace upon him. The narration is specifically ocularcentric, the Qur'an persisting on the centrality of the Sign that it is now retrieving cautiously in Joseph's dream. The Sign is pregnant to the point that the Qur'an delegates it to its own interpretative retrieval and spells it out right here in the middle of Joseph's telling his father of his dream: "Verily in Joseph and his brethren are signs (of Allah's Sovereignty) for the inquiring."[30] Joseph as Sign and Seer is the Qur'an's dream of Itself, the carefully crafted return of its repressed. Joseph is the return of the Qur'anic repressed precisely as the Sign of its most anxiety-provoking absence—namely, the absence of the Face of the Unseen, the site of Its recognition, and the Signature of Its not being there. The Unseen is not seen by our eyes, and the Unseen returns precisely as a mockery of our eyes, their inability to see when they are wide open, and thus the return of the Qur'anic repressed, Joseph, seeing with his eyes wide shut.

As the return of the Qur'anic repressed, Joseph is *signaled* out not only by his extraordinarily perceptive eyes and by God having selected him but also by his having been endowed with the power to interpret the dreams that he sees. "Thus thy Lord will prefer thee and will teach thee the interpretation of events, and will perfect His grace upon thee and upon the family of Jacob as He perfected it upon thy forefather, Abraham and Isaac. Lo! thy Lord is Knower, Wise."[31] *Interpretation* is to deliver the Sign into the realm of the Signifier, through the site of the *Revelatory* Signature, and let it loose to mean. Interpretation (the Qur'anic *ta'wil*) is the architectonic edifice of hermeneutically burying the repression of the absence of the Sign in the Qur'anic memory. Joseph is *signaled* out, retrieved from Qur'anic memory, as the return of the Qur'anic repressed by being identified as a dream interpreter, both seeing the Sign and delivering it into the realm of Signifier, the mutation and the mutant at the same time. Joseph is even more poignantly the designated Sign of the absent Face by the Qur'an being emphatic about his story being the very Sign (*ayatun*) for "the inquiring" (*li-l-sa'iliyn*).

The perilous anxiety of narrative exposure of the actively repressed is immediately evident in the *danger* to which Joseph, as the momentary and strategically conditioned retrieval of the Sign, is exposed. Joseph's jealous brothers at once begin to conspire against him. This is the *peril* to which the Qur'anic memory exposes itself by retrieving its carefully repressed. One brother suggests killing him, while the other proposes to throw him into the depth of a pit. Throw him into the depth of a pit they do, and then they come weeping to their father, saying, "O our father! We went racing one with another, and left Joseph by our things, and the wolf devoured him, and thou believest not our saying when we speak the truth."[32]

Joseph's brothers blame the wolf and produce his bloodstained shirt as evidence. Jacob has no choice but patience. Meanwhile Joseph is discovered by a water-drawer from a caravan on its way to Egypt and rescued from his subterranean dungeon. Joseph is sold very cheaply into slavery in Egypt. His owner, the Prince of Egypt, entrusts him to his wife Zoleikha and asks her to treat him honorably so that perhaps they can adopt him as a son. The Qur'anic narrative is very emphatic here as to the particularly evil way in which Joseph is treated. He is cast into a pit by his brothers out of jealousy and malevolence. He is rescued by the Divine Will, but he is sold very cheaply into slavery out of ignorance of who he really is. But the Qur'an is equally emphatic as to what God has in store for Joseph. God speaks in the first person, in the Majestic We Narrative: "Thus we established Joseph in the land that We might teach him the interpretation of events. And Allah was predominant in His career, but most of mankind know not."[33] The repressed returns but under the full control and protective custody of the Unseen, the Narrator. It is precisely from the Unseen that Joseph will learn the "interpretation of events" (*ta'wil al-ahadith*) through which he will deliver the realm of the suppressed and absent Sign to that of the promised Signification. This transmission is under the direct "teaching" of the Unseen, the Narrator: "And when he reached his prime We gave him wisdom and knowledge. Thus We reward the good."[34]

What is about to happen to Joseph is the narrative plot to retrieve the Qur'anic repression of the Sign, which began with Joseph's eyes (vision) and now extends into his entire Face (beauty).[35] Zoleikha, the wife of Joseph's master, falls madly in love with Joseph and asks "of him an evil act. She bolted the doors and said: Come!"[36] Joseph refuses. But "[s]he verily desired him, and he would have desired her if it had not been that he saw the argument of his Lord."[37] The ocularcentricism of the Qur'anic language is unmistakable here. That Joseph "saw the argument of his Lord" (*ra'a burhana rabbahu*) reveals the fortification of an organic, but exposed, link between the Sign ("saw") and the Signification ("the argument") so categorically repressed in the Qur'anic Narrative and yet here anxiously signaled in the assertion that "Lo! he was of Our chosen slaves."[38]

Joseph is chased around the house by the enraptured woman until they are suddenly confronted at the door by her husband. She immediately accuses Joseph of having attacked her intending to rape her and demands that he be properly punished. Joseph retorts back that it was she who was attacking him, while one of the witnesses proposes to the angry husband that if Joseph's shirt is torn from behind then it was she who was attacking him and if his shirt is torn from the front then it was he who was attacking her. Al-Razi has a crucial commentary here as to who the witness to this event was. He reports on the authority of some earlier commentators that when the Egyptian prince asks Joseph if he has any witnesses he says that an infant in the cradle witnessed the whole event and that the infant would testify on his behalf: "The Prince asked how could an infant in the cradle be a witness. He (Joseph) said, 'The infant would testify on my behalf.' They approached the infant's cradle. Joseph, Peace be Upon Him, said, 'You infant tell us what you saw.' By God's command the infant began to talk and spoke in complete sentences."[39] The report is in perfect harmony with the Qur'an's exposing Joseph as the pre-Significatory Sign, now placing the very Sight of a preverbal infant as the proof of his innocence. The Egyptian prince sees that Joseph's shirt is torn from behind and admonishes his wife: "Lo! the guile of you is very great."[40] The harassment of Joseph, as the Sign exposed, here reaches its culmination. Joseph is persecuted not only because of his vision and his ability to interpret—from Sign to Signifier—but because of the beauty of his Face, the Sign manifest, which becomes even more evident in the next turn of events.

The news of the wife of the Egyptian prince and her slave boy spreads throughout the city. "And women in the city said: The ruler's wife is asking of her slave-boy an ill-deed. Indeed he has smitten her to the heart with love. We behold her in plain aberration."[41] What the wife of the Egyptian prince does in response to this damaging gossip is quite extraordinary: "And when she heard of their sly talk, she sent to them and prepared for them a cushioned couch (to lie on at the feast) and gave to every one of them a knife and said (to Joseph): come out unto them! And when they saw him they exalted him and cut their hands, exclaiming: Allah Blameless! This is not a human being. This is no other than some gracious angel."[42]

This is a crucial moment in the history of the Qur'anic repressed. Joseph, as the returned repressed, is the Face manifest. He is the visual exhibition of the Truth that the Qur'anic narrative must ipso facto verbalize (devisualize and deface) in order to claim. In perhaps the most critical (and the most dangerous) moment of its self-exposure, the Qur'an in effect discloses its self-negational anxiety by putting a Face to its repressed absence of the Sign. If the Qur'an in its entirety is the active and aggressive mutation of the absence of the Sign into the presence of the Signifier (and thus the Signatory Site of its Metaphysics of Presence predicated on a debilitating Absence) so that in its pointing, inevitably, to a Signified it can implicate a Transcendental Signified as a simulacrum of the Sign, Joseph, then, is the sublimation of that simulacrum to a foster-Sign. The narrative is extraordinarily and rather dangerously sensual and erotic. There are accounts of how some medieval radical Islamic heterodox factions, such as the Maymuniyya among the Kharijites, refused to include the chapter on Joseph in their version of the Qur'an and considered it blasphemous.[43] Medieval Qur'anic commentaries are exceptionally explicit in their specific articulation of the sexual innuendoes of the text. The phrase "And when they saw him they exalted him" in 12:31, for example, is read by al-Razi, on authority of the very father of Qur'anic commentators Ibn 'Abbas, as meaning the women having instantaneous "menstruation" (*hayd*), or perhaps more accurately *orgasm*, when they see Joseph.[44] The account of menstruation may still be true. In the commentary of Abu al-Fadl Rashid al-Dîn al-Maybudi, *Kashf al-Asrar wa 'Uddat al-'Abrar* (composed in 520/1126), there is a report that among the Egyptian women there was one preadolescent girl who suddenly had her first menstruation when she saw Joseph. She prayed to God Almighty and pleaded with Him to save her from embarrassment. It was at this moment that God made all women simultaneously menstruate and cut their hands so that their blood would mix and prevent that young girl's embarrassment.[45] The anxiety of the Maymuniyya, however, reveals something far more serious than the strong sexual connotations of the chapter. In this chapter much more than a woman's sexual prowess is at stake. "And when they saw him they exalted him and cut their hands" is precisely the point where the *anxiety* of the Qur'anic Unseen in *not* having a Face becomes the *danger* of if we were to see the Face.[46] "[E]xclaiming: Allah Blameless! This is not a human being. This is no other than some gracious angel" is the closest that the Qur'an can possibly come in approximating Joseph's beautiful face to the repressed absence of the Face of the Unseen—*the unauthored Author of the Text that is authoring itself.*

Notice the difference between this Qur'anic repression of the Sign because of the invisibility of the Face of the Unseen, returning as repression in the

Face of Joseph, and the view rooted in Christian Christology and the Face of the Christ as Sign that prompts Kevin Hart to suggest that

> A discourse is metaphysical, then, if the concept is fashioned as a moment of pure presence, *and the sign as representing the concept in its absence.* Within these terms, *the sign fails to represent the concept purely and simply;* it introduces the complicating elements of materiality and difference which *serve to delay and defer the expected recovery of the concept.* This, accordingly, is the basis of the case for valuing the concept over the sign. However, argues Derrida, *the sign's failure is structurally determined,* and this is the starting-point for his case against the metaphysics of presence.[47]

It is illogical first to establish a mission for the Sign to Signify, an assignment to which no Sign has ever a claim, and then blame it for not delivering a promise it has never made. Hart's semiotic confusion is rooted in his Christian Christology. He falsely extends the constitution of the Face of Jesus Christ, as *Re-Presenting* God, from Christian Christology to poststructuralist philosophy. The misappropriation is a bad form of faith; it secularizes into philosophy the Christian punishment of the (non)believers for having failed to read Christ as the Sign/Son of God. Hart's problem is rooted in Derrida's. Not just Derrida but Husserl himself harbors a theory of the Sign entirely Christological in its hidden assumptions. The distinction that Husserl made between two kinds of Signs, the "Expressive" and the "Indicative," is at the root of Derrida's reading of the Sign:[48] "By definition there can be no sign without signification, no signifying without the signified."[49] The first part of this sentence is completely and exclusively Christian, the second part universal. Signs universally *signate*, which is to say they exude the surfacy signness of their being signs. They signify absolutely nothing. Signs never signify. Signifiers signify. Signs are forced—politically, culturally, metaphysically—to *mutate* into Signifiers, sensibilities into intelligibilities, before they can correspond to a signified and thus signify. The initial Husserlian division of the Sign into the "expressive" and the "indicative" is itself a fallacy entirely rooted in the Christological confusion of the Sign, doctrinally mandated to attribute to the Face of Christ a *meaning* that non-Christian philosophers have no grounds to assume and every reason to doubt. There is a Christian unconscious to the European philosophy for which even its Jewish practitioners, from Husserl to Derrida, have a blind spot, busy as they have been being too European to mind their Hebraic disposition.

Having proved her point to the gossiping Egyptian women, Zoleikha conspires to condemn and incarcerate Joseph. Joseph seeks refuge from the wiles of Zoleikha in prison and prefers to be incarcerated rather than subjected to such trials. According to the Qur'an, the revelation of Joseph's Face immediately results in the recognition, "after they had seen the signs," "to imprison him for a time."[50] The logical inconsistency that we read here, that Joseph is imprisoned though proven innocent, is overcompensated by the semiotic necessity of Joseph being imprisoned after the revelation of the beauty of his

Face results in the bloodbath of women slicing themselves, enraptured by the beauty of his Face.

In prison, Joseph becomes famous for his ability to interpret the dreams of his cellmates. While interpreting their dreams, Joseph uses the occasion to proselytize for the One True Religion of the Solitary God, admonishing against polytheism. Among Joseph's monotheistic admonitions is the curious insistence that "[t]hose whom ye worship beside Him are but names which ye have named, ye and your fathers. Allah hath revealed no sanction of them."[51] The narrative claim of the Qur'an at this point is of course that by and in Joseph's face, Allah has in effect revealed His hitherto Unseen Face, and thus He is now in a position to denounce all other deities as merely "names which ye have named, ye and your fathers." The return of the repressed is here used to full advantage by declassifying faith in Allah as yet another faith in a Name and rather classifying it as a Faith in a Face—namely, the supreme repression of the Qur'anic narrative anchorage. In Joseph's Face, the Faith in Allah is no longer a Faith in just a Name. It is a Faith in a Face. Al-Razi's commentary here is crucial:

> "O my two fellow-prisoners!" O my two friends in jail, "Are diverse lords better," are scattered gods better or God the Almighty. He told them so because they had idols in the prison which they worshipped and to which they prostrated. The reason he called them "diverse" is that they came in all shapes and forms, big, small, and medium, made of various things . . . "These, as they are, are helpless and impotent, while God Almighty is but One, without any match, rival, similitude, or equal. He is Omnipotent and Almighty, and can do whatever He wants." Then he admonished them for their practices and told them of the corruption of their belief, telling them that "if you think hard you are not praying to anything but names that you and your ancestors have given them, which is to say, you call these idols god, while a god is that which deserves obedience. But before a god practices magnanimity he would not deserve worshipping, and if he were not omnipotent he would not be able to grant such magnanimity, nor would he be able to do so, and unless he be alive he could do none of these things. These are all inanimate objects. Calling them gods is not but a meaningless name. The reason is that the name is not the named. Because if the name were the named, then by virtue of calling them god they would be god and it would be proper to worship them, and they would have been god by attributes, and yet that is impossible."[52]

Joseph sees and interprets his way out of prison. Two of his cellmates have a dream and come to him and ask for his interpretation. He interprets their dreams and predicts that one of them will soon be executed while the other released. Then he asks the one who is soon to be released to mention him to the Prince of Egypt. The man is released, but Satan makes him forget to mention Joseph to his master, so Joseph continues to be incarcerated for some time longer—the "Sign" concealed. Finally, the Prince of Egypt has a dream that no one can interpret. The former cellmate of Joseph's finally remembers him and goes to his cell and asks him for the interpretation of the dream that the prince has seen. Joseph informs him of the seven years of agricultural prosperity to ensue before a seven-year cycle of draught and famine. Joseph proceeds to instruct the man of the proper measures that should be taken against the calamitous seven years. The Prince of Egypt asks for the interpreter of his dream to be summoned to the court. Joseph refuses and insists to clear his good name first. He sends a message to the prince asking him to summon the women who had cut their hands when seeing him in public and ask them the circumstances of their predicament. The prince does as Joseph demands and is informed by the women in general and by Zoleikha in particular that Joseph is completely innocent and that he has been wronged by their guile.

Joseph returns to the Prince of Egypt, completely exonerated and restored in the dignity of his name, and assumes a high position of respect and authority. Joseph asks the prince to put him in charge of storehouses, and he assumes complete responsibility for managing the famine crisis that faces the Egyptians. As the hardship of the famine begins to assert itself, people from around the kingdom and its vicinity flock to Egypt in search of sustenance, among them Joseph's brothers who do not know that the man in charge of the Prince of Egypt's storehouses is none other than their own kid brother whom they had cast into a well. Joseph denies them any provisions until they go back and bring a young brother of his they had left behind. The Qur'an does not name this other brother, but medieval Qur'anic commentaries identify him as Benjamin, Joseph's brother from the same mother.[53] Joseph's brothers return to Kanaan and convince Jacob to let them take Benjamin to Egypt. Jacob reluctantly concedes. Joseph's 11 brothers go back to Egypt in the hope of getting more provisions. Joseph pulls a trick on his brothers: he reveals his identity to his full brother, surreptitiously hides a measuring cup in Benjamin's bag, then publicly announces it stolen as a ploy to keep his brother in Egypt. The other brothers are forced to go back to Kanaan and give the sad news to their father. Their father, distressed, puts his trust in God and sends them back to Egypt, where Joseph reveals his identity to them and gives them his shirt to take to his father and put on his eyes so that his sight is returned. They do as told. Jacob, his wife, and his children come to Egypt and prostrate to Joseph, at which point Joseph tells his father that this was the fulfillment of his dream, when 11 stars and the sun and the moon were prostrating to him.

The originary position of Joseph as Sign giving birth to a sustained generation of Signifiers is perhaps nowhere presented as succinctly and pointedly as in his conversation with his brother Benjamin, as reported by al-Razi. Benjamin grows up in Joseph's complete absence and as Joseph's surrogate to their father Jacob. While in Egypt, the following conversation takes place between Joseph and Benjamin:

Joseph: What is your name?
Benjamin: Ibn Yamin.
Joseph: What does Ibn Yamin mean?

Benjamin: The Afflicted Son.
Joseph: Why did they call you that?
Benjamin: Because when I was born my mother died [literally, *pish e khoday shod*: "went to God."]
Joseph: Who was your mother?
Benjamin: Rahil bent Layan bent Nakhur.
Joseph: Do you have any children?
Benjamin: I have ten sons.
Joseph: What are their Names?
Benjamin: One is Bal'a, one Akhira, one Ashkal, one Akhiya, one Akhbar, one Nu'man, one Awrad, one Aris, one Hay'im, and one Maythim.
Joseph: What kind of names are these?
Benjamin: I have drawn the etymology [*eshteqaq*] of these names from the conditions [*ahwal*] of my brother Joseph. Bal'a because he disappeared, "the earth swallowed him." As if the earth swallowed him. Akhira because he was the first-born child to my mother. Ashkal because he looked like me and was from the same parents as I am and was as old as I am. Akhiya because he was the best of us wherever he was. Nu'man because he was graceful and most dear to our parents. Awrad because he was like a red rose among us. Aris because he was like a leader and a master to us. Hay'im because our hope and aspiration is that he is alive. Maythim because if we were to see him again our happiness will be complete.[54]

This is a crucial conversation between Joseph and his *alter ego*, and it matches, echoes, and perfectly complements the destruction of the idols in the prison scene. In effect, while Joseph is in prison and smashing (de-Facing) the idols (Signs), his alter ego (notice that Benjamin says that Joseph and he are identical in looks, age, and parenthood) is giving birth to his namesakes, who are deriving their names from Joseph's predicament. Thus in the very act of Joseph's life there is a gradual *manifestation* of his Names as Signifiers as he relentlessly destroys (de-Faces) the evident idols, Signs.

We also need to notice the simultaneous fate of Joseph's father Jacob, as his alter ego Benjamin is in effect manifesting him in absentia. The Qur'anic *Re-Presentation* of Joseph as the "Sign," the return of its repressed under the protective custody of the Unseen so as to *Reveal* Itself ever so cautiously, is commensurate with Jacob, as the prophetic voice of his people, losing his sight. Jacob loses his sight in the absence of Joseph's Face: "and his eyes were whitened with the sorrow that he was suppressing."[55] Jacob must be blinded while Joseph *reveals* himself, because his blindness is the prelude to a new kind of (in)sight; he is blinded in order to see better, to be able to see the Sign of the Unseen, though ordinarily the Unseen cannot be seen. The blindness of Jacob is the suspension of seeing with the physical eyes so that he can begin to see with his eyes wide shut. It is in the certainty of that inner perception with eyes wide shut that Jacob can assure his other sons "despair not of the Spirit of Allah."[56] Jacob can now see with his eyes wide shut things that other people cannot see with their eyes wide open. The Sign of the Unseen, in Jacob and Joseph's dream, categorically resists mutation into a Signifier, because being mutated into a Signifier is to be seen, and the Qur'anic Unseen cannot be seen.

This resistance to mutation into Signifier points to a more universal insight about the nature of Sign. The categorical resistance of Sign to its mutation into the Signifier is equally evident when the "difference" between Sign and its Christologically based presumption of pointing to a Signified is noted. Here is the case according to Kevin Hart:

> Since it always functions in the absence of a presence, the sign has no self-presence by which its intelligible content can withstand the accidents of empirical differences. The sign always works with two modes of repetition: its task, as understood metaphysically, is to repeat its originating presence, in order that the intelligible be repeated in the sensible. But the sign, since it is a sign, is also open to being repeated, so the sensible mark can always be repeated outside its original context. Indeed, the sign cannot be what it is without this possibility of repetition. The first mode of repetition seeks to preserve the sign's intelligible content, while the second mode of repetition puts the identity of that intelligible content in jeopardy. And the problem is that the sign can never put that second mode of repetition out of play: the metaphysical task of the sign is forever stymied by the sign itself.[57]

This is a brilliant semiological moment when the Sign is putting up a stiff resistance to its Christianized metaphysicalization. The Christian in Kevin Hart thrives in the Husserlian distinction between the "Expressive" and the "Indicative" by giving two "modes" to the signal singularity of the Sign and fallaciously assigning to Sign an "intelligible content," but the pagan philosopher in him sees the plain fact that when the Sign is just "Itself" it signifies nothing and thus has no ulterior "mode" other than being a presignificatory Sign. Derrida himself perfectly recognizes the trap in which not just Husserl but Saussure has also fallen. In his 1968 interview with Julia Kristeva, he notes that "[t]here is at least one moment at which Saussure must renounce drawing all the conclusions from the critical work he has undertaken, and that is the not fortuitous moment when he resigns himself to using the word 'sign,' lacking anything better. After having justified the introduction of the words 'signified' and 'signifier,' Saussure writes: 'As for sign, if we retain it, it is because we find nothing else to replace it, everyday language suggesting no other.'"[58] It is most peculiar that Saussure expects "everyday language" to suggest something other than the word "Sign" as the verbal site of the organic link between the Signifier and the Signified. In a moment of irresistible crosshermeneutic weakness, Derrida concurs with Saussure in acknowledging this inability of "everyday language": "And, in effect, it is difficult to see how one could evacuate the *sign* when one has begun by proposing the opposition signified/signifier."[59] One need not *evacuate* the sign, if the *sign* is seen in the irreducible facticity of its signness, which is ipso facto and *always-already* empty. In *Speech and Phenomena*, too, Derrida again falls into this trap and keeps oscillating among French, German, and even English to narrow in on the possibility of the oxymoronic "meaningful signs."[60] But in *Positions* he does come clean and categorically recognizes that "'everyday language' is not innocent or neutral. It is the language of Western [he should more accurately say Christian] metaphysics, and it carries with it not only a considerable number of presuppositions of all types, but also presuppositions inseparable from metaphysics, which, although little attended to, are knotted into a system."[61] But ultimately, even Derrida cannot see the Sign as pre-Significatory. One may in fact argue that Derrida's whole deconstructive project is predicated on presuming as valid the entirely unexamined, Christian Christologically predicated, Husserlian dichotomy between the "Expressive" and the "Indicative" *functions* of Signs, thus failing to see the already mutated transition of the Sign into the Signifier by that very dichotomy, then making a federal case out of the residue of significations that the Sign *ought to* and yet "fails" to make. The reason that Christian theology is so positively elated with Derrida, especially the "negative theology," is these continued Christian Christological predicates of the Face of the Transcendental Signified being evident in the Sign/Son of God. The unabashed, violent, and categorical monotheism of the Qur'an (and the Hebrew Bible) denies that possibility, has to keep the Face of the Unseen unseen, and therefore tacitly recognize that Signs signify nothing before they are aggressively mutated into Signifiers, and thus it must begin "In the *Name* of God . . ."

Once Joseph has properly revealed himself, as the Sign of the Unseen, he restores his father's eyes, enabling him, on behalf of everyone in sight, to see the Sign: "Go with this shirt of mine," Joseph says to his brothers, "and lay it on my father's face, he will become a seer; and come to me with all your folk."[62] Prior to Jacob's gaining his (in)sight, the Qur'an is emphatic that he could not see but he could *smell* Joseph: "When the caravan departed their father had said: Truly I am conscious of the breath of Joseph, though ye call me dotard. (Those around him) said: By Allah, lo! thou art in thine old aberration."[63] Jacob is of course right and his family wrong: "Then, when the bearer of glad tidings came, he laid it on his face and he became a seer once more. He said: Said I not unto you that I know from Allah that which ye know not?"[64] The extension of Joseph's body, his shirt, restores his father's eyes before he can see him. The crucial point here is that no one actually "sees" Joseph before his father comes to Egypt, prostrates to him, and Joseph tells him the true meaning of his childhood dream. It is true that his ten brothers see him repeatedly before their father does. But they do not know that he is Joseph, so in effect they have not seen him. The only brother, a full brother, who actually sees Joseph and to whom Joseph reveals his identity, Benjamin, is really a figurative character and none other than Joseph's alter ego, Joseph himself, had the Unseen not decided to summon and turn him into Its own Sign. Benjamin had become Joseph so that Joseph could, in the depth of the darkness of the well, enter the realm of the Unseen and there become the Sign.

Lest the point be lost as to what exactly it is that the Unseen has just *revealed*, the Qur'an makes it perfectly clear: "This is of the tidings of the

Unseen which We inspire in thee (Muhammad)."[65] Having just sighted the Sign, the Unseen is now ready to move for the final act: "How many a portent is there in the heavens and the earth which they pass by with face averted. And most of them believe not in Allah except that they attribute partners (unto Him)."[66] Here we see the crucial crisis of ipseity that the vision of the Unseen ought to address. Having constituted Joseph's face as the Sign—and the Face—of the Unseen, the Unseen can now categorically state that the heavens and the earth are full of such Signs and that people simply do not see them. Having just restored Jacob's sight, the hope is that he and everyone else will now be able to see the Sign of Joseph's Face. But the complaint that "[a]nd most of them believe not in Allah except that they attribute partners (unto Him)" gives away the anxiety of the Unseen *not* to be seen on par with visible idols of the sort that Joseph smashed and ridiculed while in prison. The final testament of Faith becomes "Say: This is my Way: I call on Allah with sure knowledge, I and whosoever followeth me—Glory be to Allah!—and I am not of the idolaters."[67]

Idolatry is the insistence on the visible Sign, while Joseph's Face is the return of the Qur'anic repressed triumphant, abrogating the visible Sign for the Face of the Unseen.

A Sign Is No Signifier

Sights of the Sign: Paganism practiced.

The resistance of Sign in the Qur'an to its aggressive transmutation into the Signifier finds ample evidence in the ancient practice of Arab paganism. We still have much to learn from that resistance, given a philosophical language unconsciously Christian in its Semiology/Christology. Notice that already in Charles Sanders Peirce himself we see this confusion between the Sign and the Signifier: "A sign is an object which stands for another to some mind."[68] As an object, the Sign stands for nothing other than itself, unless and until it is violently mutated, its autonomy transgressed, and *made* into a Signifier, at which point—and only at which point—it "stands for" something else "to some mind." Thus even a particular mutation of a Sign, say a Cross, into a Signifier, say the Crucifixion of Jesus Christ the Son of God, is limited to a particular Christological doctrine. The Sign of the Cross *Itself* means nothing to a Muslim or a Hindu unless and until it has doctrinally been mutated into yet another kind of Signifier in those religious cultures. Thus Peirce's assertion that "a sign must have some real connection with the thing it signifies so that when the object is present or is so as the sign signifies it to be, the sign shall so signify it and otherwise not" suffers not only from a collapsing of the Sign into the Signifier but also from a universalization of the particular mutation of a Sign into a Signifier, a habit to which Christological Christianity is particularly wont.[69] Hegel's semiology, however, is acutely aware of the violence that the transmutation of the Sign into the Signifier involves. "The sign," Hegel proposed, "is some immediate intuition, representing *a totally different import* from what naturally belongs to it; it is the *pyramid* into which a foreign soul has been conveyed, and where it is conserved."[70] It is crucial here to note that the *soul* that the Egyptian Pharaonic culture force-migrates into the Sign of the pyramid thus turning it into a Signifier of immortality is very different from the *soul* that Hegel's own constitutionally Christian culture force-migrates into that same Sign. Derrida shrewdly notes and capitalizes on this crucial moment and asserts, "This is why the immediate intuition of the signifier [which he still confuses with the Sign] represents *an entirely other content* than that which it has for itself, entirely other than that whose full presence refers only to itself."[71] Hegel clearly sees the irreducible character of the Sign when he compares it to a Symbol: "Therefore it is a different thing when a sign is to be a *symbol.* The lion, for example, is taken as a symbol of magnanimity, the fox for cunning, the circle for eternity, the triangle for Trinity."[72] Symbolization of the Sign is just one particular case of a more universal violence perpetrated on the Sign by forcing it to become a Signifier and point to a Signified and thus, ipso facto, necessitate a Transcendental Signified that holds the whole game together. In and of themselves, lions, foxes, and circles *mean* nothing. They are just visual sights: Signs.

The Qur'anic narrative is manifestly conscious of this threat to its metaphysics. If Joseph is the return of the Qur'anic repressed triumphant, signs of resistance to that triumph are abundant through the Qur'an itself. As the Qur'an suppresses the Sign, transmutes it into the Signifier of the Name, and finally reappropriates it as the simulacrum of the pseudo-Sign of Joseph's Face, the visible Signs—the Signs of the evident, drawn, and sculpted—are making stiff resistances. Like his great ancestor Abraham, Joseph is an idol smasher: a destroyer of Signs, the Facial agency of the Signifier. There is a scene in which Zoleikha is seducing Joseph when the Qur'anic commentators tells us that "Zoleikha gets up and puts a veil on the head of the idol [that was in her private chambers]. Joseph asked: 'What is this you just did?' She said: 'I am ashamed of the idol. It was looking at us.' Joseph said: 'You are ashamed of an idol who cannot hear or see and yet I am not to be ashamed from He who created everything and knows everything, hears and sees and can benefit and damage everything?'"[73] This is an extraordinary instance because the face of the idol is covered exactly at the moment when Joseph's Face is revealed in Zoleikha's description of his beauty.[74] We have a repetition of this situation in the prison where Joseph admonishes his cellmates for practicing idolatry and smashes their idols.[75] In the end, Zoleikha destroys the idols she worships, becomes a true Muslim, and after the death of her husband marries Joseph, worshipping the God that Joseph's Face *Re-Presents* instead. All this points to the principal nemesis of Joseph's Sign: the Signs of the idols, the visible, evident Signs. Signs of resistance to their transmutations into Signifiers, so that a whole culture of sacred signification (now code-named *Islam*) is made possible, are evident throughout the Qur'an itself. The Qur'anic admonition "And most of them believe not in Allah except that they attribute partners (unto Him)"[76] already points to the pagan practice of worshipping the deity *allah* not as a Supreme Qur'anic Unseen but as what historians of pre-Islamic Arabia call a "high god" among many others.[77] The Qur'anic transmutation of the evident Sign into the Unseen Signifier is immediately rooted in the transition of Arabia from a practicing pagan community into a monotheistic *ummah*. The Qur'anic narrative is categorically directed against the insurrection of the pagan Signs resisting their upward mobility toward signifying something metaphysical and beyond themselves.

The term *shirk* (to constitute companions for God) and *mushrik* (those who do so) are the most loathsome in the Qur'anic self-assertion. Constituting companions for *allah* begins by acknowledging his superiority *but* then leveling him with other pagan deities or, more accurately, pulling His transmutation into a Transcendental Signified down and back to the originary pagan Sign visible in the Face of its evidence. Here is a critical passage:

> And if thou wert to ask them: Who created the heavens and the earth, and constrained the sun and the moon (to their appointed work)? they would say: Allah . . . And if thou wert to ask them: Who causeth water to come down from the sky, and therewith reviveth the earth after its death? they verily would say: Allah . . . And when they mount upon the ships they pray to Allah, making their faith pure for Him only, but when He bringeth them safe to land, behold! they ascribe partners (unto Him).[78]

The battle here is far more definitive than between an emerging monotheism and a resistant polytheism. The real battle is between the pagan persistence of that polytheism in the primacy of the Sign and its aggressive transmutation, in the absence of an evident Divine Face, into a Signifier so that it can implicate Allah as the Transcendental Signified. Here is the evidence of that real battle: "And verily: if thou shoudst ask them: Who created the heavens and the earth? they will say: Allah. Say: Bethink you then of those ye worship beside Allah, if Allah willed some hurt for me, could they remove from me His hurt; or if He willed some mercy for me, could they restrain His mercy? Say: Allah is my all. In Him do (all) the trusting put their trust."[79]

The power-basing between Allah and the other deities is predicated on the sublimation of His power in upward metaphysical mobility, an abstraction of the pagan evidence of His Facial Sign into His Signifier Name, and ultimately His Constitution as a Transcendental Signifier to which all Signs and Signifiers point. The reason that in Joseph's story we read Joseph admonishing his pagan cellmates for worshipping idols and dismissing the idols—"Those whom ye worship beside Him are but names which ye have named, ye and your fathers. Allah hath revealed no sanction for them. The decision rests with Allah only, Who hath commanded you that ye worship none save Him. This is the right religion, but most men know not"[80]—is precisely this insistence that the new practice of *Naming* ought to be the exclusive prerogative of "the right religion" and not shared by other deities. In the absence of God's Face, by designating Him as the Unseen the would-be Sign of His metaphysical Existence is mutated from its actual pagan Sign into the Signifier of His Name, so that by pointing to its inevitable Named it can constitute the sublimated deity into the Supreme Transcendental Signified. Once the active and aggressive mutation of the Sign into the Signifier is accomplished, the Metaphysics of the Presence in the exclusionary domain of the Divine Transcendental Signified is categorically and constitutionally established: "Say: Unto Whom (belongeth) the earth and whosoever is therein, if you have knowledge? They will say: Allah. Say: Will ye not then remember? Say: Who is Lord of the seven heavens, and Lord of the tremendous Throne? They will say: Unto Allah (all that belongeth). Say: Will ye not then keep duty (unto Him)? Say: In Whose hand is the dominion over all things and He protecteth, while against Him there is no protection, if ye have knowledge? They will say: Unto Allah (all that belongeth). Say: How then are ye bewitched? Nay, but We have brought them the Truth, and lo! they are liars."[81] "Bewitched" (*tusharuna*) and "liars" (*kadhibuna*) are now the designators of the just-about-to-be defeated pagan persistence of the Sign, while "the Truth" (*al-Haqq*) is the now always-already achieved Transcendental Signified.

The deathblow to practiced paganism, the sight of the Sign metaphysically transmuted into a "vision" of the Unseen, occurs in chapter 53 of the Qur'an, a narrative event that cyclically complements chapter 12 and the appearance of the figure of Joseph. Here the central figure is Prophet Muhammad himself. Chapter 53, the Surah *Al-Najm* ("The Star"), as an early Meccan Surah—that is to say pronounced at a time when Meccan paganism is receiving its severest shock—is emphatic, cataclysmic, and explosive in its opening utterance: "By the Star when it setteth."[82] The sixth/twelfth century Qur'anic commentator al-Tabarsi summarizes his predecessors and suggests that here God swears by the Qur'an "which was revealed like stars upon the prophet, God's Peace and Benedictions be upon him, in [a span of] twenty-three years."[83] The Meccans, though, did not take this announcement so lightly, we know from other commentators, nor read it so figuratively. When the son of Abu Lahab, to whom the Prophet's daughter was married, heard this verse he was so offended—because he thought the Prophet had offended the Deity of Star—that he divorced the Prophet's daughter.[84] The reading of subsequent commentators is quite crucial because it clearly establishes the narrative text of the Qur'an and the act of *Revelation* against the Signal authority of the Meccan idols. The cataclysmic, though inviting and reassuring, announcement then proceeds to assure Muhammad's listeners that "[y]our comrade erreth not, nor is deceived; Nor doth he speak of his own desire."[85] It is precisely in the language and logic of that *Revelation* that the Qur'an ensures its readers that Muhammad is now "speaking" on behalf of One Higher, Transcendental Authority, furthered and removed from the Signal site of pagan practice: "It is naught save an inspiration that is inspired."[86] The language of "inspiration" (*wahy*) and "the inspired" (*yuha'*), which can equally be read as "revelation" and "the revealed," is the Qur'anic narrative site that constitutionally mutates the signal sight of the practiced paganism. With the phrase "Which one of mighty powers hath taught him, One vigorous;"[87] even if we accept the account of the commentators that it refers to Archangel Gabriel,[88] although the term *'allamahu* ("hath taught him") could very well refer to God,[89] the reference to the Unseen as the Supreme Transcendental Signified is now complete.

The next move is the active constitution of the very act of *Revelation* as the mode of the Unseen *manifesting* itself not in Signs but in Words, Signifiers that must point to their Signifieds and thus ipso facto implicate One Absolute and Final Transcendental Signified. Archangel Gabriel is the agent of that *revelatory* act: "One vigorous; and he grew clear to view / When he was on the uppermost horizon. Then he drew nigh and came down / Till he was (distant) two bows' length or even nearer, and He revealed unto His slave that which He revealed."[90] Al-Tabarsi insists that Gabriel "appeared to Muhammad, God's Peace and Benediction be upon Him, in the *face* that was created for him," and that he "appeared with the *face* of human beings."[91] The "conversation" between Muhammad and Gabriel is closely intimate. They come to "two bows' length or even nearer" of each other, and the act of *Revelation* is through the intermediary of the Archangel via the very "breath" of the Unseen.[92]

Upon this moment of *Revelation*, the language of the Qur'an, the Re-Cited, becomes thoroughly ocularcentric, emphasizing the Prophet's *seeing* Archangel Gabriel: "The heart lied not (in seeing) what it saw. Will ye then dispute with him concerning what he seeth?"[93] The disputation is of course by the pagan Meccans who simply refuse to succumb the sight of their visual evidence of the Sign to its mutation into the site of the Signifier, in this case Archangel Gabriel *revealing* the Word of God. Just One Word from God the Unseen and the entire autonomy of the Sign is forfeited for good. It is precisely for this reason that the Qur'an accuses the pre-Islamic Meccans of "ignorance" (*jahiliyyah*)—namely, ignorance of the Qur'anic God, its Transcendental Signified—as the pagans were adamant in upholding the sight of the Signs they visually saw in the Faces (and the bodies) of their idols.[94]

The final move is the arrangement of a visitation, here and now, there and then, between Muhammad and the Unseen. On behalf of all the skeptics, humanity at large, and the visual beholders of the Sign, Muhammad is now actually *to see* the Unseen and get the whole predicament over with: "And verily he saw him yet another time / By the lote-tree of the utmost boundary, Nigh unto which is the Garden of Abode. When that which shroudeth did enshroud the lote-tree, the eye turned not aside nor yet was overbold. Verily he saw one of the greatest revelations of his Lord."[95] These verses are the origin of one of the greatest visual dramas in Islamic counter/visual culture: the instance of seeing the Unseen. Many medieval Muslim commentators have of course taken this visitation metaphorically and read the passage "The heart lied not (in seeing) what it saw" to mean that Muhammad saw God in "his heart." But many other commentators have equally insisted on a very literal reading of the passage, insisting that "God Almighty raised Muhammad's body to the heavens, while alive and perfectly healthy, until he saw what he saw in the Heavenly Abode with his [physical] eyes. And this was not in his dream . . . [There is a] difference between seeing while awake and seeing in a dream. Seeing while awake is really to comprehend [*idrakahu*] with the [physical] eyes, while seeing in dream is to imagine [*tasawwur*] in the heart, as in the presumption [*tawahhum*] of comprehension, with the sensation [*hassah*] of seeing."[96]

The Meccan paganists put up a staunch resistance to believing the very possibility of this visitation, on which depended their entirely ocularcentric practice of paganism and the primacy of the Sign.

> It is reported that when in the morning of his return [from his nocturnal trip to the Heavens] the Prophet, God's Peace and Benediction be upon Him, reported of the first earthly part of his trip to Jerusalem, his companions were elated and the news soon spread throughout Mecca. Abu Bakr the Righteous [a close companion of the Prophet] was absent that day and had not seen the Holy Prophet. When Abu Jahl [one of the staunchest and most powerful enemies of the Prophet] heard of this news, he told himself, "If there were to be only one reason to dissuade Abu Bakr from remaining a follower of Muhammad then that reason will have to be this impossible news." So he got up and went to see Abu Bakr. He told him: "O Son of Abu Qahafah, this friend of yours Muhammad tells of such an impossibility that no reasonable man could possibly believe. He says: 'Yesterday I have left this mosque [in Mecca] and gone to Jerusalem and then returned that very evening.' O Abu Bakr, can you believe that a man would be able in one night to leave Mecca for Jerusalem and then come back that very evening? That is about a months worth of travel for a caravan and a man on his feet. If you believe this impossible news, then no doubt there is something wrong with your wits." Abu Bakr the Righteous conveyed to him an answer in utmost precision and perspicacity. He said: "If he said it, then it is true." Abu Jahl was thoroughly disappointed in him. Abu Bakr rushed to the Prophet and before sitting down he asked him in utter sincerity and in utmost devotion: "O Prophet of God, tell me of your journey yesterday." The Prophet said: "O Abu Bakr, yesterday Gabriel came and brought me Buraq [the steed on which the Prophet ascended to the Heavens] and took me to Jerusalem where I saw the souls of the pure prophets and the lords of the Higher Heavens. I led them all towards the Heavenly realm until we reached the High Heavens where I saw the Signs of the Almighty [*Ayat e Kubra'*]. And then that very night I returned to Mecca." Abu Bakr said: "You are telling the truth, O Messenger of God. I swear by that God Who sent you in truth that as you have been taken while awake, in your form and person, in this journey from a [physical] place to another, my soul has similarly journeyed towards your companionship. Your journey was in form and matter, while mine in your service in soul and secret. Mine in your service is in dream, while yours in awakenness, with the approval of [God] the Truth." As this conversation was proceeding, the Trustful Gabriel ascended and brought this verse: "And whoso bringeth the truth and believeth therein [—such are the dutiful]" [The Qur'an: 39: 33]. From this day forward the title of Abu Bakr once again became "The Trustful" and until the hour of Judgment the people of the True Path and Consensus [i.e., the Majority of Muslims, with the exception of the Shi'ites] believe in

> his leadership [because he succeeded the prophet as the first caliph], because of his believing in the Nocturnal Journey [of the Prophet's mi'raj].[97]

Al-Maybudi, who reports this incident in his Qur'anic commentary, gives us a brilliant ocularcentric explanation as to why it was that God decided to bring Muhammad to His Heavenly Abode:

> Another explanation [as to why Prophet Muhammad was taken to the Heavenly abode] is that the Mission which He had bestowed [upon the Prophet] would be bestowed by virtue of Vision [*Mushahidah*] and Sight [*Nadhar*] and not by virtue of Hearing [*Sama'*] and Utterance [*Khabar*]. *Because Utterance [Khabar] is not like Visual Observation [al-Mu'ayinah].* So that when the Prophet described the blessings of Paradise and the torments of Hell he would be able to say, "I Saw it," and not just "I heard it." Because that is logically more persuasive, it convinces more effectively and powerfully.[98]

Many Muslim commentators are very adamant that this nocturnal journey and visitation with the Unseen did not take place in the Prophet's dream but in perfect awakenness, and that it was in his physical body that he was taken on this journey.[99] What we actually read in 53:18 is a clear visualization of the encounter: "Verily he saw one of the greater revelations of his Lord." The Qur'an in fact gives a very accurate positioning of the Prophet's eyes in 53:17: "The eye turned not aside nor yet was overbold." What happens at this moment is the effective visualization of the Invisible, the Unseen seen. The effect is cataclysmic. The Sign is in effect reclaimed, reappropriated, and yet kept at the unattainable distance of the Transcendental Signified. As Transcendental Signified, the Unseen is of course first and foremost phonocentrically signified through the Qur'anic Voice. But, and here is the Qur'anic ocularcentric claim that puts an end to all other claims, once thus constituted, the Qur'anic Transcendental Signified is paralyzingly conscious of the pagan persistence of the Sign making a mockery of its mutation into the Signifier that makes the whole Faith possible. By the Prophet's visitation of the Invisible, the Transcendental Signified now signals Itself as the Sign, incapacitating all other Signs except Itself.

In Surah *al-Najm* proper, immediately after the description of the Prophet's nocturnal visitation to the Heavenly Abode, we have the famous references to the three Meccan deities of Al-Lat, Al-'Uzza', and Manat: "Have ye thought upon Al-Lat and Al-'Uzza/And Manat, the third, the other? Are yours the males and His the females? That indeed were an unfair divisions!"[100] The principal function of these verses here, coming immediately after the most emphatic attempt at removing the Achilles Heel of the invisibility of the Unseen is once and for all castigating the downward pull of the pre-Islamic Arab paganism toward the Sign.

The Qur'anic reference to pagan deities has been the subject of considerable attention. A number of Orientalist scholars have noted the repetition of references in the Qur'an to "the daughters of God."[101] From these references the particular shape of the pagan pantheon has been estimated. The specific emphasis of 53:19–22, "have ye thought upon Al-Lat and Al-'Uzza/And Manat, the third, the other? Are yours the males and His the females? That indeed were an unfair division!" is taken as evidence of God being particular not to have any "daughters." But the Qur'anic dissimulation of God from pagan practices is not limited to withdrawing any possibility of His having daughters. He is equally characterized by not having sons, as in the case against Christ being considered his son:

> O People of the Scripture! Do not exaggerate in your religion nor utter aught concerning Allah save the truth. The Messiah, Jesus son of Mary, was only a messenger of Allah, and His word which He conveyed unto Mary, and a spirit from Him. So believe in Allah and His messengers, and say not "Three"—Cease! (it is) better for you!—Allah is only One God. Far is it removed from His Transcendent Majesty that He should have a son. He is all that is in the heavens and all that is in the earth. And Allah is sufficient as Defender.[102]

In fact, God the Unseen is categorically exempted from being born or giving birth: "Say: He is Allah, the One! Allah, the eternally Besought of all! He begetteth not nor was begotten. And there is none comparable unto him."[103]

There are also controversies about the occasion and variations of these four verses, referring to pagan deities as they do and exempting God the Unseen of having any similarity to them. On the authority of some early Muslim commentators, including al-Tabari, some Orientalist scholars have argued that the first two verses of this section were initially followed by two other verses acknowledging the power of these pagan deities to intercede on behalf of their believers.[104] Muslim scholars, on the other hand (with few exceptions) categorically deny such a possibility.[105] The order of the verses as they are purported to have been are as follows:

> Have you considered al-Lat and al-'Uzza
> and Manat, the third, the other?
> These are the intermediaries exalted,
> whose intercession is to be hoped for.
> Such as they do not forget.[106]

The contention is that the Prophet first acceded to the pressure of Meccan paganists and thought of acknowledging their deities and thus considered three major idols—al-Lat, al-'Uzza, and Manat—as the "daughters" of God, incorporating them, as it were, into the emerging cosmogony. W. Montgomery Watt, as an advocate of this view among the Orientalist scholars, suggests,

> The first thing to be said about the story is that it cannot be a sheer invention. Muhammad must at some point have recited as part of the Qur'an the verses which were later rejected as satanic in origin. No Muslim could

> possibly have invented such a story about Muhammad, and no reputable Muslim scholar would have accepted it from a non-Muslim unless fully convinced of its truth. The Muslims of today tend to reject the story since it contradicts their idealized picture of Muhammad; but, on the other hand it could be taken as evidence that Muhammad was "a human being like themselves" ([The Qur'an:] 41.6; etc.).[107]

Muslim scholars, recognizing fully the difference between the humanity of their Prophet and the sanctity of the Infallible Text that is believed to be the very Voice of God and as such at the root of their revealed faith, think otherwise. They maintain that

> [a] number of European scholars and Orientalists who do not believe in revelation and the mission of the Prophet of Islam have maintained, without any research and in utter ignorance, that the rallying cry of the Quraysh [a Meccan Tribe into which the Prophet was born] idolaters which was uttered by them before the appearance of Islam and in the course of their pilgrimage rituals . . . was a verse of the Qur'an. They have based themselves on an inaccurate and vague report by [the Early Muslim historian] Muhammad ibn 'Umar al-Waqidî (130/747–207/822), without paying any attention to the account of Hisham [ibn Muhammad al-Kalbi, the author of Kitab al-Asnam, one of the earliest sources on pre-Islamic Arab paganism]. Waqidi's account is not considered to be accurate by any other Muslim scholar before or after al-Waqidî except Muhammad ibn Jarir al-Tabari who was avaricious in collecting every account, whatever it might be, and who took this account from al-Waqidî and included it in his [Qur'anic] commentary without accepting or rejecting it.[108]

The controversy between Orientalist and Muslim scholars entirely misses the triumphant victory of Qur'anic *Revelation* over the very *idea* of paganism. What is important is that in Surah *al-Najm*, the pagan insistence on the primacy of the Sign, of the Visible sight of their idols, is putting its last resistance to its aggressive and final transmutation into Signifier so that the entire Qur'anic narrative triumphs on its substitution of the Voice for the Vision, the Ear for the Eye, the Sound for the Sight: the Blinding of the Eye and the opening of the Ear.

Triumph of logocentricism—reassessed.

As the inaugural moment of a culture, the Qur'an is the narrative manifesto of a globalizing abstraction wherein the particulars of a tribally diverse configuration of the real are aggressively transmuted to become the Transcendental Universals of a Cosmic Order. In the process of this globalizing abstraction of particulars—from tribal to Cosmic, from Patrimonial *Gemeinschaft* to Patriarchal *Geselleschaft*—the local iconic deities with identifiable Faces, as recognizable Signs, yield collectively to a Supreme Abrahamic Monotheism over which presides an Absolute Deity, the Allah with no Face to see, Divinity the Unseen, the Decisive suppresser of the Sign. The active Qur'anic transmutation of the pagan Sign into narrative Signifier, on the site of the Sacred Signature of *Revelation*, is no historical accident. It corresponds to the social transformation of Arabia from a scattered body of nomadic tribes into a cohesive community of commercial capitalism. The anonymity of the supertribe, the Islamic Ummah, as the site of the emerging faith, is represented by the Metaphysical Abstraction of all scattered Signs into Sacred Signifiers so that in their pointing to their designated Signifieds they would collectively implicate a Transcendental Signified, code-Named the Unseen. The Muslim faithful thus become those who in the absence of the Face, *yu'minun bi-al-ghayb*—"believe in the Unseen."

The commercial consolidation of Arabia, foregrounded by the tribal incorporation of the peninsula, paved the way for a new social organization ideologically predicated on a more global, and globalizing, cosmogony. As Arabia became integral to a globalizing logic of the commercial capital in the region, tribal deities began to yield to a corresponding Universe of Abstractions, the multiplicity of their identifiable Signs succumbing to the monotheism of a singular body of Signification.[109] The normative systematization of diverse pagan practices was a precondition to pave the way for an economic federation that would facilitate the caravan commerce between Syria and Yemen. The result was a *Revelatory* consolidation of a metaphysical taxonomy, complete with its theology (ordered under the supreme authority of Allah the Unseen), prophetology (concluded with the charismatic authority of Muhammad), cosmology (centered on earth as the testing ground of a covenant contracted in the Garden of Eden), and angelology (mitigated through the intermediary function of Archangel Gabriel). The result is the aggressive transmutation of an iconic semiotics into a textual hermeneutics, whereby the centrality of the Sign is categorically condemned in a colossal celebration of a Sacred Act of Signification. The visual Sign yields to the verbal Signifier, as individual iconic idols submit to the supreme metaphysical authority of One God, who is now the Unseen. The systematization of the metaphysical cosmogony goes hand in hand with the universalization of the logic of commercial capital, both demanding that the defiant and anarchic signs of idols and tribes yield their rebellious visual disposition to the almighty power of a singular mode of verbal signification, now code-named "Islam."

The repression of the sign is successful but not final. While the chapter on Joseph is the most revealing moment in the Qur'anic self-exposure of its anxiety of having de-Faced an iconic culture by subjecting it to a Transcendental Logocentricism, the Surah *al-Najm*, particularly the story of the Prophet's nocturnal journey to the Heavenly Abode, balanced by the aggressive denunciation of three prominent pagan idols, points to a crucial juncture when the iconic culture carries its resistance to Metaphysical Transcendentalization into the pages of the Qur'an. It is not of course accidental that the story of the Prophet's journey to see the Unseen precedes the moment when we have one of the strongest categorical condemnations of paganism in the Qur'an. Nor is it accidental that this moment of categorical and final break with practiced paganism at least appears to have had a momentary concession to paganism. Any concession to paganism, however, is so categorically against the very logic of the Qur'anic *Re-Citation* of the Truth as the supreme Signifier/ Transcendental Signified that it is hard to take it seriously if we are not to contradict the very driving energy of *Revelation* that informs and sustains the Sacred Narrative. The Qur'an could not have conceded to paganism in the slightest way without completely contradicting its constitutional, Text-long condemnation of idolatry, a necessary precondition for its aggressive mutation of the pagan Sign into the monotheistic Signifier. Far more important, the Qur'anic reference to the three pagan deities points to the identification of a particularly weak moment when the metaphysical Transcendentalization of visual icons into verbal logos is severely resisted by pagan practices. The resistance, however, is doomed. By chapter 53 in the Text, Surah *al-Najm* (in whatever order we may read the 124 chapters of the Qur'an, chronological or otherwise), the iconic culture is aggressively *metalogosed* (metamorphosed from Sign to Signifier, from sight to sound, from the visual focus to audile logos, from Face to Name) thoroughly, almost simultaneously with the successive defeats that the Prophet inflicted on the Meccan establishment at the Battle of Badr in 624, the Battle of Uhud in 625, the Battle of Ditch in 627, the Pact of al-Hudaybiyah in 628, and finally his triumphant entry into Mecca to smash all the idols at Ka'bah on January 11, 630. The material expansion of historical forces needed and welcomed the appearance of a new universalizing metaphysics, a potent metaphysical economy of signification, and the transcendental globalization of the tribal.

The Qur'an is the manifesto of a universal globalization of the sacred against the native autonomy of tribal paganism. The Qur'anic rhetoric against paganism, dismissing the whole cultural practice of it as a period of "Ignorance" (*Jahiliyyah*), is foregrounded by and in its cataclysmic constitution *and* globalization of the sacred that it presumes and resumes from the Biblical narrative at large. Precisely like Christianity centuries earlier, Islam is the global universalization of the Judaic particular. Judaic universalism, implanted in its tribal particularism, remained always *de jure* and never *de facto*. Christianity brought that *de jure* to *de facto* in the North, Islam in the South. The difference between Judaism and all other particular tribal patriarchies is the active transmutation of the Sign in the Hebrew Bible into the Signifier of YHWH, unpronounceable, a Sign pretending to be a Signifier, a Signifier strategically concealing its aggressive mutation of the (non)Sign it *Re-Presents*. In the Hebrew Bible, and in its renarration in the Arabic Qur'an, we witness the birth of a literary faith in the violent *metalogosization* of the creative imagination, from Sign to Signifier, from Face to Name. In its Southern and Northern forms, the varieties of Eurasian and Afroasian paganism remained singularly semiotic, logistically particular. Christianity and Islam borrowed the Biblical mutation of the Sign into Signifier and ran it to its universal and globalizing conclusions: The collapse of the sign into signifier, of the particular into the universal, of the material into the abstract, of the semiotic into the hermeneutic, and ultimately of the aesthetics of the visible sign into the metaphysics of the presented signifier to cover its categorical contingency on a primal absence. The active hostility between Islam and Christianity throughout medieval and modern history is in constitutional metaphysical terms, because they are two universalizing versions of a common particular—though with a critical difference: Christ for the Qur'an is the *Emissary* (Signifier), not the *Son* (Sign) of God.

Evident in the Qur'an are both its self-conscious awareness of an active repression of the Sign so that in the absence of the Face of the Unseen His Voice can author the Faith, an anxiety that is best evident in the chapter on Joseph, and the vestiges of the last ditch resistances by the tribal cosmogonics of idolic Signs to their active mutation into a universal metaphysics of signifiers pointing submissively to One, Final, Absolute, Transcendental Signified. In 45:24, "And they say: There is naught but our life of the world; we die and we live, and naught destroyeth us save time; when they have no knowledge whatsoever of (all) that; they do but guess," we have a textual witness to the minimalism of the tribal cosmogonics of the evident, life at its Face value. Resistance to the very idea of an "afterlife" is the categorical resistance to the *Sign of the evident* being collapsed and transmuted into the *Signature of the promised*. Time (*dahr*) is the narrative evidence of the visible—day and night, the sun, the moon, and stars, the circulatory constitution of the seasonal visitation of the evident, the perishable, and the renewable.

The Qur'anic manifesto documents the revelatory moment when the Unseen forcefully replaces the visible. The most evident symbolics of the signs violently condemned by the Qur'an are such tribal idols as al-Lat, al-'Uzza', and Manat, all of which had shrines in Mecca, at-Ta'if, Nakhla, and many other places. In 71:23, "And they have said: Forsake not your gods. Forsake not Wadd, nor Suwa', nor Yaghuth and Ya'uq and Nasr," we know of five other idols. These idols were constitutional to the tribal life and were immediately identified with the *images* that their believers carried with them, as we know, for example, was the case with Abu Sufyan, a prominent opponent of the Prophet in early Islamic history, who carried the image of al-Lat and al-'Uzza' while on the expedition of Uhud against the nascent Muslim community.[110] In 4:76, "Those who believe do battle for the cause of Allah; and those who disbelieve do battle for the cause of idols. So fight the minions of the devil. Lo! the devil's strategy is ever weak," we probably read a reference to this incident. The gradual assimilation of tribal deities as *banat Allah* in 16:57, 17:40, and 37:149, among many others, and then as angels in 34:4, pave the way for the formation of a Monotheist cosmology, the cosmogonic predicate of an emerging theo-ontology, over which the Transcendental Unseen presides.

By the late sixth century on the Christian calendar, the caravan route in Western Arabia between the ports of Yemen on the Indian Ocean and the fertile lands between the Byzantine and the Sassanid empires at the Mediterranean had a catalytic impact on changing the economic infrastructure of Arabia from nomadic pastoralism to commercial capitalism. Mecca was both a trading terminal and a religious sanctuary.[111] The Arabs traded their goods, praised their gods, and practiced their paganism at one and the same time. The gradual move from nomadic pastoralism to commercial capitalism results in the collapse of *'asabiyyah*, or group solidarity in tribal terms, and a process of communal disintegration begins to become evident.[112] Whereas nomadic pastoralism was conducive to strong group affiliation, the rise of commercial capitalism began to create a powerful merchant class no longer having any use for outdated loyalties. As ancient tribal solidarities began to thaw and the new merchant class began to partake in a thriving commercial capitalism on the borders of the two superpowers of the time (the Byzantines and the Sassanids), Islam emerged as the defining ideology of a new globalizing *Weltanschauung*, taking Judaism as its narrative paradigm, Christianity as its mode of ideological production, and the Byzantines and the Sassanids as its imperial model. The violent antipaganism of the Qur'an is the battle cry of the new order. The aggressive transmutation of iconic tribal signs into verbal metaphysical signifiers is the simultaneous metaphoric correspondence that acknowledges and accommodates the massive subterranean changes in the moral and political order of social life. The visible face of the pagan deities begin to disappear, dissolve into thin air, and from the Heavens the Voice of the Unseen is heard and begins to Re-Cite:

> Read: In the name of thy Lord Who createth,
> Createth man from a clot.
> Read: and thy Lord is the Most Bounteous,"[113]

This is the moment of the Name triumphant, the Face forever Unseen, the Voice eloquent, captivating, a historical epoch collapsing, another emerging, and sign submitting to signification. "In every case," it is true, "the voice is closest to the signified."[114] But by then the battle has been already fought and lost (and won). The sign has failed, the signifier triumphant. The Face is veiled. The Voice is loquacious. The Man thus alerted into creation now also reads, re-cites, from The Book, His Book, echoing the Voice, now as in posteternity, in the Presence of the Absence, the Unseen:

> And every man's augury have We fastened to his own neck,
> and We shall bring for him on the Day of Resurrection a book which he will find wide open.
> (And it will be said unto him): Read thy Book.
> Thy soul sufficeth as reckoner against thee this day.[115]

"All signifiers, and first and foremost the written signifier, are derivative with regard to what would wed the voice indissolubly to the mind or to the thought of the signified sense, indeed to the thing itself . . . from its sense thought in the logos or in the infinite understanding of God."[116] But this is "God" as in the Transcendental Signified beyond recognition, the Sign suppressed, and the Signifier combatant triumphant. The Voice of God in the Qur'anic *Re-Citation* is wedded immediately to God's Mind, to His Thought, to the Thing Itself. He Speaks. Gabriel conveys. Muhammad listens, repeats, and then writes. Because Muhammad *writes*, God speaks with His Voice *but* Teaches with the *Pen*:

Read: And thy Lord is the Most Bounteous,
Who teacheth by the pen,
Teacheth man that which he knows not.[117]

There is no privileging of the spoken word over the written here. The evident, drawn, sculpted Sign is repressed into the vocal Signifier first, but it is then sublimated into the written word, the simulacrum of the Sign. The written word is substitutional for the repressed Sign, thus the Qur'an both represses *and* resurrects the Sign in the shape of the *written* word. "All signifiers . . . are derivative" is correct, though *derivative* in the sense that they are the mutated Signs. But "and first and foremost the written signifier" confuses the act, betrays the Christian Christological presupposition, so much so that when we get to "The written signifier is always technical and representative" we have lost the trail. And by the time we reach "The notion of the Sign always implies within itself the distinction between signifier and signified," we know we have lost the key. And no feeble attempt at a subordinate clause, "even if, as Saussure argues, they are distinguished simply as the two faces of one and the same leaf," can do the trick. The Signifier and the Signified are the King and the Queen of a usurped territory once the unruly domain of the triumphantly chaotic Sign. Transcendental Signified is the God to which this King and Queen pray in order to rule with impunity over the incessantly rebellious Sign.

This is what happens in the Qur'an, the *Re-Citation*:

Evident, drawn, sculpted, the Sign is suppressed (destruction of paganism). The Sign is narratively transmuted into the Signifier, the Name: "In the Name . . ." The Name is born: Allah. The immediate Attribute is the denial of the Vision: Allah the Unseen. The Signifier begins to signify, pointing upward, directing away from the scene of the signature. The signification game has started on the site of the Unseen. The Signified is Transcendentalized. The game is over. The repressed Sign, however, returns: Joseph and his beautiful Face. Joseph is the return of the repressed triumphantly repressed. The battle resumes. The pagans are *named* and denounced, and Muhammad is summoned *to see* The Unseen. Why? Because "the Mission which He had bestowed [upon the Prophet] would be bestowed by virtue of Vision [*Mushahidah*] and Sight [*Nadhar*] and not by virtue of Hearing [*Sama'*] and Utterance [*Khabar*]. Because Utterance [*Khabar*] is not like Visual Observation [*al-Mu'ayinah*]. So that when the Prophet described the blessings of Paradise and the torments of Hell he would be able to say, 'I Saw it,' and not just 'I heard it.' Because that is logically more persuasive, it convinces more effectively and powerfully."[118] *Mi'raj*, the nocturnal journey of the Prophet who hears God speak to see the Unseen revealed, is the revision of the return of the repressed, the Sign denied, for One Final Repression. The Written Word, the Book, the Signifier counterfeiting the Sign, is the Final manifesto: The Qur'an, Muslims believe, is the miracle of their Faith—in the Absence of the Face.

In the Absence of the Face, thus, I have had to speak—and write.

REPRESSING VISION

The *suicidal body* has a long and lasting memory: It is in the air it breathes. It remembers.

We concluded that because God the Unseen cannot be seen, *seeing* is Qur'anically repressed—via a *revelatory* act that *reveals* (a misnomer that belies the tension) the verbal in order to repress the visual. But the repression of *seeing* is never completely successful in the sacred Text and systematically resurfaces and agitates the claim of revelation. This agitation is at the energetic core of the Qur'an as a text and Islam as a faith. God the Unseen is believed, in a sacred *Hadith*, to have held a mirror in front of His Face and called what he saw *insan* (human). The Qur'an, meanwhile, insists that *"[e]verything will perish save His [God's] Countenance."* In the Qur'anic repression of the Facial absence of the Divine Unseen, the historical person (as the extension of the Qur'anic *insan*—or *human*) becomes biologically complacent because we too cannot see our own face—and thus the *rebellious Sign* is mutated into a *lobotomized signifier* by a violent metaphysical act. Twice in the course of the Qur'anic revelation does the repressed return—once as Joseph's face, surfacing as the Face of the Unseen having come down for a visit, and again when Prophet Muhammad ascends to the Seventh Heaven to face and see the Face of the Unseen.

Thus bracketed, the Qur'anic Unseen is the unauthored Author of the Text that is authoring itself. Among the *Text* of the Qur'an, its Unseen *Author*, and the believing *Reader* thus surfaces a triangular hermeneutics. Who is the Author, who the Reader, and what the Text? Because the fear of the Sign is real (and the figure of the Christ-Son has not alleviated the terror of the Unseen-Father), in the Qur'an the *writing* is privileged, not the *speech*. Islam is a *written* religion, not a *spoken* faith, with a primacy given to *reading*, not to *speaking*, to *Pen*, and not to the tongue. In the Qur'an (68:2), the Unseen God swears *"By the pen and that which they write (therewith)"*—likewise, the sacred Text instructs (96: 13) *"In the name of thy Lord Who createth, / Createth man from a clot. / Read: and thy Lord is the Most Bounteous . . ."* The following is at the commencement of the revelation and also at the conclusion of life (17:13–14): *"And every man's augury have We fastened to his own neck, / and We shall bring for him on the Day of Resurrection a book which he will find wide open. / (And it will be said unto him): Read thy Book. / Thy soul sufficeth as reckoner against thee this day."*

On the surface of the Text thus emerges a conversation between the Unseen Author and the blinded Reader. The conversation inevitably assumes a hermeneutic privileging of *law* and *reason*—the prerequisite of an architectonics of collective amnesia of the absented Face of the Unseen. Now, what is *mysticism*? It is the defiance of the *nomos* of the law (*Shari'ah*) and the *logos* of the reason (*Falsafah*). Once again, what is *mysticism*? It is the extreme identification of the blinded sight of the *Reader* with the Unseen Face of the *Author*. Hold the mirror between the Face of the Unseen and what the Unseen sees in the mirror constant, for instance! Now read Rumi:

Rumi tells the story of a friend of Joseph's (a Divine Emissary, perhaps the Divinity Itself) who comes to see him and cannot think of any better gift to bring for him than a mirror.[119] Joseph is rich in every respect, and the friend cannot make a fool out of himself by taking "coal to Newcastle" or "cumin to Kerman." The moral of the story?

> He took out the mirror from under his arm—
> For those who are beautiful like the mirror.
> What is the mirror of Being? Not-Being:
> Then take the not-Being (for a gift) if you are not a fool!
> Being can only be seen in not-Being,
> As the rich can only be generous to the poor![120]

If the Face of the Unseen is holding that mirror and looks into it and sees *man*, then what is *man*? How could an Invisible Face see anything in a mirror other than invisibility? Doubly blinded—the mirror image of a Hidden Face—the blinded reader's extreme identification with the Unseen Author reverses the gaze and becomes nothing. Mystical self-annihilation (*fana'*) is such extreme identification with the Unseen that it makes man—a divine reflection—invisible, disintegrated into nothingness.

If the commercial capitalism of sixth century Arabia force-fed the *defiant signs* to *reluctant signifiers* and made a world religion possible, global capitalism at the commencement of the twenty-first century is now releasing the repressed signs for good, making them available for either a new rise of *the global paganism of the body* or else its *mystical self-annihilation*—or perhaps both. *Martyrological mysticism* grabs hold of the sign of the body and takes the medieval notion of *fana'* (annihilation) to the extremities of its misplaced concreteness, as *postmodern capitalism* grabs hold of the selfsame sign of the body and genetically reengineers it. As the *suicidal body* self-explodes and disintegrates itself, the *narcissist body* celebrates itself and seeks perpetual youth. Both the *genetically reengineered* bodies and the *mystically martyred* are active denials of death, one at the heart of capitalist postmodernity, the other at its peripheralized brutality—a center and periphery now forever brought together and collapsed on the exploded site of the World Trade Center, the Ground Zero of a new imperial calendar code-named 9/11.

Chapter 3

Bodiless Faces

"A pity you never met the old Commandant!—But," the officer interrupted himself, "I am rambling on, and here stands his apparatus before us. It consists, as you see, of three parts. In the course of time each of these parts has acquired a kind of popular nickname. The lower one is called the 'Bed,' the upper one the 'Designer,' and this one here in the middle that moves up and down is called the 'Harrow.'" "The Harrow?" asked the explorer . . . "Yes, the Harrow," said the officer, "a good name for it."

—Franz Kafka, *In the Penal Colony* (1914)

Defiant signs make for very *reluctant signifiers*, and whether they run along with a *globalized paganism of the body* or opt for a *mystical self-annihilation* strapped head to toe with layers of dynamite, they announce the visual evidence of a *corpus anarchicum* that is yet to be fully comprehended. In the following chapter, I would like to trace some of the clandestine conversations between faces and their corresponding bodies when they must resort to subterranean measures under the severe circumstances of a theocracy. The dialogical negotiations that ensue embrace the anamnesis of every cultural formation: a recollecting of past events now made compellingly present. The bodily memories invested in faces sustain the vernacular languages that bodies speak in defiance of the Latinized tyranny of their presiding cultures. When bodies are denied visibility and their memories repressed, faces act as their archival repositories, telling their forbidden tales. In this chapter, I would like to trace the tensions and discrepancies created between the *overinvested memory of faces* and the *deeply divested recollection of their bodies.* In those tensions and discrepancies, a visual form of beheading, we see aesthetically documented the serious indices of the politically mutilated bodies.

Like Ghostly Apparitions

They appear on the screen like ghostly apparitions. Colorful and evanescent, like lit lanterns hung from invisible strings of motion, they dissolve into thick layers of incandescent darkness. They move, from side to side, from top to bottom, dreamlike goblins stirred by an inexplicable vivacity, a confident sensuality at once inviting and repellent, accessible and out of reach. These bodiless faces are beautifully feminine, palpably sensual, fully expressive of an expansive topography of emotions, and yet, just like a mutated form of mermaid, they unexpectedly lead to absented bodies, to masses of shapeless deformity, falsifying figures not their own. Invested richly in the finite but minutely detailed geography of these faces is a world of perpetual motion, of relentless attention, and of intelligence informing their gaze. If every other person has the continental vastness of a whole body with which to receive and respond to the world, these faces are brutally cut off from the rest of their bodies—cut off, that is, by layers and then more layers of dark and prohibitive scarves, wrapped-around shawls, baggy shirts, oversized trousers, voluminous skirts, out-reaching overalls, and above them all the sad solitude of a mobile wardrobe forced redundantly to conceal, to capture, to inhibit, and to prohibit.

The defiant intelligence of these faces is contested in their absented bodies.

Behold the forcefully absented presence of Iranian women on the wide but ever narrower screen of an "Islamic cinema," the post-Islamic-revolution impossibility of being feminine, the censorial brutality of mutated bodies, carefully cut off and concealed from faces that must now speak and envision, act and convey, the entire task of a denied body. Their presences absented by force, these bodies dissolve, by the sheer physical reality of their concealment, into ever-darker dungeons of veils covering veils covering more layers of mystifying shades of darkness. Upon this mass of darkness move expressive faces full of energy and zest, intelligence and beauty, sensuality and eroticism. There is something extremely disturbing about these faces, not because they lack the bodies they need, but because they miss the bodies they own.

Bodies and Faces

Faces that belong to habitually uncovered bodies are different from faces that are the extension of bodies accustomed to veiling. Bodies that are covered only by the logic and rhetoric of seasons, fashions, tastes, and (im)pieties of one sort or another give birth to faces that are courageous, cultured, and ready to confront the unexpected accidentalities of life. Bodies that have grown involuntarily under the protective custody of veils, however, can only produce faces that are hesitant, halting, and ashamed for no evident reason. Bodies that have grown up negotiating a presence for themselves in a culture produce faces that exude confidence, earned in hard-won battles against the gaze of *others*. Bodies forcefully concealed from the gaze of such *others* grow into shapeless masses that can only produce uncultivated faces, faces that know nothing for sure about their public place. The Sartrian existential anxiety of "the Look," whereby we become self-consciously aware of ourselves, is radically eliminated when the body is not "Being seen by the Other" and as a result the body never cultivates a presence for itself in public. The battle of the body and the gaze is denied to the person who has the protective shield of the veil. Untested by this brutal battle, a body atrophies into lazy corners of self-denial and in turn gives birth to an inexplicably hesitant face. Veiling women forcefully is not just to segregate socially but, far more importantly, to disempower them politically by denying their bodies accumulated memories. Bodies are the embodiment of otherwise scattered memories.

The history of a body that grows in active conversation with the world invests an understated pride in its face, a subdued trust in its place in the public space, a self-assurance of gestures and moves, an unforeseen and aggressive faith in victory. An exposed body invests a repertoire of victorious memories in the face that represents it. But the active and repressed memories of a body matured but not cultivated (both against her will) under the placid opaqueness of a baggy cover inducts a face full of hidden and evident anxieties, a face arrested in its cultivation of gestures, emotions, sensibilities, and even fears and fantasies. There is a life-affirming vivaciousness in faces that rest on bodies voluntarily exposed and confident of their places in the world. There is an active alertness in faces that represent confident and exposed bodies. An animated suggestiveness charges the nooks and crannies of these faces. Faces of bodies grown involuntarily accustomed to veils, on the other hand, are sights of a perpetual and inexplicable embarrassment, an apology in the making, an impatient waiting to exit the world and enter the veil. A body forcefully denied the physical exercise of social presence can only support a face equally ill at ease at the mere suggestion of an accidental gaze. Being looked and gazed at is the routine exercise that invests enough confidence in a body to produce an unselfconscious face. Being denied the necessary exercise of that look and that gaze, a body grows fat and lazy, comfortable only in the privacy of the mandatory veils and walls. For those of us born to veiling mothers, we remember very well how their proud confidence in our private quarters instantly faded away at the mere suggestion of a public space, of the intrusion of a *na-mahram*, where and when that selfsame face, having never mastered the craft of public encounter, would seek protection behind a *chador*. Rabble-rousing children always sought refuge from the wrath of their mothers in the open space of the street where they knew she could not chase and hunt them down. The selfsame mothers of the Reza Shah period, however, gave birth to daughters of his son Mohammad Reza Shah's monarchy, young girls who grew outside the veil, their bodies exposed to natural and social elements, their souls cultivated in daily dialogue with the world. Their bodies exposed, socialized, cultured, and confident, their faces, in turn, matured into an intelligent and sharp beauty, a precision in their sight, a piercing gaze, a provocative shrewdness that deeply animated their budding sensuality. Forced veiling preempts bodily memories. Patriarchal societies that demand and exact veiling fear and preempt the social persona awaiting emergence from that veil.

One of the most disturbing aspects of Iranian cinema in the aftermath of Islamist censorship is watching cultivated faces of women whose bodies have obviously grown outside the veil be denied their bodies. There is a disconcerting incongruence between these faces and the shabby deformities that stand for their absented bodies. The critical intelligence of these faces is mutilated by the bodies they naturally own but are politically denied.[1] Forced veiling is a politics of exclusion, a sociology of denial, a culture of the muscular atrophy of bodily memory barring the feminine body at the gate of social intercourse, where her vision of herself in public is blinded. The Pahlavi monarchy forced women out of their tradition to manufacture Kemalist modernity for Iran. The Islamic Republic forced that very same lost tradition on the grandchildren of those forcefully exposed grandmothers. The result was the same, abusing women's bodies to either overexpose or underexpose to the public gaze, thus denying their bodies social intercourse.

TRUTH AND VEILING

Cultures that force-veil their women posit a fearful reading of *truth*. They abstract their readings of reality to approximate their reigning metaphysics. The metamorphic nature of truth/woman as dual metaphor found its way even into the postmetaphysical language of Nietzsche who opened *Beyond Good and Evil* with the disarming rhetoric, "Supposing Truth to be a woman—what then?"[2] To force-veil women is to necessitate a hermeneutic of unveiling *the truth* in a culture of perpetual interpretation. In his *Sufism: Veil and Quintessence*, Frithjof Schuon was the first to theorize the link in Islamic metaphysics between *veiling* and *truth*: "Direct and naked truth is both too precious and too dangerous, it intoxicates and it kills, and it runs the risk of being profaned and of inciting revolts; it is like wine which must be sealed, and which Islam prohibits, or like woman who must be covered, and whom Islam veils."[3] He further elaborates:

> According to tradition, the *houris* wear seventy dresses, but at the same time these are transparent and one can see the marrow flowing in their bones, "like liquid and luminous honey," we are told; the dresses symbolize the beauties of veiling, and thus of the formal or "liturgical" aspects of beauty, while the marrow represents the uncreated essence, which is none other than an aspect of the Divine Substance, or a kind of emanation from a beatific Divine Quality. That is to say that God makes Himself perceptible through all that is in Paradise; but the connection between the relativity of the created and the absoluteness of the Essence requires an indefinite play of veiling and unveiling, of formal coagulation and compensatory transparence.[4]

The *danger* that Schuon detects in the Islamic *truth* is the fear of its naked exposition, the anxiety of its not being there. The juridical Islam prohibits wine and veils women because in one dwells the Dionysian joy of laughter and in the other the festive celebration of life. Sealed bottles of wine and covered faces and bodies of women warrant, facilitate, and implicate a transcendental *truth* that must perpetually be sought after in sobriety and asceticism, in seriousness and denial, and yet never totally attained. Correspondingly, as the best *truth* is the one that is never totally revealed, the best wine is the one that does not intoxicate and the best woman the most chaste. As the supreme countermetaphysics of juridical nomocentricism, Islamic Sufism celebrated a theo-erotic language in which the beauty of the masculine or feminine face and the ecstasy of drinking wine became its two principal leitmotifs. Trapped, though, in the overriding Islamic metaphysics, Sufism, too, would further abstract the earthly woman into an *Eternal Beloved*, and wine into *not the real wine*. Thus developed two metamorphic concepts in mystical metaphysics: *Haqiqat* (Truth) and *Majaz* (Metaphor). What we see in the world is not the real thing: It is the *majaz*, a metaphoric reference to the real thing, the *haqiqat*, which is otherworldly.

This metaphysics of veiling is counterintuitive; if truth and veiled women are identical, then like truth that must be hermeneutically unveiled, covered women are also to be unveiled. Juridically veiling women, like presuming Truth to be hidden, is therefore tantamount to concealing them, as in hermeneutically unveiling the truth of an assertion. But why should the feminine body be the metaphysical site of telling or not telling the truth? Whence the metaphor, wherefore the similitude? Forcibly veiling women (as in the Islamic Republic) is the politics of power practiced. Severing the island of their face from the territory of their body is to mutilate the consistency of the memory that holds them together. Forcibly veiling women's bodies is to deny them the daily exercises of accumulating bodily memories, disallow them public access to temporal experience, and bar them from the spatial awareness of time, the teleology of their own narrative. The veiled feminine body is the palimpsestic template of any body that is metaphorically depleted of the organicity of its accumulated memory and thus made vacant for an injection of any idea—as a thin red line drawn over a tabula rasa.

THE ANXIETY OF SURFACE

It is in the postrevolutionary Iranian cinema that the metaphysical mandate of veiling, as a supreme hermeneutics of truth-telling, has had its most effective presence. All its political symbolics fully cashed in on a successful revolution, this metaphysics is now fully utilizing the semiotic culture at its disposal to reconceal its core claim to telling the *truth*. Fully exposed in the course of a revolutionary reconstitution of the Iranian political culture, Islamic metaphysics must now reinvent itself in a new aesthetics. As to why the practice of veiling woman must be pursued with the same passionate intensity on the screen as in the streets and alleys of cities, we need to read the metaphysical claim to One Supreme Truth against the recent history of unveiling (*kashf-e hejab*) in Iran.

As the colonially mitigated project of capitalist modernity commenced its hesitant history in nineteenth-century Iran, the unveiling of women gradually assumed a social and cultural dimension in the wake of the Constitutional Revolution of 1906–1911. While poets, social reformists, political activists, and revolutionary figures contributed massively to the unveiling of urban women, the state-sponsored modernization schemes of Reza Shah (1924–1941) lent a powerful momentum to the movement. The forceful, and at times brutal, unveiling of women in the 1930s and 1940s gradually subsided during the reign of Mohammad Reza Shah (1941–1979) and ultimately settled at a point where generational and class demarcations separated the veiled and unveiled women. From the 1950s to the dawn of the Islamic Revolution in the late 1970s, a metamorphic line separated unveiled Iranian women—from members of the royal family down to certain segments of the lower-middle-class bourgeoisie—from the veiled women among the religiously observant members of the middle class to the lower class and the poor. Quite a number of other factors had a significant impact on this bifurcation. Generational differences led to situations in which mothers and grandmothers in certain families veiled themselves and their daughters and granddaughters did not. In addition, veiling was a principally urban phenomenon. In northern, western, eastern, and southern parts of Iran, among the Gilakis, Kurds, Turkmens, Baluchs, and the southern tribes and communities, the practice of veiling is to this day almost nonexistent.

While during the Pahlavi monarchy the image of an unveiled woman became the supreme symbol of state-sponsored modernity, since the Islamic Revolution the veiled woman gradually emerged as the paramount picture of the cultural foregrounding of the cataclysmic event. The Islamic Revolution reversed and repeated the dictatorial atrocities of Reza Shah. While Reza Shah brutally forced Iranian women out of their customary habit in order to project his image of modernity (the same way that the racist proclivities of the French government is today forcing Muslim women in France to unveil), the Islamic Republic, about half a century later, forced them back into a dress code they had all but forgotten. It took about half a century for Iranian mothers to produce a generation of daughters confident and graceful in their bodily and facial gestures outside the veil. The Islamic Revolution occurred precisely at a time when that generation of confident daughters was about to deposit the fetishized idea of the *veil* as a marker of piety in the museums of their cultural history. A strict *Islamic* dress code, however, forced women who had liberated their bodies from the confinements of the veil back into their mothers' habits while raising a new generation of young girls who cannot even remember a life outside the veil. The pathological fixation of governments with veiling (Iran) or unveiling (France) women has scarcely anything to do with so-called *Islamism* or *secularism* and everything to do with the mutation of the human body into the principal site of political violence. In both cases the veil has been fetishized—in one as a marker of piety (without which you cannot be a pious person) and in the other as a sign of religious fanaticism (with which you cannot be modern). In both cases the fetishization of the veil conceals the identical fixation with the control and conquest of the (female) body as the *terra incognita* of revolt against the power of the state.

The image of women in the current Iranian cinema is entirely dedicated to this veiled and veiling ideal, the cultural imperative of metaphysics of concealment. Between the jargon of authenticity ("Islamic Tradition") and a colonially mitigated modernity (the state-sponsored modernization), the fate of Iranian women has had to fluctuate. The assumption that veiling—from the Iranian *chador* to Afghan *burka* to Arab *hejab* to a whole slew of similar garments when forcibly used and abused to bar women from occupying the public sphere—is the *traditional* habit of Muslim women is wrong. Asian and African women—from South Asia to Central Africa, from Malaysia to China—have practiced their Islam with perfect piety and dignity and without anything remotely similar to the *chador*, *burka*, or *hejab*. The political brutality of banning the use of the chador under Reza Shah and mandating it under Khomeini is the historical evidence that such *traditions* are invented by force and exacted by terror by way of forcing or denying a garment in order to control the body beneath it as the solitary site of state violence used to ascertain the state's power and legitimacy.

Whether for Reza Shah's *modernization* or during Khomeini's *Islamization*, the feminine (and by extension human) body has remained the solitary site of political contestation, a palimpsestic template on which cultural scriptures are to be written and rewritten, inscribed and overridden. Whether veiled or unveiled, what remains constant about the feminine (and by extension human) body is the metaphorical depletion of its own accumulated memory and the systematic investment of a state-sponsored recollection of historical claims in its vacated space. The *larger* and more grandiloquent the political claims of a monarchical or revolutionary agenda, a colonial or anticolonial program, the more exacting their demands on the *limited* territory of the human body as the principal location of their respective repertoires of symbolic legitimacy.

The Vivid Lantern of Emotions in Search of a Body

Whether in comedy, drama, or a cinema of subversive creativity, the image of Iranian women is now emerging as the haunting head of a bodiless figure tilting and panning from side to side, the vivid lantern of emotions in search of a body to sustain and nourish it.

Mehdi Fakhimzadeh's *The Spouse* (*Hamsar*; 1994), for example, is a fairly successful comic adventure in the battle of sexes that subtextually manages to become a remarkable valorization of women in their mandatory garb but also an emphatic reminder that what the officials term "Islamic veiling" (*hejab-e Islami*) has now been successfully normalized. When the varying beauty of these women exudes itself even through these thick veils, the veils are visually aestheticized beyond history and revolution. What is particularly paradoxical here is that the vibrant and vivacious presence of these women ironically defies the officially imposed dress code and manages to give a semblance of normalcy to an otherwise perfectly manufactured appearance. Fatemeh Motamed Aria has now emerged as the leading Iranian actress while maintaining a remarkable versatility in the range of characters she portrays. It is precisely in her versatility, however, that the ease and the grace with which the mandatory garb has been normalized become evident. Whether she portrays the sprightly and agile pharmaceutical employee in Mehdi Fakhimzadeh's *The Spouse*, the poverty-stricken but remarkably noble Nobar Kordani in Rakhshan Bani-Etemad's *The Blue-Veiled* (*Rusari-abi*; 1995), the flamboyantly mad Simin in Mohsen Makhmalbaf's *The Actor* (*Honarpisheh*; 1993), or any one of a host of other characters, Fatemeh Motamed Aria is the sort of public persona that the reigning ideologues of an Islamic Republic can tolerate, or, perhaps more accurately, that Iranian filmmakers have been able to weasel out of the Islamic Republic's censorship.

Here is of course where cinema must lie. Pictures and videotapes of private parties that are sent out of the country reveal an entirely different picture of Iranian women in their post–Islamic Revolution appearance. In these images, one sees a more consistent continuity with a history of colonial modernity to which both Reza Shah and Ayatollah Khomeini are powerful intrusions. Older and more pious mothers and grandmothers may be more comfortable with more layers of clothing, while their daughters and granddaughters with less. There is a colorful combination of individual tastes and choices, personal preferences, varying degrees of piety, and oscillating claims to beauty. But this is all behind closed doors or else for the private viewing of members of the family abroad. The public personae that the Islamic ideologues wish to portray, and brutally exact, find their most effective characterizations in films produced or sponsored by the Ministry of Guidance. An Orwellian nightmare come true, "The Ministry of Guidance" in effect uses the effervescent creativity of filmmakers to normalize this manufactured picture of an ideal woman. Some splendid attention as a result of this restriction is being paid to local variations on female dress by a number of filmmakers. Since the *chador* is an essentially urban phenomenon, costume that is comfortably customary to any number of Iranian localities is increasingly used by filmmakers as an attractive alternative to the official dress codes. The character of Na'i in Bahram Beizai's *Bashu: The Little Stranger* (*Bashu: Gharibeh-ye Kuchak*; 1986) wears perhaps the most visually visceral example of northern Iranian dress common among women active on rice paddies. The same is true about Tahereh Ladanian in Kiarostami's *Through the Olive Trees* (*Zir-e Derakhtan-e Zeytun*; 1994). Southern Iranian female clothing is splendidly exhibited in, among many other films, Ebrahim Mokhtari's *Zinat* (1994) and Kiumars Pour Ahmad's *For the Sake of Hanieh* (*Beh Khater-e Hanieh*; 1995). In Kamal Tabrizi's *End of Childhood* (*Payan-e Kudaki*; 1994), a vivacious example of Kurdish clothing is used for the leading female character as is a more modest variation of it in Bahman Qobadi's astonishing debut, *A Time for Drunken Horse* (*Zamani bara-ye Masti Asb-ha*; 2000). What Dariush Mehrjui does in *Hamoun* (1993) is even more brilliant. In one of her creative urges, the turbulent Mahshid becomes a fashion designer and surrounds herself with the most fantastic collection of brave and blatant fabrics and models bright, boisterous, and colorfully turbulent dresses. In *Gabbeh* (1997), Mohsen Makhmalbaf revels in a rainbow of color in a tribal setting to combat the official darkness of women's dressing. In his *Silence* (*Sokut*;

1999), Makhmalbaf goes to Tajikistan, where he has a feast with the gloriously colorful local dresses that women wear. In his *Kandahar* (2001), he even uses the burka against its intended purpose and adopts it to frame (rather than hide) Nafas's beauty.

Behind the officially mandated dress code operative in Fakhimzadeh's *The Spouse*, he examines the relations of power operative in a marriage and its interaction with society at large. Comic situations are created when perfectly serious issues result in tension between a husband and wife who work for a pharmaceutical company where, under certain circumstances, she becomes his superior. What is visually paramount in this film, however, is the very physical presence of strikingly beautiful women in positions of authority (one woman even plays the key role of a detective) whose expressive faces move on nonexistent bodies. A visually disturbing set of disequilibria emerges in which we see rough-looking but full-bodied men interact with beautiful but bodiless faces. These faces are expressive, articulate, persuasive, and fully and energetically present in their surrounding space, and yet they are suspended in midair, as it were; no body supports them, nor do they seem to lack a body. They persuasively suggest a body, which they are then brutally denied. Thus they appear as if hanging, like puppets in old-fashioned Persian puppet shows, from conspicuously absent strings. The scenes are particularly disconcerting because these expressive faces move, run, pause, lead a car chase, laugh, cry, and do every other thing that a full-bodied face does with the unselfconscious confidence of faces that belong to bodies that have grown outside the veil. This paralyzing paradox is the most striking aspect of the image of Iranian women in their current (officially regulated) cinema.

As evident in the current Iranian cinema, the bodies of women have been the principal site of demarcation of colonial modernity. From Reza Shah early in the twentieth century to Ayatollah Khomeini late in the same century, the veiling or unveiling of women has been the single most visible sign of the state's claim to progressive politics or revolutionary asceticism.[5] Both the Iranian adaptation of *secular modernity* and the Islamic articulation of a *revolutionary ideology* have opted to mark and navigate their respective claims to power, and thus violence, on the bodies of women. There is nothing *Islamic* or *un-Islamic* about veiling or unveiling except an ideological articulation of power that zeroes in on the *human body* as the principal site of its self-legitimizing violence. In this, Reza Shah and Khomeini are identical, as are the Islamic Republic of Iran and the secular republic of France—both insisting that women should dress in one way or another. The central issue is neither veiling nor unveiling, neither piety nor impiety; the central issue is the amorphous nature of *power* and the necessity of its citing itself on a tangible territory. The more effusive the nature of the transnational state that must correspond itself with an increasingly amorphous capital, the more the human body presents itself as the solitary site of the state's self-legitimizing violence. The Islamic Republic of Iran forces veiling in order to deny its women citizens the daily exposure of their body to the social gaze through which they will gain moral confidence and historical agency. The self-proclaimed secular republic of

France bans veiling because it has made a religion out of what it calls *laïcité* (and its historians and theologians have convinced themselves that this was in fact a Christian contribution to their culture).[6] As Etienne Balibar has critically noted, the European (in particular the French) reinvention of *secularism* "is brandished as a shield against other forms of religious universalism (above all Islam) antagonistic with Christianity, and becomes an instrument to protect 'domestic' cults."[7] The systematic and official harassment of Muslim women in Europe in particular is quintessential to the project that Balibar calls "We, The People of Europe"—with or without a question mark. That very project targeted its Jewish victims at one catastrophic corner of its history and now is narrowing in on its Muslim population. Common to all these projects—both in and out of the so-called *Islamic world*—is the repression of the defiant sign of the body and its forceful mutation into a site of political violence—for or against the state.

HOMELESS EMOTIONS

It is not only *political totalitarianism* that seeks to occupy and dominate the body; so does a mind-numbing *metaphysical absolutism*. Bodiless faces, full of homeless emotions, become the supreme signs of a metaphysical culture perpetually in search of an absolute and absolutist *truth* and radically abstracting itself beyond matter and space. The bodiless faces of Iranian women in their current cinema—cut off from the bodies they must naturally raise, represent, and ultimately occupy—are now the abstracted banners of an essentialist metaphysics once again seeking to transcend the real, the matter, the here, the irreducible facticity of being. As matters of contingent reality are consistently suppressed in a metaphysics of absolutist *truth*, so are physical bodies of women cut off from their faces. These faces, however, are to be kept hidden, concealed, their window into the soul they represent closed. Thus exposed, they reveal too much. Abstracted from realities that materially inform and animate them, they neither accumulate nor are permitted to speak from their bodily memories. The task of a metaphysically modulated cinema is to empty these faces of those bodily memories, forcing them back not just behind veils but into abstractions, into a memoryless self-forgetfulness. The bodies of women thus mutate into totalities of the real, their imposed veils the categorical imperative of a faith at odds with a materially exposed world it cannot fathom. It must resist. The result is the oddity of perfectly occupied faces on doubly vacated bodies.

One of the most powerful visualizations of this relentless *metaphysical absolutism* is to be seen in Dariush Mehrjui's *Pari* (1995). Based on J. D. Salinger's *Franny and Zooey* (1961), *Pari* is a hauntingly Bergmanesque film that in its extremely successful mélange of the beautiful central character, her staunch determination, and the passionate intensity of her neomysticism scares the living daylights out of any conception of reason. From her point of view, *Pari* demonizes the university setting, the professorate, and the mundane banalities of young intellectuals and then draws the world into a mystical act of self-signification that precisely because of its nightmarish beauty is deeply disturbing. The living world of Pari, the lead character, and her brother Dadashi is collapsed into the *metaphoric world* that Pari's neomysticism ceaselessly dreams. The ultimate test of this film is whether Dadashi's turn from *mysticism* to *acting* can match Pari's opposite turn from *acting* to *mysticism*. One can read the penultimate sequence as a reconciliation of the two, but there still remain many disturbing areas. In *Pari*, Dariush Mehrjui has plunged deeply into a self-effacing mysticism that is at once pathologically outdated and calamitously dangerous, erasing the physical evidence of the human body on a spiral of numinous metaphysics of self-annihilation.

What is particularly disturbing in this film is the radical oscillation between a search for, and a conviction in, an eternal and absolute truth for Pari (Niki Karimi) and an empty dwelling in life-as-acting for Dadashi. The intellectual flirtations of the two older brothers, role models for their younger siblings, have led one to a ceremonial suicide and the other to a useless and pathetic isolationism. But the dominant character in the narrative, by virtue of her stunning beauty, eloquent verbosity, absolutist convictions, and single-minded determination, is Pari: a driven mystical visionary who has recurrent nightmares of being forcefully drowned in a small pool; who has a passion for writing with chalk on a blackboard; who storms out of the class of a pretentiously idiotic professor; who sees nothing but confusion, anarchy, and despair in her house (which is in an absolute state of chaos, presumably being renovated); and who abandons her home in Tehran and seeks solace, salvation, and *truth* in the Shaykh Lotfollah Mosque in Isfahan. The embodiment of her *truth* manifest is a strikingly handsome male apparition in the figure of Christ (blond, blue eyes, mystical) who hangs himself upside down from his ankle into a well in the middle of a ruinous and abandoned dwelling and then recites the Qur'an from the first to the last chapter. That Christly figure is there to negate everything about Pari's fiancé in Isfahan, a superciliously pretentious pseudointellectual who gobbles up hearty portions of chelow-kabab while Pari tells him of her most intimate fears, hopes, anxieties, and confusions. The fact that Pari has to seek refuge in the restaurant's washroom to find peace and tranquility and there and then sees the figuratively Christ-figure face of her dearly beloved truth manifest would have exuded its banality had it not been for the intensity and brilliance of Niki Karimi's convincing portrayal of Pari.

Oscillating between life as an act (*bazi*) and life as a quest (*soluk*), Dariush Mehrjui's Pari and Dadashi play out the two gut-wrenching extremities of life at the center of the glorious confusion of which Abbas Kiarostami and Mohsen Makhmalbaf's cinemas have sought to look, be, laugh, cry, and live differently. Mehrjui's superlative cinema, his numbingly beautiful shots, helps create and sustain the two extremities of *truth* and *theatricality*, or *mysticism* and *make-believe*, occasioned by radically pompous intellectuality. Mehrjui's cinema, visually far more learned and contemplative than that of many of his contemporaries, is best suited to reveal the extremities of Iranian cultural tendencies toward *truth-seeking mysticism* and *make-believe acting*.

But the power of *Pari* is precisely in his narrative mutation from *observation of* into *coimagination with* the mystical. That is by far the most dangerous trap that has morally paralyzed this once a great visionary of Iranian cinema. Kiarostami's cinema, operative on a radical modification of the very tempo of our visual encounters with the real, pushes both these extremities aside in order to create or detect a cleavage as if opening a door into a vastly rich and new way of looking at things. In a space thus carved, the binary oppositions evident in the dominant culture and depicted in Mehrjui's cinema collapse into an undefined, undeniable, perfectly palpable, and thus enabling vision of life. Pari and Dadashi, Sister Moon and Brother Sun, represent the two extremities of a cultural alternation between *absolute truth* and *absolute lie*. More petrifying than Dadashi's acting the moral imperatives of life as *many varieties of lies* is Pari's frightening search for *one singular truth* that defines and embraces everything. It is precisely the sort of passionate intensity so evident in Pari that culturally predisposes a people to violent metaphysics, monstrous abstractions, and ultimately to authoritarian monarchies, totalitarian theocracies, and above all the depletion of the historical person from the factual evidence of bodily memories.

Pari's face is the haunting apparition of a pale persistence in abstraction. "The face," proposes Paolo Fabbri in his "Deformities of the Face," "is the place of identification and distinction. The moral guarantor of our persistence in being, of our subjective identity, the face can also suffer from the loss of all modesty and reserve."[8] In the case of Pari, her face expresses nothing but a pale abstraction that reveals her violent persistence on an absolute and unconditional *truth*. "Appearance," again according to Fabbri, "is also an artifice, the ceremonial locus for recognition and transfiguration."[9] Pari's "appearance" speaks nothing but a cultivated proclivity toward abstraction running amuck. Here is a face cut off from her bodily memories. Despite her stunning beauty, Pari (Niki Karimi) is mysteriously asexual. There is a fictive allusiveness about her face, a ghostly shade, which thrives on negating reality in search of an abstracted *truth*. It may be true that "[o]ur face is not a code for connecting the heraldry of expression to the zodiac of emotions," but, as Fabbri himself in fact suggests, "what is left for us, once it has been declared that we cannot know the face?"[10] From Pari's face nothing can be learned. This is a face that shows how the veiling of its body has successfully extended its concealing force up toward the head. The face is pale, emotionless, and without presence, on it the brutal marks of an incurably metaphysical culture, violent to the core of its self-abstracting being. But while a thick and multilayered tyranny of a baggy cloth conceals Pari's body, her face is totally exposed and yet even more fully depleted—a face that speaks nothing of the horrors that it must have seen or will see.

In "Behind the Mirror: Notes from the Portrait in the Twentieth Century," Günter Metken reads Walter Benjamin's 1933 essay "Experience and Poverty" as an overarching comment on portraiture in the twentieth century. Coming back from their harrowing experiences on the front, soldiers of the First World War became the very epiphany of unseen horrors. "Their faces were the only means they had for communicating their experiences at the front."[11] But then in *Pari*, a revolution, a war, and two decades of the most harrowing experiences in the life of a people are absent from the blinding flatness on the face of an otherwise strikingly beautiful woman. Emptied of its worldly memories by an atrocious republic of terror, Pari's body has disappeared behind layers of unwanted veils, while Mehrjui's camera gives a helping hand and effaces her face of all its indexical expressions, mesmerized as she is with *one final absolute truth that explains everything*. In Pari's bodiless face we are trapped in a vision without memory, a beauty without sensuality, an idea without substance, a culture without history, an illusion without conviction. Pari's face is a sacred site to which no pilgrim has paid any visit.

Perfectly evident in Pari is the predisposition of a veiling culture for overarching abstractions, for *Truth* in so capital a letter that it will scare every lowercase doubt out of the vocabulary. Her haunting beauty informs her veiling face and covered body, and both become the quest incarnate of an entire metaphysical culture in search of absolute *God-terms*, of one singular *truth* that reveals, defines, sustains, and overrides everything. A violent metaphysics of "Searching for Truth" is hauntingly evident in the veiled and veiling face of Pari. A woman in abstraction, Pari can never live except in generic terms; can never love but a metaphoric figure; and can never make love except to the shapes, colors, and fantasies of her own making. Pari is the nightmare of a culture of abstraction that had it not been for Abbas Kiarostami, Mohsen Makhmalbaf, Marziyeh Meshkini, and their gloriously real cameras would have totally forgotten how to live. The character of Pari is a disastrous rendezvous between the theocratic politics of a violent metaphysics and the lethargic mysticism of a disillusioned artist.

Pari's mystical quest for absolutist truth empties her mind of all enduring realities, while her brother Dadashi's acting out one version of one truth after another (without any conviction in any one of them) empties his body of all lasting experiences. They are thus where their two elder brothers were years ago; as their elder brothers are where they will be soon: one the walking embodiment of a useless banality (a disillusioned intellectual who has retreated to a village); the other at once the victim and the perpetrator of a ritual suicide by self-immolation. The eldest brother of these four has committed suicide by setting himself ritually on fire, and burning himself, along with the house, to death.

From Disillusioned Artists to Their Critics

Disillusioned artists may in turn anticipate their misguided critics. The wealth of evidence that the Iranian cinema of the last two decades has produced in exposing the particular anxieties of a culture of metaphysical terror requires a very careful attention, particularly under the circumstances of this by far most exciting artistic adventure in recent memory now being subjected to a succession of careless and random readings.

In his study "Veiled Vision/Powerful Presences: Women in Post-revolutionary Iranian Cinema," Hamid Naficy, a leading expert, has pointed out how "the practice of veiling women motivates people to search for hidden, inner meanings in all they see, hear, receive in daily interaction with others; to interpret constantly all products of social interactions, while trying to conceal their own intentions at the same time."[12] To be sure, Naficy is here on the verge of a crucial insight into the working of Iranian cultural anxiety. His theorization of the act of veiling, however, predicated on the categorical proposition that "Iranian hermeneutics is based on the primacy of hiding the core values (that is, of veiling) and of distrusting manifest meanings (that is, vision)," is flawed.[13] That flaw has a cause and a consequence. The cause of it is Naficy's collapse into such unfortunate Orientalist categorizations as, "[i]n many non-western societies with strong hierarchical and group contextual relationships, including Iran, the self is not fully individuated or unified as it is purported to be in the West, but is thought to be familial and communal, that is, defining itself foremost as part of one's family and community."[14] If "the self" is only "purported to be" fully "individuated or unified . . . in the West," then that supposition cannot be a measure of its absence or lack in "non-western" locations. If it is more than "purported" and is believed to be actually the case, and thus its suggestion as a measure of its absence in the unfortunate "non-western" premises, then we have a seriously damaged mind behind the colonized intelligence. Under circumstances that the critical constitution of "the Self" in conditions of coloniality is yet to be fully theorized, Naficy's categorical statement is not only false but, coming from an Iranian, rather unfortunate.[15] An anthropologically disguised, Orientalist reading of Iranian character traits in both linguistic and cultural terms, into whose trap Naficy falls, is traceable to William O. Beeman's *Language, Status, and Power in Iran*.[16] This analytically ludicrous, thinly disguised racist reading of Iranian architectural practices of *biruni/andaruni*, which are also linked to the Islamic mystical notions of *zaher* and *baten*, inevitably distorts the untheorized historical practices into substantiating old-fashioned Orientalist readings of the Oriental as insidious, beguiling, and corrupt. Naficy accepts Beeman's conclusion without the slightest critical consideration.[17] This uncritical acceptance sends Naficy in perilous directions.

The result of this uncritical partaking in Orientalist assumptions is a confusion of the causes of Islamic hermeneutics with its consequences. The sort of hermeneutics that is textually traceable to Qur'anic and Hadith exegesis points not to "the primacy of hiding the core values," as Naficy has assumed, but, quite to the contrary, to the *act* of unveiling the always-already veiled or *decoding* the always-already codified. This hermeneutics of the physical disclosure of the metaphysical concealment does not point to "distrusting manifest meanings" but in fact points to *producing* such meanings by way of implicating a hidden *truth*. The metaphysical foregrounding of the Islamic aspect of Iranian culture, which of course does not exhaust its multifaceted and polyvocal disposition, is neither "hiding the core values" nor "distrusting manifest meanings" but posits a hermeneutic assumption that there is a hidden truth *waiting* to be discovered. On the site of that *expectation* dwells the whole paradoxical self-fulfillment of Islamic metaphysics, which as all other acts of metaphysics is a *promise* that thrives in its *not* being delivered. There is a crucial difference here between a metaphysical assumption that Islamically informs the practice of veiling as concealment and the Orientalist assumption of a cultural proclivity to distrust the manifested and revealed and thus hide one's intention, which is an only slightly veiled way of saying that Iranians are constitutionally suspicious and pathologically duplicitous.

There is a supplementary flaw in Naficy's field of observation. Such attempts at theorization of veiling as a cultural practice fall flat on their face, because the contemporary grasp of the Iranian *visual present* is articulated at the heavy cost of its *literary past*. Naficy confuses the public and private spheres by ascribing to the "Iranian hermeneutics" an essentialized binary opposition between a cherished concealment of the hidden truths and a distrusted rejection of the manifested vision. This is historically inaccurate and theoretically flawed. What is textually evident in the Qur'an and the Hadith masternarratives, and hermeneutically realized by libraries of commentaries, is the act of dialectical discovery that holds the *a priori* hidden *truth* and the *a posteriori* vision of it epistemically together. The entire genre of *Kashf al-Mahjub*, not just the two most famous texts by al-Sajistani in the fourth/tenth century and al-Hujwiri in the fifth/eleventh, points precisely to this dialectic of discovery. What is happening in the contemporary Iranian cinema is the paradoxical relocation of an already revealed *truth* back to its veiled condition, a paradox that ultimately fails because while Islamicized bodies must politically yield to a veiling of *truth*, the cultivated fact of the faces that those bodies inform aesthetically reveals an already exposed countertruth. The politics of sexuality operative in the construction of this "Islamic body" needs a far more serious attention than offered it by critics and scholars interested in Iranian cinema. That politics is constitutional to the jargon of authenticity ("the traditional Iranian woman") that survives any overthrow of a monarchy and perfectly matches any Islamic Republic.[18]

Repeated attempts at reading the act of veiling in the contemporary Iranian cinema are consistently crippled by the distorting consequences of the conventional and unexamined bifurcation postulated between "non-Western societies" and "the West." It is simply astonishing for anyone with the remotest claim to critical thinking to continue to operate in between these empty vacuous abstractions. Figments of the Orientalist imagination, these terms have for the longest time essentialized/vilified otherwise radically subversive details that make a mockery of any such power-basing terms of convenience and confusion. There are as many forces conducive to / inhibitive of "individuating selves" in Cairo, Tehran, Bombay, Beijing, and Seoul as there are in New York, London, Paris, or Munich. This is so even if we reduce these perpetually evolving cultures to their religious parameters, which is an incredibly odd thing to do in a mode of critical thinking with a claim to *poststructuralism* and *postmodernism*. So where precisely is this "West," and where on earth must one stand to be in "the non-West"? "Islam" is as much conducive to / inhibitive of "familial and communal" proclivities as Judaism and Christianity. But all these are unexamined, essentialist, foundational, and metaphysical ways of thinking about historical cultures that fly in the face of their changing material realities and porous boundaries. Over the last two hundred years, the condition of coloniality in much of the world, including the subaltern conditions in the so-called "West" itself, has created and constituted a mode of subjectivity in between colonially constituted modernity and the jargon of authenticity it has engendered and called "traditions," which cannot be reduced to such power-basing abstractions as "the West" and "the non-West." Instead of giving *native* credence to such colonial constructs, we need to understand the inflected presence of these cultures on the colonial outpost, where a far more revolutionary art awaits theorizing. Unless we begin to see the fabrication of the very idea of "the West" as an ideological by-product of the project of colonial modernity, with specific roots in a particular period of history, the Hegelian teleological assumptions are bound to make *slaves* of us all to the *master* narratives of colonial officers, whether they had a Bible, a gun, or a dictionary of local languages in hand.

There is a myriad of evidence that the fact and phenomenon of veiling can be creatively used to work *against* the presumption of hidden meanings. As a perfect example of how the very practice of veiling, embedded in a mythological narrative of prehistory, can be used effectively in subverting a culture of absolutist assumptions and/or a "hermeneutics of hidden meaning" one can look at Bahram Beizai's cinema in general but *The Ballad of Tara* (*Cherikeh-ye Tara*; 1977) or *Bashu: The Little Stranger* in particular. In *The Ballad of Tara*, Beizai crafts a mythological narrative, a *veiled* mode of telling, in which the very gendered idea of *woman* is radically reexamined. From the very first image, Tara is seen as part and parcel of a perpetually life-giving nature: She rides proudly on a horse-drawn carriage, holding the reins with confidence, her two children by her side, the very picture of mother earth. The woman as earth, nature, fertility, and perpetual life-giver is portrayed here mythically at a moment that she has lost two of her men: a husband and a father. She is being courted by four men: by a half-crazed boy; by the brother of her murdered husband who is probably his murderer and who is madly in love with her and whose name is Ashub (Chaos); by Qelich who, like her, is earthly and digs water from the depths of the earth; and then by *The Historical Man* who has been sent back from history to this its premoment in order to get back his sword and falls in love with Tara.

The mythological narrative, or the "veiled" mode of telling a prehistoric tale, is here fully charged to undo the historically narrated ideal of Truth as Veiled Woman. Beizai in effect retrieves the reigning cultural parameters back to their prehistoric moment of conception so that he can begin to renegotiate their validity. But this very act has to be performed in the veiling mode of mythological storytelling. Violence is by far the single most important factor in this visual renegotiation of cultural imperatives. Whatever Tara has inherited from her grandfather she distributes to everybody in the village, much to their delight, even the sword, which is brought back to her immediately because of the fear of its being haunted. She is given back the sword, but she does not know quite what to do with it. She tries to chop wood with it, cut vegetables, or use it as a doorstop. She throws it out into the sea, much to the anger of "The Historical Man," but the sea returns the sword, much to her surprise. She begins to discover the use of the sword when a wild dog attacks her and her children. "The Historical Man" is out to get his sword back to defend his honor, but while in this premoment of history he falls in love with Tara and cannot leave and go back to history until he is assured that Qelich is also in love with Tara. All these mythological modes of storytelling are squarely at the service of Beizai's ingenious recasting of the Persian mythical imagination, which he believes to be squarely at the roots of the contemporary predicament of being an Iranian. He might be misguided in that assumption or overbearing in his treatment of that mythological imagination. But the cast of his cinematic cosmovision is integral to his creative critique of his contemporary culture.

Veiling his cinematic vision in a mythological language, Beizai in effect subverts time and narrative in a way that enables his story to find and demonstrate its own internal logic and rhetoric. That *logic* is foregrounded in a mythological premoment in which Beizai can redefine not just the *idea* of woman hitherto invented patriarchally but with it the entire course of human history. Beizai's judicious use of veiling, as in fact his adaptation of Iranian passion play (*Ta'ziyeh*) motifs, helps him create that premoment that is constitutional to his mythological narrative. But this entire narrative strategy is constructed and geared toward Beizai's intended redefinition of the very idea of femininity in culture: a reflection at once critical and constructive, mythological and real, retrospective and liberating.

The crucial distinction that we must make here is between the nameless ideologues who as self-appointed custodians of public morality are trying to *Islamicize* Iranian cinema, and as such become the agents of censorship in "the Ministry of Guidance," and visionary filmmakers like Bahram Beizai who are the master practitioners of an art that is at once critical and empowering, revealing and liberating. The troubling aspect of such generic assumptions as "the practice of veiling women motivates people to search for hidden, inner meanings in all they see, hear, receive in daily interaction with others; to interpret constantly all products of social interactions, while trying to conceal their own intentions at the same time" is that in effect they wed the worst remnants of colonial Orientalism with the absolutist definitions that theocracies give to an otherwise multifaceted culture.[19] The same culture, the same "Iranian hermeneutics," holds as its crucial components such liberating forces as the cinema of Bahram Beizai. It is not from the outside of a culture but from within its very constitutional forces, the *mythos* that sustains its *logos*, that a liberating aesthetics can map out the terms of its emancipation. Because it is a dead and deadening discourse, Orientalism has always defined cultures in terms of their repressive institutions and has remained constitutionally ignorant of their defiant forces. As to why a contemporary critic from within a culture should partake in such reactionary and repressive assumptions, it really baffles the mind.

Between disillusioned artists and misguided critics, cultures can create and sustain the particular terms of their own moral entrapments, bodily denials, memorial self-abstention, and agential repressions. The recent cinema of Dariush Mehrjui, best represented in his *Pari*, has at once generated and solicited a mode of *mystical absolutism* and *cultural essentialism* that aestheticizes a manner of bodily veiling that denies the active accumulation of historical memory, eliminates the categorical significance of the social space, bars the spatial awareness of time and texture, and thus altogether empties the physical body of its own narrative devices, making it instrumental to anything but its own will to live.

Between Poetry and Censorship

The innate forces of a liberating vision that breaks loose of this creative entrapment in an aesthetics of *mystical annihilation* getting dangerously close to the factual evidence of the body is under the control of the filmmakers themselves. What the ideologues of the Islamic Republic and its censorial forces do not understand is that the terms of no aesthetics can possibly be legislated. There are always unintended consequences to a work of art. Not just the censorial scissors of the Islamic ideologues but the filmmakers themselves can be fully in control of what is being issued from their dialectical fear of each other. The fate of Iranian cinema, Mohsen Makhmalbaf once said, is being determined between poetry and censorship. Once the poetics that sustains this cinema elevates it, the censorship that stifles it suppresses it. From the midst of that dialectic of reciprocity, Iranian cinema is being reimagined, and with it is being negotiated the very cast of Iranian cultural presence in the world. Though its principal architects are known, no single artist is in full control of this emancipatory movement, and not even the Gestapo itself could derail its momentum. As Mary Sheriff has argued in her study of "Fragonard's Erotic Mothers and the Politics of Reproduction," there is always a certain uneasiness about a picture as a text *sui generis* and the sort of political purposes it is meant to serve: "The image [, she points out,] stubbornly resists any straightforward reading, even one based on a sensitive appraisal of the gender or class biases of the painting's audience(s). For both ambiguous and ironic works, it is crucial that the internal dynamics of the painting direct the reading and that the multiple interactions between ostensible subject, subtext(s), and formal structure govern how the interpreter conceives the relationship between the painted image and either the social practice it represents or the social ideal it helps to create."[20] What Rakhshan Bani-Etemad achieves in her *The Blue-Veiled*, a good example of transvaluative representation, is in effect a radical reconstitution of the nature of love affairs permitted in a cinema that an Islamic Republic can take. One need not here report or elaborate on the sort of behind-the-scenes, anecdotal stories that the director herself relates in order to secure permission for certain scenes of intimacy between her two lead characters. Already evident in the released film itself are the signs of a rich cinematic technique at the service of a successful transvaluation of love and affection permissible by the censor. To manage to exude sensuality from the face and figure of a poor woman garbed in working class versions of the *chador* and roundly rough and rugged in her demeanor is now among the hallmark features of Iranian cinema. *The Blue-Veiled* is an effective transformation of the classical melodramatic genre of rich man meets poor girl into a cinema that radically redefines the cliché into a potent cultural catalyst. In *The Blue-veiled*, Bani-Etemad canvases a constellation of trains, train tracks, roads, highways, and long chimneys, all translucently marked by the panning and tilting movements of her camera, to suggest the vertical and horizontal lines of a geography of regimentation that she then sublates to graft the range of rigid sentiments operative in a repressively routinized culture.

The Blue-Veiled is a forbidden love story between a rich and powerful widower and a poor and dignified young woman. But paramount in the telling of this story is the question of how exactly a woman director could tell a love story in an Islamic Republic. The sheer fact of a woman telling a love story on a wide and voluptuous screen in a land of veiled faces, concealed bodies, and denied sensualities is perhaps the most significant aspect of Bani-Etemad's cinematic career. In order to tell her story, she has reached deep into the most recent and distant memories of her cultural repertoire. Her semiotic sense of names, shapes, objects, and colors assumes mythical proportions when it comes to the point of visually insinuating moments of intimacy between a man and a woman permitted on an Islamic screen. The night that the marriage between Rasul Rahmani and Nobar Kordani is to be consummated, the least and the most she can weasel through the censor is the image of two pairs of feet dancing naked on the wet floor of a courtyard affectionately dimmed in an early evening dusk. This image pales in comparison with a Titianesque portrait of Rasul Rahmani sitting with his white shirt, his back against the wall of a sparsely lit courtyard. On his lap is the sleeping head of his young wife's even younger sister. As he gently caresses the young girl's hair, Nobar, his bride, prepares a voluptuous tray of fresh fruit. Here Bani-Etemad employs the significance of the name she has given her heroine. "Nobar" means "fresh fruit." Placing the trayful of fresh fruit at the feet of her groom, Nobar offers the visual substitution of herself, the fruit of her body, to Rasul, her husband. Rarely can a scene be so innocent and yet so provocatively sensuous. When we see Nobar the following morning, her beautiful face exudes a radiant happiness, the empty pool at the center of her courtyard now full of fresh, life-giving water, around the pool vases of passionately red geraniums, one of them plucked by her younger sister and accidentally dropped into the pool. *Veiling* here is no longer inhibitive; it is no means of concealing the truth or disguising reality. Here *veiling* is turned into the very instrument of revelation. Cultural parameters can never be tyrannically legislated or metaphysically mandated. Art defies not just the theocracies that it subverts but the philosophies that it sublates.

ABSENTING THE OTHER

Beyond the control of filmmakers like Beizai and Bani-Etemad, the mandated practice of veiling in Iranian cinema aesthetically visualizes what a theocracy has metaphysically mandated. The result is a constitutional abstraction of the idea and presence of "the Other," to the point that Sartre's existential anxiety, that "I exist for myself as a body known by Other," is no longer viable.[21] In all essentializing strategies of violent metaphysics, every individuated possibility of "the self" is negated via an active reversal of all existential "others." If not in active and critical dialogue with individuated "others," all potential "selves" cannot but be essentialized into ahistorical abstractions. "With the appearance of the Other's look," Sartre observed, "I experience the revelation of my being-as-object; that is, of my transcendence as transcended."[22] But that cannot occur unless we have the preliminary possibility of a directed gaze of "the Other" at the exposed body of an individuated "self." Substitution of veiled abstractions for existential "others" is the most immediate strategy at the disposal of all metaphysics to abort that possibility. Absolutist metaphysics, Islamic or otherwise, thrives on abstractions and insists on essentialized categories that even in apparent opposition to the sacred cannot but strengthen its premise. The fate of the individual, as a result, is always a negotiated settlement between the dominant abstractions of the sacred and the emancipatory strategies of art. Between *the metaphysics of the sacred* and *the aesthetics of the surface*, the two dialectical ends of every form of art, the variegated topography of reality yields its alternative shades.

Consider, for example, the function of invoking classical Shi'i leitmotifs in the making of an Islamically modulated cinema. Playing with variations on the Karbala theme has provided many Iranian filmmakers with much opportunity for dramatic renarrations of tragedy, sacrifice, and redemptive suffering, all of which are squarely at the service of a metaphysical celebration of martyrdom powerfully predicated on an abstracted idea of a distanced "Gaze" substituting an existential "Other." Kiumars Pour-Ahmad's *For the Sake of Hanieh* is a good example of this genre. The active remembrance of the Karbala leitmotif in *For the Sake of Hanieh* is the visual celebration of all martyrological leitmotifs in Iranian/Islamic culture. When the father of a southern family in Bushehr dies while playing dammam (a kind of drum played on both ends while hanging from the neck), his young son's ambition becomes to take his father's place as the drummer during the Muharram ceremony. The new role of the young boy, Bashiroo, also requires that he provide for *his* family by doing various odd jobs. Returning from one of these tasks, he drops the money he has earned on the ground where his mother is sitting. Offended by this disrespectful gesture, the mother slaps Bashiroo in the face and tells him that he has to come and offer his earnings to his mother respectfully, "like a man." Pour-Ahmad relies heavily on the visual remembrance of *thirst*, central to the renewed memory of the Karbala motif, and makes sure that Bashiroo's repeated attempts to drink water are thwarted by various events.

Bodily affliction of a young girl, the manly devotions of a young boy, a closely knit community of believers, and then a sustained set of miraculous deeds and expectations mark Pour-Ahmad's active resuscitation of the memorable leitmotifs of the Karbala paradigm, suggesting a preeternal gaze that decides the everlasting terms of humanity at large. *For the Sake of Hanieh* is the outcome of an essentializing metaphysics compatible with a culture of veiling. "In particular," we have known since Sartre, "I feel myself touched by the Other in my factual existence; it is my being-there-for-others for which I am responsible. This being-there is precisely the body."[23] That *body*, dialectically negotiated with the world that is already evident in the gaze of "the Other," is denied in a culture of concealment that substitutes the everlasting glare of "the Sacred" for the existential gaze of "the Other." Whereas Beizai's cinema plots to renarrate and historicize the *mythos* of his culture, and Bani-Etemad's cinema seeks ways of subverting its essentialized *sacred* assumptions, Pour-Ahmad's effectively sustains them.

FORMING BODILESS FACES

Between these two opposing modes of attending to the current perils and promises of the Iranian cinema, the fate of its postrevolutionary aesthetics is being determined. What these bodiless faces have learned to do is to begin to point beyond themselves, to show something similar to what Anne Deneys in "The Political Economy of the Body in the *Liaisons dangeureuses* of Choderlos de Laclos" calls "the discourse of libertines."[24] As opposed to the "natural" or "naive" language, the "libertines" language in *Liaisons dangeureuses* "elaborates a particular economy in signs in which a 'sign' or 'signifier' no longer corresponds to a true 'sentiment' or to any moral 'signified,' in opposition to what happens in natural language. In this economy the sign becomes a mask, a false pretense whose only finality is to mystify the other. Libertine discourse is no longer 'expressive;' it is a discourse of exchange."[25] In a cinema regulated by an Islamic Republic, this means taking the innate and constitutional parameters of *veiling* and using them against their intended purposes.

One of the most brilliant examples of this mode of subversive signification of the dominant metaphors is to be seen in Mohsen Makhmalbaf's *The Bread and the Flowerpot* (*Nun va Goldun*; 1996).[26] What Makhmalbaf achieves in this film is a moment of cinematic brilliance where the routine gesture of a young girl pulling the right side of her veil up to cover her face from strangers is used with measured tempo to come to a precise crescendo in the very last, and very beautiful, shot of the film—with exactly the opposite effects of what a veil is supposed to do.

The Bread and the Flowerpot is the fictive reconstruction of an actual event in the life of Makhmalbaf himself when at the age of 17 he conspired with his friends to stab a policeman and steal his gun. With a measured maturity now worked to perfection in his cinematic vision, Makhmalbaf looks back at this event assaying the silent brutalities of a culture of violence. The young girl who is to play the role of Makhmalbaf's cousin and coconspirator holds the right side of her veil up throughout the film in order to negotiate a public measure of modesty and privacy for herself. Makhmalbaf takes this innocent gesture and does something visually subversive with it. The gesture is inevitable, mandatory, and compulsive under the ascetic rules of the Islamic censor. The gesture, as Makhmalbaf carefully demonstrates throughout the film, is dismissive, barring the intruding eyes from looking at the beautiful face of the young girl. In the very last shot, the young girl is supposed to go up to the policeman and ask him what time it is so that young Makhmalbaf's has time to stab him and steal his gun. In the meantime, the policeman has just found out that contrary to his imagination the young girl is not really interested in him but is a coconspirator in a plot to kill him. While the old Makhmalbaf is directing his young self to stab the policeman and steal his gun, his young self is hopelessly resisting doing so, sobs in confusion and refusal, and in desperation buys a loaf of bread to conceal his knife while approaching the policeman. In the meantime, while the former policeman is directing his young self to forget about the flowerpot he had intended to give to the young girl but instead draw his gun and shoot her, his young self, a mirror image of Makhmalbaf's, is equally reluctant to commit a violent act.

In one of the most brilliantly directed and choreographed sequences in Iranian cinema—with balletic repetitions, melodic accents, and close-ups of breathtaking precision and subtlety—the young girl approaches the policeman, turns her face away from him and toward the camera, which now can penetrate into the inner sanctum of her budding sensuality, while lifting up the right side of her veil. The camera freezes here. We now have a close-up of her face with perfect framing of her black veil and white face. Her round face is the circular center of a rectangular portrait of innocent beauty. Her extended hand pulling up the veil creates a pitch-black curtain around that circular center, while her black eyes and eyebrows accentuate the dark, underlining the whiteness of the face. A portrait of uncommon beauty is now in full view of the camera.

The camera now dwells on the close-up of this graceful portrait with the repeated question of the young girl to the policeman, "Excuse me officer, what time is it?" The repeated close-up of the young girl's face, draped by her extended arm pulling up the curtain of her veil, has the multiple functions of allowing not only the camera to cultivate the exuding beauty, the budding sensuality of that face, but also the young Makhmalbaf and the young policeman to contemplate the nature of the violence they are about to commit. The moment is a moment of suicidal assassination—certain death on both sides, or else. The young Makhmalbaf approaches with a naked knife in his hand concealed beneath a loaf of fresh bread, while the young policeman has a small flowerpot in one hand and his ready gun in the other. "Excuse me officer, what time is it" asks the sensual face, the extended arm, the embracing veil that has now accepted the camera into the full embrace of her bosom. As the camera is about to freeze, into the frame come from the young policeman's side a pot of flowers and from the young Makhmalbaf a loaf of bread.

"This entire film is really just a postcard," Makhmalbaf once said in the course of a conversation in mid-August 1996 in Locarno, where *The Bread and the Flowerpot* had its first international screening. In that last frozen shot—a loving "postcard" from the maturing Makhmalbaf nearing in age his deuteronomical number of punishment—the routine gesture of young women covering their faces is redefined, aesthetically cultivated into a signal not of exclusion but inclusion, not of dismissal but of invitation, not the death of the body but the life of the face. In that frozen shot, Makhmalbaf's loving "postcard" to his youth, is collected life, beauty, and bread. Here is where the gentle hand of an artist transforms the most brutal measures of denying life and love into precisely the opposite of those cruel measures. "The notion of bodily resurrection," as Caroline Walker Bynum concludes her examination of it in Western Christianity, "is a concept of sublime courage and optimism. It locates redemption there where ultimate horror also resides—in pain, mutilation, death, and decay."[27] No *metaphysics of resurrection* is needed where an *aesthetics of redemption* can sublimate violence into love.

The possibility of a metamorphosis of the *metaphysics of veiling* into an *aesthetic of sensuality* is particularly susceptible to the sort of political parameters that sustain an Islamic revolution. As Lynn Hunt has demonstrated in "The Many Bodies of Marie Antoinette: Political Pornography and the Problem of the Feminine in the French Revolution," the homosocial ideals of masculinity in the French Revolution required not only "the violent rejection of aristocratic degeneracy" but, more important, opposition to any "intrusion of the feminine into the public."[28] As she puts it, "the republican brothers who had overthrown the king and taken upon themselves his mantle did not want their sisters to follow their lead."[29] The postrevolutionary Iranian cinema is now the contested ground of precisely a similar negotiation for the very idea of femininity. Is the body of the feminine to be delegated to the oblivious nonpresence of the veil, or is it to be brought back to the central space of the renegotiated public? In this particularly significant respect, what such films as Kamal Tabrizi's *End of Childhood* or Kiumars Pour Ahmad's *For the Sake of Hanieh* perpetuate in the Shi'i memory of Persian patriarchy, Mohsen Makhmalbaf's disquieting tragicomedy, *The Actor* (*Honarpisheh*; 1993), successfully disrupts. *The Actor* is narrated with such visual precision and balance that Makhmalbaf's Felliniesque camera always suspends the audience between the two conflicting emotions of laughter and sorrow, viewing comedy and witnessing tragedy. A comedian husband and a wife driven to madness by the communal expectation of her having a (preferably male) child become the centerpiece of a deeply moving meditation on the nature of reason and madness, love and sacrifice, private anguish and public despair. In this beautifully crafted antitale that for 86 minutes carries the audience through a rollercoaster of conflicting emotions, the act of veiling is used to conceal and reveal emotions and sentiments otherwise emotively inaccessible.

What is particularly powerful in this film is Makhmalbaf's almost vicious inventiveness to break loose the customary boundaries of comedy and tragedy, sanity and madness, reason and unreason, life and art, art and decadence, and, perhaps most subversively of all, masculinity and femininity. All these are done first and foremost with a rambunctiously agitated camera with an uncanny ability to generate and sustain creative confusion, irresolvable tension, asphyxiating anxiety, and above all the debilitating terror of not knowing whether one is to laugh or cry, embrace or escape, kneel down or run away. The character of the dumb gypsy girl is central to a flamboyant carnivalesque use of native dressing to cover the young body of a woman without concealing her mute sexuality. Makhmalbaf manages visually to generate a ménage-a-trois among the gypsy girl and the couple at the center of the film. There are even moments of daring homoeroticism between the gypsy girl and Simin that could have only escaped censorship through the sheer power of their inventiveness. Makhmalbaf succeeds in visually conveying the idea of two female characters *marrying* each other and even one making the other, metaphorically and visually, *pregnant*.

From the depth of the cause comes also its cure—in terms domestic to the pain, with no morality in attendance. The body denied in its death, the body remembered in its life—and this not in the politics of its suicidal despair but in the aesthetics of its celebration of hope.

The Serenity of a Distanced Gaze

How far can these *aesthetic* manipulations of the *metaphysical* go? The culture that must sustain a metaphysics of an absolute singular truth that is concealed from the naked eye must, necessarily, cover feminine faces that challenge the serenity of a distanced gaze. Thus *sharm*, *haya*, and *ab-e ru*—all variations on the compelling concepts of "shame," "modesty," and "respect"—become the codes of public conduct. A hermeneutics of duality thus emerges between *surat* ("face" or "form") and *sirat* ("character" or "content"), between *zaher* ("appearance" or "outside") and *batin* ("essence" or "inside"). In this culture, facilitated by all its visual and iconic forces, prohibition of the naked, of the exposed, is the cultural codification of the metaphysics of truth-telling. Supposition of *truth* as naked necessitates the *veiling* of it beyond the reach of the material life. Thus is constituted a rhetoric of *Kashf al-Mahjub*, of revealing what is by necessity hidden. Al-Hujwiri, the fifth/eleventh century author of *Kashf al-Mahjub*, in fact narrates a whole treatise on the principal doctrinal beliefs of Muslims on the epistemic thrust of "revealing the veiled" truth of the Knowledge of God, His Unity, Faith in His Existence, Ritual Purity, Repentance, Prayer, and the Love of God.[30] Under these circumstances, voyeurism becomes the supreme fear of a culture of concealment. Disfiguring (covering) bodies and defacing (veiling) faces are the most immediate ways in which a culture of concealment serves its presiding metaphysics of *one hidden truth*. Islam's is the metaphysics of "Those who believe in the unseen."[31] The nature of "revelation" in this metaphysics is that "[t]hese are announcements relating to the unseen which We reveal to you, you did not know them—(neither) you nor your people—before this."[32] The first and foremost assumption in this metaphysics is that there is a Supreme Revealer "[a]nd with Him are the keys of the unseen treasures—none knows them but He."[33] The more powerful the presiding power of this metaphysics of *One Unseen Seer*, the more a culture of bodily transfiguration, an aesthetics of facial mutation, is necessitated.

The exposed head of a woman seems to constitute a threat to a patriarchal order. The threat is functionally reminiscent of the danger that medieval theorists of patriarchal monarchy saw in two royal claims on one land. Medieval theorists of power believed that "mystical or political body of the kingdom *(corpus mysticum sive politicum regni)*" must be subject to "one head" of the state. Moreover, "since a two-headed society would be monstrous and anarchic, the Pope is merely a secondary head, a *caput secundarium*."[34] The exposition of the head, its theatricality, equally reveals the ocularcentricism of all prophetic visions of the sacred. The privileging of *vision* in the Islamic metaphysics, of God as the Unseen Seer, makes *ocularcentricism* a principal component of the Islamic culture of concealment. As the metaphor of the Unseen is central to the Islamic metaphysics, constituting and yet paradoxically veiling the vision becomes the operative energy of an Islamic aesthetic. As Martin Jay's placement of Sartre and Merleau-Ponty in the poststructuralist history of antiocularcentricism demonstrates, the substitution of cinematic theories for experience shares a profound affinity with phenomenology and its emphasis on meaning and expression.[35] Cinema as an experience, in and of itself, is an ocularcentric event. Combined with a theocentric metaphysics, it cannot but doubly negate the existentially cultivated bodies and faces. In the foundational thinking that an Islamic metaphysics constitutes, *truth* must therefore be concealed with the same logic and rhetoric with which women should be covered. By privileging and yet prohibiting vision, the ocularcentricism embedded in this metaphysics equates *truth* with *concealment*, as it does *exposure* to *untruth*. The exposure is to be mistrusted because "[t]he life of this world is made to seem fair to those who disbelieve"[36] and "[t]he love of desires, of women and sons and hoarded treasures of gold and silver and well bred horses and tilled land and cattle is made to seem fair to men; this is the provision of the life of this world."[37]

If an essentialized truth must be concealed, then extended from a cultivated body, an exposed face reveals the existentialized dialectic of reality, the anxiety of being in the world. Cultures veil their women to claim concealment for a presumed *quintessence*. A *quintessence*, however, is constituted, narratively presumed, doctrinally believed to be. The rhetoric of *Kashf al-Mahjub*, *revealing that which is hidden*, is there to claim that there is a concealed *truth* waiting to be *discovered*. Suppose nothing is hidden behind the veil. What then? Abu Ya'qub Sajistani, the fourth/tenth century author of another treatise also called *Kashf al-Mahjub*, believes that "[t]ruth is hidden because of Satan and his descendants, and yet they are revealed to the friends of God and His Chosen ones."[38] Veiling is based on the metaphysical assumption of an essentially mysterious, perpetually inaccessible, always distanced, and transcendentally concealed *truth*. Suppose we do not share that assumption. What then? Unveiled faces are testimonial exhibitions of lived realities, of the contingency of all convictions, of the necessity of dialogue. What we see in the Islamically slanted Iranian cinema are existentialized faces hanging over essentialized bodies. These faces are the victory of a dialectic of alterity; those bodies are the defeat of a metaphysics of identity. Precisely because those faces reveal too much, subverting any metaphysics of absolute truth too radically, the latest news from the censor bureau of the Islamic Republic was that close-ups of female faces were absolutely forbidden. But in the fateful battle between the Islamic Republic and the Iranian cinema, the choice between the victor and the vanquished is not a matter of political preference; it is a manner of aesthetic predilection.

Chapter 4

Bordercrossings

He took the explorer's hand and guided it over the Bed. "It's specially prepared cotton wool, that's why it looks so different; I'll tell you presently what it's for."

—Franz Kafka, *In the Penal Colony* (1914)

In the last chapter, I sought to find specific examples from the current Iranian cinema of a concealed kind of correspondences between *exposed faces* and *concealed bodies*. By doing so I had hoped to discern the dialogical negotiations between faces and their respective bodies to subvert the metaphysical prevention of their bodily memories. As I suggested in that chapter, my proposal is that *bodily memories* invested in the faces they sustain are constitutional to the grammatical coherence of the vernacular languages a body can speak in defiance of the Latinized tyranny of the presiding culture that tells them to do or be one thing or another. In that chapter, the visionary filmmakers I examined were limited to the banalities of an Islamic Republic, and as such they were located on a space in which the particulars of the *bodily memory* are subject to systematic amnesia. In search of a corrective lens, my intention in the following chapter, which is a sustained reflection on the works of Shirin Neshat, is to see how she has managed to restore to body its originary entropy. Shirin Neshat operates with a much wider margin of possibilities, and her visual reflections on the body are exceptionally successful in retrieving its anarchic defiance of all acts of legislative semantics coming its way. In that act of anarchic defiance, I propose, Shirin Neshat has spotted the location where the *metaphoric body* is at once self-annihilative and self-celebratory.

Veiling and Revealing

The kind of visual art that Shirin Neshat has now brought to perfection receives much of its energy from that ambiguous borderline where *veiling* and *revealing* converse. The equivocality of that borderline is where the body flirtatiously rubs itself against its commanding culture. When we look at that borderline the way Shirin Neshat pictures it, we realize that it is always through the violent terror of *naming* that cultures regulate their mandates. *Naming* (of bodily organs, birth certificates, and all in between) is the most immediate form of *veiling* whereby a culture controls the effervescent defiance of the body. Shirin Neshat has trained her camera with such precision of insight that the negotiated and settled differences between the overriding culture and the submissive body are once again agitated and brought back to the negotiating table. To be able to do that, an artist needs a judicious presence in a transgressive space. Creatively to dwell in that space and yet use it with impeccable control is what distinguishes a great artist from a mere globetrotting dilettante. To what Shirin Neshat owes the spectacular control of her vision is impossible fully to articulate. What is immediately evident, however, is the visual evidence of her successfully tapping into the volcanic junctures of her fragmented cultures, the normative crossings of good and evil, beautiful and repellent, feminine and masculine, controlling and releasing, seduction and solemnity—thus taking us all back to the festive occasion of (in)articulate presence in the premoment of our historical agency.

Shirin Neshat has persistently dwelled on that borderline and infiltrated the modified museum spaces of a global bewilderment in order to *demuseumize* her received, now retrieved, culture; the result is the sublation of one critical cultural moment into the neighborhood of a global aesthetics. Shirin Neshat is an aesthetic tactician of uncommon precision, brevity the soul of her visual wit, bordercrossing her tenuous, attenuated trademark. She is and will always remain, true to her visual transgressions, an illegal immigrant on *both sides* of the border: the political and the aesthetic.

By far the most powerful set of binary oppositions now visually collapsing in Shirin Neshat's work is *sanctity* and *sensuality*. The lifted hand that points to the lips at once allows for the fingers to silence the lips while letting the lips kiss the fingers. The ascetics of silence and the erotics of kissing are here the subtextual prelude of a hand that pictures the two iconographic opposites of *sanctity*—the supreme Shi'i invocation "Ya Qamar-e Bani Hashem"—and *sensuality*—one of the most famous poems of Forough Farrokhzad. Masculine Shi'ism as ascetic inhibition and feminine poetics as sensual emancipation here embrace each other in the back of a single hand. In this single move, Shirin Neshat embraces the (im)possibilities of two iconographic inhibitions. Through their matrix of inhibitions, cultures make it impossible for the juridically mandated pieties to border with the suppressed and denied sensuality. An *ascetics of denial* is at the roots of the *jurisprudence of piety* operative in Shirin Neshat's paternal culture. In the same culture, however, the subversive *theo-eroticism* of Persian Sufism has always experimented with the (im)possibilities of that border. While in the realm of the literary from Mawlana Jalal al-Din Rumi's *mystical poetics* in the seventh/thirteenth century to Sohrab Sepehri's *ascetic realism* in the twentieth we have witnessed destabilizing encounters of the *sensual* with the *sacred*, in visual terms we have never seen what it means to have the two universes collide. It is through her extraordinarily perceptive grasp of the nature of feminine piety in an Iranian/Islamic universe that Shirin Neshat can detect and convey the seductive energy of the clasp when the sacred and the sensual meet. The palpable love and affection with which Shirin Neshat embraces such evident opposites is one crucial source of the precision of her visual bordercrossings. The *prophetic* and the *poetic*, the *sacred* and the *sensual*, and ultimately *home* and *exile* collapse into an overwhelming embrace summoned by Shirin Neshat's loving hands, seen and shot through her unfailingly sensual gaze.

Equally evident in this measured awareness of the colliding energies of her inherited culture is Shirin Neshat's pictorial oscillation between *controlling* the visual while *releasing* the sensual. This precision of balance can visually transform the clasping of two maternal hands into an embracing vaginal hold of two infantile hands in the simulation of a fetus formation. This is *the* mother-and-child in the making. In another move with similar features, she can aesthetically transform the dismissive clasp of the vaginal formation in the moment of pregnancy into the inviting openness of a womb. The aesthetic control of the visual unleashes here an energy of unsurpassed power, beyond any cultural control. Here, and through Shirin Neshat's camera, body is teaching itself how to mock the inhibited, deride the forbidden, and simulate the truth. By teaching the organs how to mock, Shirin Neshat invests the body with artful counterintelligence. Through its mocking organs, the body is now storing itself with ironic memories, restoring itself to its defiant disposition, and teaching itself how to remember things forbidden, play with fire, and dare its own forgotten elements. Shirin Neshat retrieves and chronicles the forgotten memories of the body and rescues them from the suppressed reservoir of her culture, waging them against their own God-terms, freeing the body from the prison house of its accumulated, ossified rectitude.

In the feminine body in particular, Shirin Neshat has much more enduring memories to invest. The kind of bordercrossings evident in her photographic faces begins to inject *seduction* into *sadness* and *violence* into *serenity*. How could a sad face be sensual, and how could serenity harbor violence? Beyond a furious revolution in 1979 and a catastrophic war between 1980 and 1988, the two most violent memories that animate Shirin Neshat's photography, she reaches for the innermost assumptions that divide and conquer the anxieties of revolt and the dreams of emancipation. The instant that her camera forgets how to look for the *erotics of irony* in a face, that emancipatory possibility is in danger. The glory of Shirin Neshat's photography is in her uncanny ability to turn violence into an energetic serenity and sadness into sensuality. The result is an unsettling revelation about the seductive force of violence. In this respect, she is the visual conscience and the photographic memory of an entire generation of hopes turned into fears, laughter turned into tears, and the joyous ephemerality of the body turned into the dead certainties of a culture. By picturing our present predicament with a loving gaze, Shirin Neshat has a claim on being the photographer of our past indiscretions and the dreamer of our future emancipation. She pictures *things* that have already happened but are unregistered, *things* that are yet to happen but are unforeseen; she is a visionary of the (im)possible.

It is toward an articulation of the terms of that future emancipation that Shirin Neshat's turn to the male body will have to be read. Her male bodies are the projected sites of a decidedly feminine gaze. From the secure vaginal embrace of an infantile boy to the distant figure of a full-bodied man, the masculinity of a body remains always contingent on the femininity of the gaze cast on it. Without that feminine gaze, without Shirin Neshat's seductive camera, *man* is but a name with no claim to any body. Thus her entire camerawork is the corrective lens of a culture of masculinity that has formed the male body in the absence of the publicity of a feminine gaze. Shirin Neshat's camera publicizes the private look of a feminine denial into the pronounced gaze of its positive affirmation. She is looking at the masculine body with the intensity of all the denied feminine gazes that her culture has harbored. The result is not a mere publicity of the feminine gaze. The result is destabilizing the fake confidence of the masculine body, formed and infused in the absence of a confident feminine gaze.

Shirin Neshat's body of photographic evidence registers the sustained record of successful bordercrossings. As she challenges the received repressions of all our metaphysics of denials, she invests in us all the emancipatory memories of a bodily resurrection. The strategic modulations of bordercrossings, definitive to her entire oeuvre, function like a visual ploy to intimate the possibilities of a bodily resurrection. Bodily resurrection, as a metaphysical (im)possibility, has a long and revered history in her received (Islamic) culture. But what she does with that (im)possibility is precisely where her art has a fateful rendezvous with the global implications of her metaphysical culture. On the premise of that appointment, we can see visibly how the *metaphoric body* is at once self-annihilative and self-celebratory, and how precisely in that paradox the *metaphoric body*, no longer in charge of itself, becomes conscious of its own metamorphic disposition. The result is the visual postulation of a pliable, bendable body that Shirin Neshat has teased out of its received and legislated rectitude. In the pliability of that metaphoric body we can then see how *seduction and sadness* are next-door neighbors, as are *violence and serenity*, and thus see the logic and lunacy of the seduction of violence that bodies at once harbor and harness. It is a gift of Shirin Neshat to be able to channel that *violence into piety* and that *piety into eroticism*. But that very logic of her aesthetics points to the lunacy of the politics that suggests that there is an *eroticism to piety* and a *piety to violence*—all contradictory claims that collide and collapse on the bones and banalities of the human body. As the eroticism of Shirin Neshat's feminine gaze depoliticizes the masculine bodies she photographs, we become even more conscious of the fact and fantasy that her caring camera has detected in the political violence that has already occupied that body. Shirin Neshat is the photographer of the hidden horrors that have been visited upon our bodies.

A Bodily Resurrection

Today the possibilities of the bodily resurrection that Shirin Neshat photographs are taking place in full public view and on the site of two crisscrossing passages: bodies taking their cultures to task, and cultures taking their nations to the globe. The global view though confuses the two, taking one for the other and ignoring the organic root of the two in each other. In his review of the Santa Fe biennial, Ralph Rugoff opted to showcase Shirin Neshat's video installation "Rapture" as an example of what he termed "migratory artists" crowding "circus-like surveys . . . [of] an internationalist ethic."[1] As Rugoff noted, "the international biennial has taken center stage as the dominant exhibition format for presenting new works," and even more important, showcasing "an internationalist ethic" has become "in itself a prerequisite for creating a truly contemporary art show." That may indeed be the case, but to what end? Rosa Martinez, the Spanish curator of Site Santa Fe, calls the exhibition in her New Mexico space "Looking for a Place" out of her conviction that "the most innovative art seeks to break out of institutionalized spaces." If European museums at the turn of the last *fin de siécle* in the nineteenth century were the substitute pantheons of high European bourgeoisie replacing the palaces they had vacated of power and churches they had declared dead, these international biennials at the turn of this *fin de siécle* in the twentieth century are now rightly the sites of immigrant artists no longer at home where they were born but seeking to turn the lemon of migratory labor into the lemonade of creative art.

Rugoff credits Shirin Neshat with having "developed a hybrid vernacular capable of simultaneously addressing her different audiences" and points out that many of her colleagues at the Santa Fe have failed to do so. The question, though, remains: what precisely is this "hybrid vernacular" that is capable of addressing multiple audiences? Does Shirin Neshat indeed manage to speak to more than one audience? And who might these audiences exactly be? Iranians? Migratory (the so-called diasporic) communities? Globalizing capital and labor, of the sort that *The Financial Times* chronicles? Neshat's audience(s) cannot of course be considered her compatriot Iranians inside their country because, as Rugoff rightly notes, she "cannot be shown in her native country (Iran)." As for the *globality* of Neshat's art, the term conceals much more than it reveals. What it reveals, though, is quite crucial. The globality of the predicament that embraces and informs Neshat's art supersedes such binary opposition as East-West (or Islam and the West)—terms that have for long distorted the circularity of capital and its culture. The globality of our predicament, which is nothing new, though recently aggravated, cannot any longer be collapsed into convenient but misleading categories. To be contemporary is to be global but global in terms constitutional to the circularity of capital (and labor) migration and the culture it equally forces to be migratory. The global also means the immediate suspension of all the aggressive categories that have so far forced the world into artificial encampments independent of the circular logic of capital and its commanding cultures.

As Rugoff notes of the Chinese artist Lai Guo-Qiang's installation of a twenty-foot-high lighthouse built from timber and detritus atop Site Santa Fe's building, it collapses into "repackaging their aesthetically modest work as grandiose metaphor" and as such having a claim over nothing more than "its inane pretension." This is an example of remaining within the confinements of a domesticity that fails to transcend beyond itself and reach for a "hybrid vernacular" that locates the Chinese in the globality of its post–Tiananmen Square predicament. But the example also points to entrapment in the existing paradigmatics of identitarian ethics and politics, of which not just Lai Guo-Qiang but Rugoff himself remains accused. The *inter-national* reception of an art generated within the *global* circularity of capital and culture cannot but continue the old, outdated, binary assumptions of East and West, of nations and national cultures in conversation or clash with each other. If there is to be a "hybrid vernacular," it can be neither "hybrid" nor assumed "vernacular." The "hybridity" assumes an originary authenticity that no longer is, as the "vernacular" predicates a sacramental Latin we can no longer remember or revere.

Rosa Martinez, the curator of Santa Fe 1999, is credited for having recently announced that "cultures must reinvent a new ethic of existence."[2] Whether or not such lofty credits, self-assigned by curators, are in or out of place, presumably what Martinez has in mind is for art to catch up with the migratory force of capital and labor. Neither Martinez, though, nor any one of the artists she has exhibited can "invent" anything unless the outcome corresponds to a yet-to-be-named, pictured, or narrated reality. The reality that Shirin Neshat pictures and of which her audiences are yet to be informed are always-already bordercrossing realities. These bordercrossings are locally subversive precisely because they are globally transgressive. They liberate domestically precisely because they subvert globally. In the process, they manage to do what Rosa Martinez demands them to do and "invent" an ethic of globality that at the same time liberates them locally. But they do so not because they are sitting on an Olympian mountain of aesthetic aloofness. They do so because they are responding in earnest to a cultural globality that is barely catching up with the capital that has occasioned it.

Ralph Rugoff's principle objection to Rosa Martinez is that the majority of the art works she has exhibited "seem far more concerned with declaring what their work is about, rather than showing us how they get there." The problem with such a blunt declaration, Rugoff declares, is that "exhibitions like this can do little more than celebrate internationalism for its own sake—a worthy political goal, perhaps, but utterly bankrupt as an aesthetic proposition." This damning declaration points precisely to the tension between the emerging globality of an art that still *rightly* lacks a definition and an *internationalist's* expectation of a definitive aesthetics that charts and locates that definition. The result of this tension is the condemnatory language of the art critic who declares that what we see in Santa Fe "is a latter-day Tower of Babel where the possibility of dialogue between cultures is reduced to a polyglot din. If contemporary art is truly becoming a global language, exhibitions such as this one will need to find new formats, and perhaps new ambitions, in order to do it justice." This is as charitable and sympathetic as an art critic for *The Financial Times* can get in attending such Towers of Babel. But the site of *The Financial Times* is precisely where the underlining globalization of capital and its culture is best readable and thus where its attention to the art that this globalization generates is most noteworthy. It is against that reading of the "internationalism for its own sake" that Ralph Rugoff's attraction to Shirin Neshat's work, entirely despite himself, informs the "new ethics" that Rosa Martinez expects, equally despite herself. The problem is in the configuration of the emerging cultural globality being read from an angle entirely alien to the aesthetic locality that has occasioned them, right before that locality itself is superseded by the globality it informs. The casuistry of the argument mirrors the circularity of labor and capital that has occasioned it, making an "international" perspective no longer viable, as it makes a "dialogue among cultures" entirely moot. Neither *national* nor *cultural* units of analysis can any longer hold any water against the broken dam of postnational globalization. The kind of categorical bordercrossing that Shirin Neshat's art simulates is one particularly poignant strategy of *bodily resurrection* against the tyranny of cultures and the prison house of their national identity, a cultural revolt against national cultures that actively partakes in cultural globalization. By positing an aesthetics of alterity, by placing the body against its tyrannical culture, and ultimately by staging a bodily resurrection, Shirin Neshat's work collapses her local culture into the parameters of a globality that now has to account for its own terms of terror and intimidation, depravation and poverty, tyranny and injustice. Her work, the best that this transitional bordercrossing between the local and the global can afford, projects a guerrilla tactic where the local escapes into the global and the global into the local, crisscrossing and transgressing one trap into the other, all the while keeping a defiant resurrection of the body in her camera's mind.

By now an "international aesthetics," what Rugoff seems to demand, is a contradiction in terms. But the problem is not with the false expectation of a singular "aesthetics" that can be read and visualized across the presumption of hermetically sealed cultures. The problem is rather with the falsifying assumption of *inter*-nationalism and dialogue *among* cultures. What Rugoff intuitively notes in his reading of Shirin Neshat but theoretically fails to articulate about Santa Fe in general is that we can no longer enter such exhibitions with the assumption that there are *nations* and *cultures* categorically distinct *from* each other and yet in aesthetic need of communicating *with* each other. The internal and spiraling logic of the incessantly globalizing capital and its ensuing culture has necessitated a mode of reading that can no longer be predicated on such assumptions of constitutionally different cultures and successfully policed borders. Shirin Neshat's "native homeland," which now boasts of living under an *Islamic* Republic, can hardly conceal the categorical location of that republic—from its nascent ideological formation to its institutions of legitimate authority—in the colonial bosom of the project of modernity. The entire artifact of the *Islamic ideology* is a product of an active response to the colonially mitigated project of modernity and as such a mere mirror image of it, albeit made of the distant memories of an ancient culture. The art that the globalizing capital and its corresponding cultures engender categorically defies any distinct moral or political, social or cultural, boundary. This art represents, instead, the transfiguring nature of both the material basis *and* the aesthetic parameters of that emerging world that the inner logic of capital can hardly conceal or care to deny.

Less than twenty years ago it was impossible to imagine a Shirin Neshat. Today it is impossible to imagine her out of the visual repertoire of our world. *Metaphoric bodies* had started taking their cultures to tasks, and their cultures taking their nations to the globe, long before Shirin Neshat started photographing the impieties of such bodies. The globalized audience that now attends Shirin Neshat's exhibitions reflects the already globalized body that she shares with her audience. That *globalized body* is no longer at home in any national boundary, and at the creative moments of its *self-celebrations* it can hardly conceal the critical moments of its *self-annihilation*.

THE GLOBAL GAZE

It is not just the global gaze that undertheorizes itself. The local look is equally bewildered. The criticism leveled against Shirin Neshat by some Iranians, Muslims, or in general by those who advocate the cause of the "Third World" is that she takes advantage of and thus reinforces the existing stereotypes of Muslim women and as a result perpetuates that image. She is accused of aestheticizing and thus celebrating what she ought to be criticizing and subverting. She is said to have catered to the tantalizing whims of her "Western Audience" by giving them the over-Orientalized version of what they have already imagined. Women in veils—how much more could one self-Orientalize?

All these accusations are fallacious and predicated on an outdated identitarian politics, continuing to presume a *static* world to the East and a *creative* world to the West of Shirin Neshat's logistics. The dichotomy is false and the Iranian cinema of Shirin Neshat's lifetime is the evidence. Central to Shirin Neshat's photographic imagination is the *performative* disposition of veiling. She demystifies the act of veiling via an orchestration of the face simultaneous with a choreography of the body. She overstages veiling by placing it as a pronounced social practice, the claim of the stabilizing culture on the moving body. The performative presence of Shirin Neshat's work cannot be bracketed and then accused of self-Orientalization. It is constitutional to the very act of bordercrossing she performs that she must take the culturally private to the globally public. We need a whole new conception of cultural mobilization here. With the fabricated East-West dichotomy melting away under the gaze of the globalizing capital, an Orient no longer exists to be Orientalized. Shirin Neshat's bordercrossings are a dialectics of defiance, a bodily resurrection against fabricated cultures and the prison house of their national identity, with the nation-state as the custodian of the power that reaps the benefit.

Performing the veil, as Shirin Neshat does, stages the culturally constituted body in an overwhelmingly exaggerated way, the only way that the body can be shown in its cultural contortions. The implications of that exaggerated, performative staging of the concealed body commence with the physical evidence of the body but extend all the way to the underlying metaphysics that animates the cultural constitution of the body. Prior to its aestheticization, the veil cannot conceal its own history that it was there to accompany the body, there as the canvas of the metaphysics that demands it. There is a progression in the practice of veiling from the politics of power to the metaphysics of signification. There is a choreography to the social practice of veiling that embraces the body in the politics of its control and the metaphysics of its submission. With the veil the *hands* are made inoperative, the *speech* impossible, the *face* covered, and the *body* denied. The body—carrying the face, the hands, and the voice—moves and the veil legislates on behalf of the metaphysical culture that authorizes it. The *face* that the veil covers can no longer reveal itself as a sign that signates and thus threatens all the controlling signifiers that ipso facto implicate a Transcendental Signified. The *body* that the veil denies is prohibited to substitute the soul that animates that metaphysics. The *speech* that the veil inhibits is mutated to authenticate the masculinity of the Divine Voice at the root of that metaphysics. The *hands* that the veil ties are rendered inoperative so that the act of productivity is incubated and its fruits denied.

The veiled body, as we can now see it through Shirin Neshat's revealing camera, is the walking denial of the culture, the supreme summation of its repressed denials, the negative aesthetics of its inhibitions, the shadow of its light. On the premise of the veiled body, the social practice of veiling mutates the politics of power into the metaphysics of its inevitability—immutable, absolutist, and permanent. The practice is closed-circuit, circuitous, and self-authenticating from the politics of its practice to the metaphysics of its certainty. Shirin Neshat visually interjects into that social practice and strategically disrupts that metaphysics. This she does in two simultaneously disruptive, mutually corroborative moves: in the *privacy* of her Iranian aesthetics and in the *publicity* of her global audience. The term *global* is nowhere more applicable and apt than here. Her global audience misses out on the locality of her references (ritual veiling, calligraphic poetry, Persian music, Qur'anic recitation, folkloric references), while her nativist audience equally fails to reconfigure its binary suppositions between Islam (the East) and the West, or tradition and modernity. The result is that her global audience celebrates her for the wrong reasons, while her nativist critics condemn her with a bad politics. Bringing her local aesthetics to her global audience and bypassing her international admirers and nativist critics, we can see Shirin Neshat at the forefront of an aesthetic imagination that is behind the globalizing logic of the capital but ahead of its trailing culture.

Bordercrossing left and right, Shirin Neshat stages a *bodily resurrection* in which the *face* is allowed to signate beyond the control of any Transcendental Signified, the *body* to substitute for the soul, the *speech* to be demasculated, and the *hands* to become productive in the field of the otherwise. In the absence of such Transcendental Signifieds, there cannot be any claim to any *metaphysics of presence*. Metaphoric bodies speak from both sides of their mouths, in two languages. The "I" of "I want to go home" is always somewhere else, permanently homeless. We are always-already absent, always on the other side of the border, our *metaphorized bodies* pointing to something they are not, instrumental in a function they have not articulated themselves, signified by force, signaled involuntarily, and signed in absentia and with proxies.

THE SPACE IN BETWEEN

Shirin Neshat is the artist of the space in between, of suggestions and suppositions, of a whole new cosmogony of vestiges and mementos. She gives an entirely new meaning to the idea and practice of flirting. She flirts. She flirts with danger with flare. The verbal abused, the knee-jerk reaction would be to go for the kill with the visual. But not for Shirin Neshat. She goes for the kill with the haunting instinct and patient precision of a lioness. She waits patiently and calculates with the precision of a Swiss watch where to sit, when to move, what to show, why to retreat, and when to go for the jugular. Shirin Neshat is the artist of the (un)seen, of the (not)shown, of the strongly suggested, of "Who? Me? I never said that!" She is the artist of light and shadow, the marker of the twilight location where all the suggested signs remain signaling but never significate enough to register a sentence, suggest a phrase, or issue a statement. Never a statement—always only a hint. Shirin Neshat's is an aesthetics of (im)permanence, a politics of (in)articulation.

With that arsenal of suggestive mobilization at her disposal, Shirin Neshat has singularly targeted the body as the site of her contestation. From her earliest photographic work to her latest video installations, and before and after anything else, Shirin Neshat is a visual theorist of the body. Her bodies are the sites of critical contestations with the cultures that create, seal, and sign them. Bodies are the signed and sealed signatures of a culture. In and of themselves bodies are already inscribed, constituted, defined, veiled beyond recognition. Veils are just the slightly more exaggerated veneers of the cultured bodies. Topless bikinis, even skinny dipping in nude colonies, are as much markers of cultural constitutions of the body as a fully veiled figure. Clothing of any kind, from a turban to a tie, is the cultural closure of the body, a claim on its location, demanding it to behave, exacting a tax on its rectitude. Clothing pales in comparison with how bodies in and of their nude selves are culturally constituted. Bodies are the mobile repositories of the culture they (literally) embody. From the moment of their birth, before the moment of their birth, to the moment of their death, and beyond the moment of their death, bodies are the sites of cultural contestations. Cultures demand and exact obedience from their bodies before conception and beyond the grave. A Muslim is a Muslim before his or her conception, before his or her parents are married, before his or her grandparents are born, and before his or her entire ancestry took their first breath. A Muslim is a Muslim beyond his or her grave, into the afterlife, long—very long—after he or she is dead and gone. Into the Day of Resurrection, he or she is still a Muslim, a believer of one sort or another.

Shirin Neshat is born and bred into the Iranian version of the Islamic culture. Her art is decidedly rooted in her ancestral culture, in the manner and matter of her parental faith. It is almost impossible to read and write Shirin Neshat without noticing her incessantly quoting her culture. As a visual theorist of the body, she resurrects her bodies against the culture that has historically claimed them in order to deny them. The control of the culture over body is beyond measure, predating any time, anticipating any space. In the Islamic culture, bodies are mandated and controlled before their ritual birth and beyond their ritual burial. Muslims believe that beyond their ritual birth into their faith they will die in their physical bodies and then they will be bodily resurrected on the Day of Judgment to be rewarded in Paradise for their good deeds or else be punished in Hell for their evil acts. God is the "Owner of the Day of Judgment" (The Qur'an, I: 3), "the day when every soul will find itself confronted with all that it hath done of good and all that it hath done of evil" (III: 30), "the day when (some) faces will be whitened and (some) faces will be blackened; and as for those whose faces have been blackened, it will be said unto them: Disbelieved ye after your (profession of) belief? Then taste the punishment for that ye disbelieved. As for those whose faces have been whitened, lo! In the mercy of Allah they dwell for ever" (III: 106–107). It is not just the soul and the face of the created being that are resurrected on the Day of Judgment. They will resurrect in their entire body, from their bone through their flesh to their skin: "Lo! Those who disbelieve Our revelations, We shall expose them to the Fire. As often as their skins are consumed We shall exchange them for fresh skins that they may taste the torment. Lo! Allah is ever Mighty, Wise" (IV: 56).

From this Qur'anic beginning, the question of the *corporeality* of the body and the (im)possibility of its bodily resurrection became a matter of grave theological debate among Muslims. The theological debate, however, is a subterfuge for something far more worldly and tangible, and that is the enduring claim of a commanding culture on the *corporeal reality of the defiant body.* What Shirin Neshat is doing today in the light-and-shadow reconfiguration of the human body is visually theorizing the *caro corporalis* where her ancestors have failed to sublate it verbally into *caro spiritualis.* This is a battle of wits that has raged throughout Iranian history and Islamic culture, from the dawn of Islam some 1,400 years ago down to the aftermath of the Islamic Revolution in 1979. Today, at the writing of these words, the most critical public debate in Iran is the question of public flogging and execution, with the Islamic judiciary strongly insisting that it will continue such practices irrespective of the objection of then President Khatami's government and the international outrage. The body of the Muslim subject of an Islamic Republic is the most immediate, most visible, and most politically significant site of both political and cultural claims on it. If residents of Tehran were all to evacuate their capital city for a week and go on a picnic to the Alborz Mountain, the Islamic Republic would collapse—it would have *nothing* (not just *nobody*) to rule over!

There is a history though between the commencement of the Qur'anic constitution of the human body as the punitive site of the faith and its combative predicament in an Islamic Republic. The rise of philosophical rationalism in medieval Islamic intellectual history resulted in the denial of the possibility of bodily resurrection. Al-Ghazali (d. 1111) denounced the philosophers for their belief in the eternity of the world, their denial of God's knowledge of the particulars, and their rejection of bodily resurrection on Judgment Day. Throughout Islamic history, theological and philosophical debates about bodily resurrection were in effect battles over the metaphysical mutation of the *caro corporalis* into *caro spiritualis*. The battle came to a culmination in the tenth/sixteenth century in the figure of Mulla Sadra Shirazi (d. 1641) and the establishment of the School of Isfahan. Mulla Sadra Shirazi's ambition was to bring together the best and most enduring philosophical speculations in Islamic intellectual history and wed them with the Islamic metaphysical doctrines. His efforts were so monumental and enduring that to this day the practice of Islamic philosophy has not freed itself of his influence. By the thirteenth/nineteenth century, one of his astute followers, Shaykh Ahmad Ahsa'i (d. 1826), brought his philosophical speculations on body to an unprecedented edge and founded the Shaykhi School of philosophy, named after him, which in turn resulted in by far the most revolutionary social uprising of thirteenth/nineteenth-century Iran, the Babi movement.

Shaykh Ahmad Ahsa'i faced the same problem that generations of Muslim philosophers had faced. What was he to do with the physical body? It had all the signs of generation and corruption. It comes about and it dies away, and yet the Qur'an says that these very bodies will be resurrected, brought back to life on the Day of Judgment and then praised in Paradise or punished in Hell for what these selfsame bodies had done on earth. Shaykh Ahmad Ahsa'i came up with an elaborate theory of the body to rescue it from corruption, save it for paradisiacal praise or infernal fire, and thus metaphysically prolong its endurance into a posteternity that embraced its earthly existence. Toward that end, Ahsa'i categorically divided the body into four stages of its corporeal existence. Two were related to the term *jasad*, which literally means *corpus*, and two with the term *jism*, which literally means *body*. There are, Ahsa'i surmised in his theory of the body, two stages to *jasad* and two to the *jism*.

Jasad A is our corporeal body, the body we touch and feel. This body, according to Ahsa'i, is like a garment that a person puts on and later takes off. This body in and of itself has neither enjoyment nor suffering. It is subject to neither fidelity nor rebellion.[3] This fleshly *Jasad A* can diminish or increase, a person may get sick and lose weight or else eat too much and get fat, but his essential quality, servile or rebellious, Ahsa'i insists, will remain the same. This body "is homologous to the opacity that exists in silica and potash."[4] This visibly opaque body is our *caro corporalis*.

Jasad B is our quintessential body, the body that survives, according to Ahsa'i, the decomposition of our *Jasad A* into its constituent elements when on death its fire goes to Fire, its air to Air, its water to Water, and its earth to Earth. This *Jasad B* is "the reality of the human being," Ahsa'i insists, because when *Jasad A*, our *caro corporalis*, is decomposed and destroyed, "there is finally nothing of it to be found, so that some people affirm that the human being is annihilated. Not at all! Not so! But if we say that there is a body that survives 'in the tomb,' that body is nonetheless *invisible* to earthly beings, to the people of this world, on account of the opacity that darkens their fleshly eyes and prevents them from *seeing* what is not of the same kind as themselves."[5] When it is finally the time for the soul to return to a bodily formation to be brought back to face the consequences of its actions, God causes a rain to fall from an ocean under His throne, a rain "colder than snow," which in turn causes "a universal refining process," at which point, "the members of the spiritual body *(jasad B)* of each individual join together to form an organism in perfect 'shape,' that is to say conforming to the structure the body had in this world; the elements of the neck are welded to the elements of the head, then to those of the bust and so forth . . . This spiritual body coming back to life is the body that belongs to the earth, Hurqalya. This is the body in which humans are resurrected, and with which they enter into paradise or into Hell."[6] Ahsa'i responds to the objection that his view is too philosophically anti-Islamic by asserting that what will resurrect is in fact the *caro corporalis*, but that it has been purified from its opacity and density while sustaining its identity and ipseity. This invisibly luminous body is our *caro spiritualis*.

What happens to the soul when it departs the *caro corporalis* and before it enters the *caro spiritualis*? Here is where *Jism A*, or our *terrestrial body*, becomes handy, because this is the body into which the soul moves from our corporeal body. The terrestrial body accompanies the soul to the Earthly Paradise if it is a believing soul or else to the Terrestrial Hell if it is an unbelieving soul. The Earthly Paradise, where the believing soul and its terrestrial body dwell, is located in the West of Ahsa'i's geographical imagination. The spirit of the infidel, meanwhile, accompanies its terrestrial soul at the sunrise, and at the sunset it takes refuge in *Barahut* and wanders with it during the night in the valley of sulfur in a geographically unspecified location. This is how the spirit persists until the First Blast of the Trumpet of Resurrection, at which point all the spirits are annihilated between the First and the Second Blast of the Trumpet. This cosmic pause lasts for four hundred years, and then the spirits are resuscitated into *Jism B*, or our *astral body*. This is made possible because *Jism B is* just *Jism A* purified of its opacity and density. The soul now resides in this *astral body* in the purgatory until such time that the Second Trumpet of Archangel Seraphiel summons all souls to Divine Justice, at which time they all enter their designated *Jasad B*, or their *caro spiritualis*, and attend the Day of Judgment to be burned in Hell or rewarded in Paradise.[7]

Ahsa'i's theory of the body, articulated in support and anticipation of *bodily resurrection*, can be summarized as follows:

We are born into the world in our:
Jasad A (Caro Corporalis)
Upon our death, our soul departs from our *Caro Corporalis* and enters our:
Jism A (Terrestrial Body)
After a cosmic pause and at the wake of the Day of Judgment our soul moves from our *Terrestrial Body* and enters our:
Jism B (Astral Body)
And finally on the actual Day of Judgment we are bodily resurrected out of our *Astral Body* and move into our:
Jasad B (Caro Spiritualis)

Ahsa'i's elaborate theory of the body thus divides it into a *caro corporalis* and a *caro spiritualis*, with the *terrestrial body* and the *astral body* acting as the intermediary vehicles of sustaining the soul in a state of limbo when it has exited one and not yet entered the other until such time that it is ready to meet its creator and reap the reward or suffer the consequences of its worldly deeds.

There is much to be learned from Shirin Neshat's photographic memory with Ahsa'i's theory of the body in mind—much about what her caring camera reveals and much about when she turns her face and closes her eyes. Shirin Neshat's art is nothing if not restoring the *caro spiritualis* visually where her theological ancestry failed verbally to sublate the *caro corporalis*. Partaking in an entire history of theological debates confronting the onslaught of philosophical rationalism, Ahsa'i struggled valiantly to demonstrate that *caro spiritualis* (the spiritual body that the soul ultimately occupies after leaving its primary abode, the *caro corporalis*, as it attends the Divine justice on the Day of Judgment) is *invisible* to humans because of the "opacity that darkens their fleshly eyes." The kind of photographic memory that informs Shirin Neshat teases an (in)sight out of the opacity of our fleshly eyes, making them see the otherwise invisible configuration of the *caro spiritualis*, which this time around is not a negation or sublation but in the very material texture of our *caro corporalis*. As Forough Farrokhzad was the poetic voice, Shirin Neshat is the lyrical vision of a living aesthetics of the *matter* superseding the deadly metaphysics of the soul.

Shirin Neshat is doing nothing if not making visible the invisible body, the body that Shi'i saints and Muslim scholars have compared to "the gold dust in the goldsmith's crucible. This, likewise, the eyes do not see. But the goldsmith, having washed it with water and purified it of the earth with which it was mixed, causes it to become visible."[8] Shirin Neshat's art is an alchemy of revelation, making the invisible visible, the hidden manifest, the potential possible, teasing the *caro spiritualis* out of the *caro corporalis*, the soul out of the body, the soul of the body no longer having any claim on authenticity other than being in and of the body.

In Shirin Neshat's ancestral culture, the physical body, *caro corporalis*, is metaphorically identified as an item of clothing that one wears one day and discards another. In Shaykh Ahmad Ahsa'i's words, "indeed, in regard to the human being, [the corporeal body] is, as it were, a garment thrown over him."[9] This is the "carnal coating," as Ahsa'i calls the human body, which in effect makes it visible. As soon as that carnal coating is taken off, the quintessence of the human body, its *caro spiritualis*, becomes "imperceptible to the sight of ordinary humans."[10] Shirin Neshat is the visual theorist of that imperceptibility, making it, in effect, perceptible, but not by verbally sublating the *caro corporalis* to the imperceptible supposition of a *caro spiritualis*, but instead by visually positing that spiritual body in and out of the physical body itself, teasing it out of its opacity and ipseity, its being physically there in the world.

The result is that Shirin Neshat visually succeeds where Muslim theologians have philosophically failed. They have had to theorize the body in the absence of the evidence and by repressing our defiant *caro corporalis*. She, on the contrary, visualizes in the very body of our evidence. Their theoretical failure has historically translated into a triumphant metaphysics of violence against the body. Her visual triumph has now succeeded in liberating the body from the prison house of its presumed soul. Their Platonic philosophizing presumes that the soul is incarcerated in the body in order to incarcerate the body in a cultural predisposition toward "The Soul." Her vision retrieves a transparent luminosity out of the physical body and thus liberates the body from the supposition of its holding a soul hostage. Body does not hold any soul. The supposition of a soul incarcerates the body. An entire culture of terror has been visited upon the Muslim body by Muslim theologians just because they could not Qur'anically account for bodily resurrection after death. Shirin Neshat's still and moving pictures are the manifesto of the liberation of the body from the prison house of its presumed soul, sighting, as she does, the sensual evidence of the body. Muslim theologians have created an entire culture of fear and intimidation by theorizing a *caro spiritualis* out of the evidence of our *caro corporalis*, presuming an *astral* destination to the *terrestrial* evidence of our body. Shirin Neshat deterrorizes the body out of that culture by detheorizing it out of the prison house of the soul, teasing out visually the *caro spiritualis* that is evident (as she evidences it) in the very *caro corporalis*. Muslim theologians have begun with *caro corporalis* in order to suppress, deny, and denounce it on their way to the presumed destination of a *caro spiritualis*. Shirin Neshat begins and ends, dwells in and celebrates, with and in the body of our evidence, our *caro corporalis*. Muslim theologians promised and warned of a *bodily resurrection* they could never prove. Shirin Neshat delivers a *bodily resurrection*, which is our proof.

And there—dare now—is the rub: Detecting and delivering the *caro spiritualis* from the heart of *caro corporalis*—light from the heart of its darkness—Shirin Neshat's caring camera lovingly discovers and joyously reveals in the *aesthetics* of the body, which in its *politics* cannot but explode into the bits and pieces of itself. In between that *aesthetics* and *politics* is always implicated a *metaphysics* of fragmented bodies—bodies presumed holy in the relics of their remembrances.[11] It was not accidental that in Sheikh Ahmad Ahsa'i's metaphysics of the body dwelled the politics of its most dangerous appeal to revolutionary emancipation of masses from their medieval bondage. In the received metaphysics of violence that from Judaism, through Christianity, to Islam has informed Shirin Neshat's ancestral faith, *caro spiritualis* is posited as visibly hidden, religiously repressed, and materially denied by virtue of the fact and figure of the *caro corporalis* that covers it. Shirin Neshat's caring camera gently teases out what a backpack full of dynamite may violently seek to excavate in one sudden blow—light from the heart of its darkness.

CARO SPIRITUALIS

A visual theorist of the body, over the last decade Shirin Neshat has quietly compromised the patriarchally patented theory of the *corpus*, liberating it from the prison house supposition of its *Islamic* soul, celebrating a *caro spiritualis* evident in the very body of the *caro corporalis*, and once and for all collapsing the binary opposition into itself: the body as the evidence of its own radiant luminosity—its own significance.

In two successive trilogies shot between 1998 and 2001, Shirin Neshat narrates two complementary moves launched from the privacy of a performance toward the publicity of a communal recognition before erupting in the apocalyptic landscape of a resurrection and renewal. The first trilogy consists of *Bi-Qarar* (*Turbulent*; 1998), *Owj* (*Rapture*; 1999), and *Eltehab* (*Fervor*; 2000). The second trilogy consists of *Nabz* (*Pulse*; 2001), *Fetneh* (*Possessed*; 2001), and *Safar* (*Passage*; 2001). These two trilogies are punctuated by a soliloquy, *Zamzameh* (*Soliloquy*; 1999).

In the first trilogy, Shirin Neshat *begins* (*Turbulent*) with the male articulation of a poetic presence set up against the feminine (in)articulation of a lyrical luring of reason from the logos, both performed in the enclosed atmospheric control of a stage. She then *moves* (*Rapture*) to the citadel site of a *civilitas* and *concludes* (*Fervor*) with the apocalyptic terror of a resurrection.

As in most other titles of her work, the English *Turbulent* does not quite catch the Persian *Bi-Qarar*, nor vice versa, but Shirin Neshat insists on giving them both at once, a kind of contorted "dialogue of civilizations," a bilingualism that belies the two opposing cultures at one and the same time. *Restless*, or *restive*, is a much better translation for *bi-qarar* than *turbulent*, and if the reference is to the woman character, then she is far better described as *restless* than *turbulent*. *Bi-Qarar* has a sense of erratic and anxiogenic restlessness—an impossibility to sit or stand still—perturbed by some emotion or incident. *Turbulent* describes the state, whereas *bi-qarar* hints at the (im) possibility of resting a case. *Turbulent* has forgotten all the memory of its preturbulent state. *Bi-Qarar* has all the physical evidence of its stability right in front of it, in *qarar*, which means "to have peace and stability." *Bi* negates *qarar* without erasing its compelling memory; it just puts it under erasure, writing and crossing it at the same time. And that memorial trace is critical in the reading of the piece, though now we call it *Turbulent*.

The entire piece operates on the comparison and contrast of light and shadow, male and female, and white and black: a successive binary tête-à-tête of oppositions. The male figure sings with eloquence and conviction; the female with inarticulate passion. He dresses in white and faces a crowded hall; she in black sings to an empty auditorium. He is in full public view; she is in the complete privacy of her solitude, feigning publicity. He faces the camera; she hides from the camera, and the camera has to circumambulate around her to find and face her. He is evident. She is hidden. His presence is frontal and vertical; hers is concealed and circular—the two of them (separated by the physical distance between the two screens on which they are permanently divided, permanently yearning) complimenting, contradicting, and exacerbating each other.

Right before this binary opposition can flatly collapse into a passive resignation to the masculinity of a culture and the peripheral femininity of it, something quite surreptitious begins to happen. The look of bewilderment on the male singer announces an almost inconspicuous articulation emerging from the female voice. Suddenly we realize that the masculine space is entirely occupied, actual, and fulfilled, while that of the feminine is suggestively inviting, potential, and promising. The masculine voice and vision are named and identified, while those of the female are merely noticed and palpably syncopated. The masculine space is entirely delivered, while that of the feminine is simply promised. The male space is brightly occupied; the feminine space is darkly inviting. Now if we look closer at the masculine face of confusion, suddenly the feminine circulation of a vertiginous look begins to ooze an (in)escapable (in)articulation. The parenthetical double meaning emerges as the suggestive symbol of this entire visual articulation of the feminine circular against the frontal matter-of-factness of the masculine vertical. It is not just that the male is so utterly *named* and the female so suggestively *noticed*. No, there is something far more important here. The masculine is the flat phallic of a mirror reflection; the feminine a specular depth of vaginal space. The light clothing of the masculine phallic is evident and worn out, while the dark cover of the feminine cave is pregnant and promising.

We have another problem of discrepancy between the Persian *Owj* and the English *Rapture*. *Owj* is more like *soaring*, *rising*, or *ascension* than *rapture*, unless we take this term to mean *elation*, *exaltation*, *exultation*, or even *euphoria*. But still, the dominant mood in *Owj* is *going high*, as in the rising of a wave or the soaring of an eagle—a deliberate verticality strongly implicated in the term. This is suggested both in the masculine climbing of ladders in and over the fortress and in the rising ululation of women in the desert. *Rapture* thus picks up in the open landscape where *Turbulent* left off on the enclosed stage. The crosspositioning here is between the masculine verticality of the *citadel* and the feminine flatness of the *desert*: men occupying a fortress and women emerging from a forsaken land. Men in *Rapture* are erectly occupied and women flatly inviting. The masculine fortress rises out of the feminine flatness of the desert. Men in white occupy and (pro)claim the *civilitas*, while women announce the *deserted* (im)possibilities of their origin: In the castle many cry; in the desert many whisper. Men are ordered and determined; women are chaotic and pregnant with yet to be articulated (in)ordinates. Men are in the full light of their recognition; women are in the dark concealment of their promises. Men are ceremoniously quarrelsome; women are chaotically observant. The camera looks up to the men and down on the women. Men are in the ranks and files of determined destinations; women defy the logic of any ordering. Throughout *Rapture*, men are on the move and at the end come to a vertically idle standstill, whereas women are stationary until the very end when they move to the determined horizontality of their sailing to the sea. There is a rhythm to the masculine figures on the move, and yet barely a pulse is audible from the feminine figures in the scene. The men's naked whiteness has nowhere to go; the women's covered blackness has everywhere to choose. Men are actors and women the audience. Men are agents and women the subjects. Men are fighting; women are watching.

There is a sudden rupture in *Rapture*. Almost halfway through the event, there is an abrupt rising of feminine ululation that interrupts and stops the masculine business. Men are cast into long shots and women are brought into close-ups. Males are interrupted; females are interrupting. In this second, interrupting phase, men are sitting in a circular long shot of inarticulate aggregation, while women march in a columnar intrusion. The visual event is verbally marked by a majestic Qur'anic recitation—chapter 81, verses 1–9:

> *THE OVERTHROWING*
>
> Revealed at Mecca
> In the Name of Allah, the Beneficent, the Merciful
> 1. When the sun is overthrown,
> 2. And when the stars fall,
> 3. And when the hills are moved,
> 4. And when the camels big with young are abandoned,
> 5. And when the wild beasts are herded together,
> 6. And when the seas rise,
> 7. And when souls are reunited
> 8. And when the girl-child that was buried alive is asked
> 9. For what sin she was slain,

The atmosphere of this early Meccan chapter is entirely apocalyptic, its content the famous Qur'anic condemnation of an ancient tribal practice of female infanticide. But why Qur'anic recitation, and why these particular verses? The most immediate presence of the recitation is evident in the beauty and elegance of its melodic incantation. Almost no one in Shirin Neshat's audiences in Western Europe and North America understands what the melodious recitation actually says. For them, this is an operatic aria of some unfamiliar origin. That it has an almost physical effect on the inner ear and the hidden heart of a Muslim, driving him or her to tears, invoking his or her most sacrosanct pieties, is entirely lost on the crowd that regularly attends a video installation in a gallery. But the voice is audible, commanding absolute and total attention. First and foremost, the Qur'anic recitation is eloquent beyond mere words, musical in the tonality of its every reverberation. There is a sudden and sacred silence about Shirin Neshat's vision just before the Qur'anic recitation begins; every atom of her visual vigilance is in deferential attendance for the announcement, as if these were the very first verses that were ever revealed by Archangel Gabriel to Prophet Muhammad on Mount Hira, near Mecca, in about 610 CE.

The eloquence of this Qur'anic recitation in *Rapture* is reminiscent of the poetic beauty of the masculine love song in *Turbulent*: that in Persian, this in Arabic; that from the poetic pantheon of Shirin Neshat's language and culture, this from the pious memory of her faith and religion; that from the poetic interior of Rumi, this from the revelatory rhythm of the Qur'anic landscape. But both are masculine in their eloquence, placed and positioned against the feminine (in)articulation of poetry and piety.

Beyond the eloquent announcement of the Qur'anic recitation, the apocalyptic atmosphere of the verses warns of the Day of Resurrection. *Bodily resurrection* is here not just anticipated; it is enacted. The Day of Judgment is at hand. Equally pronounced in the verses is the Qur'anic condemnation of the ancient practice of female infanticide. Here, the vocalist Sussan Deyhim's selection of the melodious Qur'anic recitation uses the sacred text of Muslims itself against its own abuses. "And when the girl-child that was buried alive is asked / For what sin she was slain," refers to the practice of female infanticide. But the factual condemnation and Qur'anic quotation are fused and mutated into a compelling visuality that takes full advantage of their melodic resonance without allowing what they mean to modify or compromise what they resonate. Shirin Neshat uses sounds—vocal or instrumental—for their reverberating effects, as they echo back and forth between the fact of their audibility and the fantasy of their undulation. The result is that the body of evidence we see exudes the terms of its own signation beyond or before any domain of signification. The body resonates not from the depth of its presumed soul but from the surface of its evident substance. This *bodily resurrection* is self-evident. From the depth of the Qur'anic memory, Shirin Neshat resurrects a *caro corporalis* that is ipso facto a *caro spiritualis*—as if bringing back to life the dead body of the young girl that the Qur'anic passage mourns. This *living aesthetics* represses a *deadly politics.*

Fervor, the third installment of this trilogy, equally operates on the borderline between light and shadow, this time regarding a would-be love affair. Shirin Neshat draws the two (male and female) figures from the shadowy configuration of their walking their way toward a religious gathering. Here, Shirin Neshat is at her visual best in gathering together the emotional energy of the ceremony, her camera in effect mimicking the ritual disposition of the event. In the central figure of the *Naqqal* (the storyteller at the borderline center of the male/female gathering), Shirin Neshat portrays the third articulation of masculine eloquence, reflecting the Qur'anic recitation in *Rapture* and the Persian singer in *Turbulent*. His eloquence, though, is frightful and terrorizing. There is in effect a progression of masculine eloquence, from poetic love in *Turbulent*, to sacred awe in *Rapture*, to apocalyptic terror in *Fervor*. In these three forms of (Islamic) elocution, Shirin Neshat both celebrates and warns, privileges and terrorizes—her vision at once enthralled and frightened. What is *beautiful* in these three masculine voices is also *frightful*, perhaps even attractive *by virtue of being* repellent.

This succession of sacred and profane emotions places this trilogy on an extraordinarily critical plane against the very composition of the culture. Anything from a beautiful love song to an awe-inspiring Qur'anic recitation to a frightful account of the Day of Judgment is here brought together under one verbal canopy of terror and intimidation, stifling, in effect, any possibility of breathing. In that suffocating moment, Shirin Neshat achieves one crucial affinity between overwhelming sensuality and the mysterious energy of piety. What exactly is the texture of *piety* that is so oozing with *sensuality*? In the figure of the woman protagonist, reminiscent of many of Shirin Neshat's earliest photographs, she captures the quintessence of *pious sensuality*: the sensuality that is in piety and the piety in sensuality. No one before Shirin Neshat has dared in her received culture to get close to and visually trespass this dangerous territory where the erotic and the sacred embrace. *Fervor* is by far her most successful articulation of that embrace, where *the carnal* and *the sacral* collapse to reveal the quintessentially sensual disposition of the sacred.[12] Through Shirin Neshat's camera we see for the first time the body resurrecting and revolting against the tyrannizing terror of an entire history and a whole culture of fear and intimidation by revealing its own inherent, innermost piety and the erotic energy that the sacred has commandeered for its own exclusive benefit. Retrieve that erotic energy from the sacred, the carnal from the sacral, and there remains nothing of substance to it. This *bodily resurrection* against the commanding cultures that claim and control it is Shirin Neshat's most daring bordercrossing—from the parking lot of *the permitted* into the open space of *the forbidden*.[13]

Shirin Neshat's second trilogy—*Pulse*, *Possessed*, and *Passage*—follows a trajectory similar to the first one's: from the privacy of a solitary reflection, to the publicity of an urban defiance, and ultimately to the apocalyptic conclusion of a death and resurrection.

Nabz (*Pulse*) depicts the temptation of a solitary woman (Shohreh Aghdashloo) in the privacy of a room whispering with the publicity of a male/female duet on the radio. The most pronounced force in *Pulse* is the pulsating rhythm of the event narrowing in on the solitary interior. The parabolic move of the camera around the room, rotating one complete round from long shot to close up back to long shot, secures the event in one swooping summation. The male/female voice-over coming from the radio (Reza Derakhshani and Sussan Deyhim) sings a famous *ghazal* of Jalal al-Din Rumi. The poem rests on the critical assertion that all humanity is trapped in bodily limitations and material boundaries. The poetic pronouncement "*Shoma hamcho asirid*" ("You are all like slaves") anticipates the announcement "*Cho zendan beshekastid / Hameh shah o amirid*" ("When you break loose of the jail (of your bodies) / You are all kings and princes.") The radio instrumentally facilitates a link between the privacy of the mournful solitude and the publicity of a poetic promise.

In *Fetneh* (*Possessed*), the solitude of that poetic moment expands and moves out into the publicity of a feminine madness in full view. The woman as the personification of madness expostulates hysteria on a blatantly public plane. The feminine figure of madness enters and disturbs the public peace as the repressed catalyst of anarchy. Once initiated by the repressed feminine madness, the fury continues even after she has left the scene. The public is in danger of disintegration once her lunacy transgresses the privacy of her bewilderment and enters the publicity of her denial. The danger is being woman, mad, and in public—thus the visual suspense of nobody initially noticing her as she enters the public domain. The suspense of these few minutes of being *in public incognito* underscores the public presence of the feminine absence. The private has now gone public and the privacy of (in)sanity is staged in the publicity of the (in)sanity, and thus (in)sanity is demarcated. Here we have entered the publicity of urbanity, after having just moved out of the privacy of solitude. The move anticipates *Passage* into the apocalyptic desert (*Sahra-ye Mahshar*), so that we can move through this trilogy from sitting in whispering solitude, then going out into the (in)sanity of the public, and from there passing into the apocalyptic desert.

The woman in her madness facing the dead end of a thick wall, with nowhere to go, intimates the prophetic figure of defiance, a messianic visionary collapsing the borderline between reason and revelation. Both the prophetic and the messianic suggestions again anticipate *Passage* as apocalyptic and resurrectionary. We have the privacy of a room anticipating the publicity of a city and leading into an apocalyptic landscape—a private contemplation whispering a public declaration and pregnant with an apocalyptic death and resurrection. The movement is tantamount to a universalization of the thematic core of the subject. The setting is the town of Essaouira in Morocco, but through the visionary sublation of Shirin Neshat, aided impeccably by Susan Deyhim's haunting music (a stunning harmony of her voice with the kamancheh and cello), the implication becomes global.

In *Safar* (*Passage*), brought home by Philip Glass's music, the trilogy comes to a closure. We have now moved from the private whispering of *Pulse* through the public (in)sanity of *Temptation* and into the apocalyptic murmur of *Passage*. With Philip Glass's haunting music announcing the forbidding event, Shirin Neshat's camera begins to play with the long-shot dead assertion of a phallic column approaching the temptation and palpitation of the vaginal grave, while a little girl is making a stone house for herself. The columnar masculinity is carrying a dead body, a dead phallic in the midst of the living and mobile, toward a circular femininity of a grave being ardently dug by a group of women. But we scarcely know or even see that. Shirin Neshat's camera (The cinematographer Qasem Ebrahimian at his absolute best) teases and flirts, suggests and hesitates, promises and barely delivers. This is the ritual preparation for a dead, deadening intercourse of a dead phallic body into a vaginal grave, the moment of birth collapsing on the moment of death, the lovemaking of a life-making made into a death-making, a beginning to an end. In this light/dark palpitation of the (im)possible, the ceremonial preparation for love/death-making, the little girl, Shirin Neshat incarnate, sits as the virginal dream of a house yet to be built. This is the scariest, and yet the most hopeful, vision of Shirin Neshat extant: resurrecting the figure of a young girl (protected from hell by a low wall) from the hellish burial of a dead Adam and a buried Eve.

The *Passage* is visually mesmerizing. The sky, sea, and sand embrace a masculine crowd in black carrying the white shroud of a dead body. The camera then cuts and curiously approaches the sky and sand's silent embrace of the feminine digging of a grave. The columnar intrusion of the masculine dead phallic into the feminine digging begins to visualize the dead, deadening copulation, a necromantic occultation of the living soul, a transgressive copulation of dead bodies. From the vicinity of its periphery, a little girl, a child, is already born out of that wedlock between dead men walking and dead women digging their graves. The little girl reenacts the digging of the grave—with stones for the digging women and a hole in between for the grave—into which she places a piece of deadwood.

The moment of the apocalypse is now upon us. This is the Day of Judgment. Lo and Behold! Ecce Homo! From under the feet of the little girl sitting, now rising, emerges the Fire of Hell. Engulfing the desert in the rising flames of an apocalyptic conflagration, the fire is about to consume the columnar masculinity and the vaginal grave, gently sparing the girl-child resurrected from the dead certainties of a culture that once buried her alive (*Rapture*). This is a nightmare of a dream, Shirin Neshat awakening and concluding with her camera imperceptibly lifting the little girl's perspective, ever so gently, just high enough for her to see the whole desert—desolate, destitute, on fire, with the dead certainties of a dated, outdated world now fully under her gaze. It is bodily resurrection from an immaculate conception.

At its core, Shirin Neshat's joyous *aesthetics* of the living body represses its most fearful remembrance of a *politics* of deadly despair. The more actively she beatifies the body, the more evidently it resonates the politics of its hidden horrors. Her visual art is the aesthetic repression of the disemboweled politics of the body now crossculturally distributed beyond its Islamic domains—thus the global resonances of her work. In her most visually compelling works, she aesthetically resurrects the politically decimated evidence of the selfsame bodies. Her beatification of the body is almost canonical and hallowed, mirroring in hope the despair of its disemboweled politics.

A visual theorist of the body, Shirin Neshat has teased out of the classically constituted conception of the *corpus* the terms of its own luminosity without subjecting it to the realm of the spirits. In no other work is this extraction of the constitutional incandescence of the body more evident than in her *Zamzameh* (*Soliloquy*). Two identical women (Shirin Neshat herself) enter a simultaneous act of remembering/reflecting, a creative anamnesis, an absolutely stunning inversion of time and narrative that collapses the *telos* of any cultural teleology into one genealogical plateau of presence. Yet again, *soliloquy* is not exactly what *zamzameh* means. These repeated discrepancies between English and Persian create a suggestive crevice in Shirin Neshat's work that tilts the visual narrative off, just a bit. *Zamzameh* means "to whisper" or "to murmur." *Soliloquy*, as "interior monologue," has quite a distance from *zamzameh. Zamzameh* is audible but inarticulate. *Soliloquy* is inaudible but articulate. They are almost exactly the opposite of each other. The burden of semantic proof, however, is on *zamzameh*, which has to be pulled quite a distance—stop being audible and start being articulate—before it can meet *soliloquy. Soliloquy* too will have to be mutated quite seriously—no longer articulate but perfectly audible—before it can metamorphose into *zamzameh*. In effect, Shirin Neshat pulls and pushes the verbal boundaries of cultures almost in the same way that she contracts and expands the visual boundaries of anamnesis in *Soliloquy*. The two identical women are placed at two opposite temporal poles: one at the extremity of the past and the other at the extremity of the present (to call these "tradition" and "modernity" is ludicrous and would rob the narrative of its far more serious twist).

While the world cries *despair*, Shirin Neshat's art pictures *hope*. Celebrating a *caro spiritualis* evident in the very body of our *caro corporalis*, thus once and for all collapsing the binary opposition into itself, requires a mode of visual narrative that categorically defies the *telos* in the metaphysical teleology of every culture. Shirin Neshat achieves that in *Soliloquy* via an ingenious act of anamnesis. The woman at the extremity of the present remembers an entire history of feminine desubjection, as her identical counterpart simultaneously *remembers* the same in *her future*. In that bizarre act of anamnesis, Shirin Neshat makes it possible for the woman at the extremity of the past to *remember her future* precisely at the same time that her selfsame counterpart remembers the same in her past. The events are simultaneous and simultaneously *targeted* against each other. The past *remembers* the future and the future *remembers* the past. The result is an act of simultaneous anamnesis that categorically contracts the critical element of time in the narrative constitution of truth. With that visually achieved, the metaphysical constitution of the culture—incubated in the temporal implications of its narrative—collapses onto itself, and the inhibitive repressions of the culture are flattened and mapped out for one critical encounter on the surface of the present, the contemporaneity of our being toward now. No history, no time, no past, no present, no memory, no forgetfulness—here we are in the full presence of the present, culture at its most immediate, irreducible, flattened out matter of factness. No mother, father, king, nor cleric has any claim on this *presently* articulated slicing out of the culture. On the flat and evened-out surface of that plane, Shirin Neshat subjects the desubjected, and as she gives agency to the feminine, the masculine is (re)articulated, there and then to degender an entire repressive operation of the culture. She gives birth to an Adam and Eve who are no longer the gendered articulations of power but the harbingers of a whole new culture of emancipation and freedom: the body resurrected as the evidence of its own radiant luminosity and its own significance, and historical agency creatively restored out of a critical resubjection of the colonial subject.

Chapter 5

Voice, Vision, and Veiling

The wrist strap broke; probably the soldier had drawn it too tight. The officer had to intervene, the soldier held up the broken piece of strap to show him. So the officer went over to him and said, his face still turned toward the explorer: "This is a very complex machine, it can't be helped that things are breaking or giving way here and there; but one must not thereby allow oneself to be diverted in one's general judgment."

—Franz Kafka, *In the Penal Colony* (1914)

In this chapter, I am principally concerned with testing a reversal of the direction of the gaze—not with what happens when we are looked at, but what happens when we are allowed to watch. I want to show how *being allowed to watch* is in fact the occasion of *being seen by oneself*, of placing the observer's body visibly in his or her own field of vision, in the world, and that this imagining of one's own body in the world is integral to cultivating a historical agency. I concluded the last chapter by arguing that at its core, Shirin Neshat's joyous *aesthetics* of the living body represses its most fearful remembrance of a *politics* of deadly despair. In this chapter, I want to see how a *bodily memory* is formed by actively imagining itself in public and whether or not it can defy its entrapment in and by political power. I said in the last chapter that the more actively Shirin Neshat beatifies the body, the more evidently it resonates the politics of its hidden horrors. In this chapter, I want to work through the specifics of a *visionary poet*, Forough Farrokhzad, and a succession of women filmmakers to see and demonstrate how their poetic perceptions ipso facto posit a farsighted recital that is never to be blinded, benighted, or banned. If Shirin Neshat's aesthetic beatification of the body is canonical and hallowed and thus mirrors in hope the despair of its disemboweled politics, as I argued in the last chapter, here I want to see how a visionary poet and the sorority of farsighted filmmakers she made possible retrieve and restore *agential memory* to a body—outlasting, perhaps, the politics of its despair and the aesthetics of its hope.

WATCHING A SOCCER GAME

On Thursday, November 15, 2001, the Iranian national soccer team met with its Irish counterpart for the second leg of a two-game World Cup qualifier playoff. The Iranian team needed every advantage they could get. The first leg of the playoff had taken place nine days earlier at Landsdown Road in Dublin, where Robbie Keane and Ian Harte had scored in each half to take a 2–0 lead on Iran. The Irish soccer fans were not going to let their national team venture unprotected into the intimidating atmosphere of any Islamic Republic alone. Thousands of Irish men and women sought to update their passports and secure their visas. On this auspicious occasion, the Islamic Republic of Iran's Soccer Federation gave three hundred Irish women special permission to watch the Iran-Ireland game, provided they cover themselves, head to toe, the way Iranian women were forced to do. The special permission was necessary because Iranian women are legally banned from entering Tehran's 100,000-seat Azadi Stadium and cheering for their national team. The official reason given for the special permission by Islamic authorities in Iran was that the Irish women did not understand Persian and as a result would not be harassed by the abusive language of male soccer fans. The reason behind the ban was that since the Islamic Revolution of 1979, Iranian women have been prohibited from entering sports stadiums because the Islamic law prevalent in the republic considers it sinful for them to look at athletes' half-naked bodies.[1]

What the soccer stadium now stood for was the functional equivalent of the grand mosque during major public ceremonies and communal rituals where women could ascend the roof (or in interior of the mosque hide behind the *mashrabiyyah*) and watch the world perform—at times, even with half-naked men beating their chest rhythmically as in the ritual commemorating the death of the third Shi'i Imam, Husayn ibn Ali. There was a difference though. From the *dark and invisible* rooftop or the *secret and hidden* space behind the *mashrabiyyah*, women could see men and imagine themselves with them in public and in the world. In either of those two ritualized spaces, women could watch men secretly and in dark denial ("Who me? No, I was not watching."). In the soccer stadium, however, women could not only watch but also show off that they were watching. With the women behind the *mashrabiyyah* or in the darkness of the rooftop, men could pretend they did not know they were being watched—one of the grandest acts of hypocrisy on which that particular public civility was based. But here the soccer players had no such luxury; women were watching them openly. In the classical case of women in the dark denial of the roof or behind the secretive *mashrabiyyah*, they could only imagine themselves to be with men in public through the furtive, secretive, transgressive *look* of their public denial—a *look* they were not supposed to have. In the grand public view of the soccer stadium, they would not partake in that grand hypocrisy; they would watch men and imagine themselves with them with that greatest of all threats to all metaphysics of fear and politics of terror: confidence.

Looking—at a football match, a movie, a person riding on a bicycle in the street, or just the rambunctious hustle-bustle of life with no particular focus—is the act of accumulating *visual memory*, in which we can then begin to *imagine* ourselves. Being looked at—and thus the ability to be able to imagine oneself in one's own field of vision—is the act of accumulating *bodily memory*, with which we can begin to *place* ourselves in the world. *Veiling*, being prevented from being seen, and *vision*, being permitted to look, are thus integral to each other. Forbidding to be looked at is directly linked to forbidding to look. Forbidding Iranian women to look at male soccer players is integral to a theocracy that must prevent its citizens from thriving under their own gaze and thus accumulating both *bodily* and *visual memory*, in which they could then imagine themselves. The tyrannical practices of an Islamic Republic are not a mere act of sexual apartheid. It is far worse than that. It is a game of power-basing between a theocracy and its desubjected subjects. Unless looked at, bodies will not develop confidant memories of themselves in public, and their memorial muscles will atrophy into insecure self-consciousness; we might as well cover them with a veil. Unless Iranian women are allowed into soccer stadiums to look at their national team and cheer for them, the Iranian soccer players will be miserable athletes. The result of the Iran-Ireland game in Tehran, under the full gaze of the Irish women looking at the Irish men and cheering their national team, and in the absence of Iranian women doing the same, was a foregone conclusion: The second leg of the Iran-Ireland playoff began under the jubilant gaze of no less than three hundred Irish women watching their national team play a classic defensive game even without the inspiring presence of Roy Keane. The Irish battled valiantly for every ball and kept Iran at bay for ninety minutes. A last minute goal for Iran jangled the nerves of the Irish a bit, but the Irish fans were never going to give up the right to play at the 2002 World Cup in Japan and Korea, a conviction they relayed to their team, which in turn resulted in a 2–1 win over Iran.

Heartbreaking as this loss was for Iranian women and men alike, the full causes and consequences of banning Iranian women from attending soccer stadiums and watching men play are far more serious. Under an Islamic Republic, Iranian women are not only barred from being looked at by being forced to veil their bodies against their will (though there are those who choose to do so and face the European fear of their habit in a reverse assertion of state power if they find themselves in France, Germany, etc.); they are equally banned from looking by being barred from soccer stadiums or any other sport that people play in comfortable clothes. The result affects both genders and is not limited to the making of bad athletes. Banning women from watching a soccer game is integral to forcibly veiling them. The former prevents them from accumulating *visual* memories, while the latter prevents them from building up *bodily* memories. The former forces a *historical blindness* on them; the latter makes them *geographically invisible*. In the absence of looking they cannot imagine themselves in the historicity of their own presence, while in want of being looked at they cannot place themselves geographically in the world. This is a built-in mechanism of a totalitarian theocracy designed for desubjecting a whole nation under the suzerainty of a medieval political culture, rendering all its people *visually blind* and *bodily invisible* ready-made objects of the powerful Panopticon of state control that denies all others vision and visibility so it can watch everything and be visible everywhere.

The particular challenge that women face in Iran is the normative template of a far more universal problem: How does the body accumulate an *agential memory* of itself so it can get up and do something autonomous, assertive, imaginative, or beyond the pales and forts of the violence-prone state? Being able to envision and thus watch oneself in one's own field of vision, in the world, is conducive to generating and sustaining *agential memory* in the body of the beholder. The alternative to such an *agential memory* is a passive, received, ready-made, conventional memory, in which the body is the obedient subject of its state of affairs. To be able to see and envision oneself in one's own field of vision and thus to accumulate a visual perception of one's own bodily memory is constitutional to an agential imagining of one's physical presence in the world. But because the constitutionally delegitimated state has lost all claim to legitimate territorial violence and opted for the human body as its principal site of power, preventing that body from accumulating an *agential memory* of itself is the state's chief *modus operandi*. This operation may assume dictatorial shapes in an Islamic Republic or else be performed by massive propaganda machineries like CNN globally, but the result is identical: the aggressive substitution of a collective subjectivity in lieu of a cultivated vision of one's *bodily presence* and *agential memory* in the world.

BUILDING VISUAL MEMORIES

But people do not just bend over and accommodate power. It is nothing short of sheer will rising against the cruelties of a belated theocracy succeeding those of a medieval monarchy squarely at the service of a predatory empire that today in Iran we have a sustained history of close to half a century of women filmmaking: a succession of visionaries defying the banning of their *body* and blinding of their *vision* to create bodily, visual, and agential memories for an entire nation in which they can imagine and place themselves. Whether condemned to a medieval monarchy or captured in a belated mullarchy, whether trapped in a Persian patriarchy or caught in an Islamic Republic, generations of Iranian women painters, photographers, filmmakers, singers, actresses, and poets have persistently sought to secure a vision of their own and a way of looking at the world, via that looking to imagine themselves in that world, by that imagining to restore to themselves the status of a knowing subject, and in that subjection to assume their historical agency.

Before and since Iranian women began making films, there is no better *voice* to hear than the poetry of Forough Farrokhzad (1935–1967) if we are to trace the aesthetic roots of their *vision*. There is a direct connection, an organic link, between the *poetic voice* of Forough Farrokhzad and the *poetic vision* that a constellation of Iranian women filmmakers have now made publicly available. Forough Farrokhzad became the repressed *voice* and the blinded *vision* of Iranian women across history that came back to haunt their domineering culture as they colored the dreams of Iran's poets and prophets. Forough Farrokhzad was neither the first nor the last Iranian woman poet. Tahereh Qorrat al-Ayn (1814–1852), Parvin E'tesami (1906–1941), and Shams Kasma'i (d. 1961) were chief among a number of leading women poets who preceded Forough Farrokhzad. Tahereh Qorrat al-Ayn was a revolutionary activist of unsurpassed courage and imagination, a gifted poet, and an extraordinarily learned woman who took the theologians and jurists of her time to task.[2] In the course of her revolutionary activities, she unveiled herself long before unveiling was even an issue in contemporary Iranian history. Parvin E'tesami was a poet of exquisite moral sensibilities and social concerns.[3] Shams Kasma'i broke loose from the rigid mandates of Persian prosody long before the founding father of modernist Persian poetry, Nima Yushij, did the same (albeit in a theoretically more sustained and systematic way). But none of them, each illustrious and accomplished in her own right, achieved Forough Farrokhzad's laser-beam access to the core of her historical representation of a repressed *voice*, restoring vision to a historical blindness. None of these distinguished poets sat down patiently and reflected on the untapped reservoir of millennia of repressed emotions and sensibilities the way Forough Farrokhzad did in the short span of only a decade, from the late 1950s to the late 1960s. "I kept looking at my surrounding world," she once said in an interview, "at things and people around me, and I looked at the principal outlines of this world, until I discovered it. When I tried to express it, I realized that I needed words, fresh words that belonged to that world. If I were to be scared I would have died. But I was not scared. I introduced the words. What do I care if these words are not yet poetic? They have life. I will make them poetic."[4]

It now appears as quite an ordinary—though ordinarily beautiful and brilliant—line, but it is nothing short of a miracle if we think through the implication of the verse when Forough Farrokhzad ever so simply says, "I come from the land of dolls." She was adamant, relentless, and unforgiving until she found her voice. She divorced her husband with the same tenacity and conviction that she ploughed through volumes of medieval poetry until she had her hands on the very pulse of her own history:

> I come from the land of dolls:
> From under the shade of paper trees
> Growing in an illustrated book,
> From dried-out seasons of aborted experiences
> In friendship and love
> Upon the dirt-alleys of innocence,
> From the years of pale alphabets
> Growing behind benches in a tubercular school,
> From that moment when children

Could spell the word "stone" on the blackboard
And the sparrows flew away from the top of the old tree.[5]

The earliest record of an Iranian woman filmmaker looking through a camera dates back to mid-1950s. Historians of Iranian cinema consider Shahla Riyahi's *Marjan* (1956) as the first occasion when a woman was identified as a filmmaker. Shahla Riyahi was already a popular actress of stage and screen by the time she made *Marjan*, but masculinist historiography has twice compromised her achievement: once by giving only her first name, a mere "Shahla," as the director,[6] and another time by completely denying that she even directed *Marjan*, asserting that she was the producer of the film and that her costar, Mohammad Ali Ja'fari, directed the film and then "the name of Shahla was also added as director on top of theater doors, and this was quite attractive for the audience, to see a woman's name as director."[7]

Shahla Riyahi was the first woman to break the psychological barrier thickly dividing the two sides of the camera. For a melodrama, Shahla Riyahi's *Marjan* has its own peculiar twists. A young gypsy girl falls in love with a teacher who has just captured her father trying to steal a sheep from the school in which he teaches. The teacher gradually leaves his village and moves to the city, followed by the young gypsy girl. She cannot find him and ends up working as a nurse in a hospital where some time later the teacher brings his young wife to deliver their child. Disappointed in her love, Marjan returns to her tribe.

Marjan was a pioneering feature in mapping out dual marginality at a time when such issues were not of any immediate concern to Iranian cinema. From the commencement of Iranian cinema in the late 1920s—when Ovanes Oganians, an Armenian Iranian, made the first Iranian feature film, *Abi and Rabi* (1929)—the annual production of films in Iran was limited to one every two years and gradually rose to about twenty a year in the mid-1950s, with all the producers, directors, and cinematographers being men. Shahla Riyahi was the first woman to cross the imaginary line and move from in front of the camera to behind it, from being looked at to looking. As such, she was the first woman filmmaker who could imagine herself in the speculum of a lens in which the world was already reflected and thus place herself (and with herself her gender) in her own field of vision. What Shahla Riyahi saw through that lens was not just herself acting as *Marjan*. Far more significantly, she placed, posed, imagined, and acted herself as Shahla Riyahi in the middle of a universe of imagination in which anything was possible. It was not Reza Shah in the 1930s but Shahla Riyahi in the 1950s who unveiled Iranian women, because it is as important to be able to see and have a *vision* as it is to be able to be seen and not be *invisible*. Shahla Riyahi was able to generate and accumulate a sustained *visual memory* of herself and the gender she represented in which she could now imagine herself—and with herself a whole nation—in the world. To be able to see and to be able to be seen are integral to each other; one generates a *visual*, the other a *bodily*, and both together an *agential* memory. The three memories collide to create a vision of the person and with that person the collectivity he or she represents in the historicity of his or her presence in the world. And it is precisely that *presence* that the state apparatus (as such and not just an Islamic Republic) has to abort in order to keep the body memoryless and submissive as the primary site of its violence.

It is crucial to remember that by the time that Shahla Riyahi made *Marjan* in 1956, Forough Farrokhzad's first collection of poems, *The Captive* (1955), had already been published. Shahla Riyahi's vision, as a result, may not have been predicated on a sustained record of women filmmakers, but it was squarely rooted in Forough Farrokhzad's poetry and the revolutionary resistances to historical blindness that she represented. Forough Farrokhzad's *poetic voice and vision* were the antecedent of the agential memory of Iranian women, resisting their enforced veiling as a means of blinding them to their own historical presence. It is a miraculous fact of modern Iranian art that the first globally celebrated woman filmmaker was also the most distinguished poet of her generation. Forough Farrokhzad is the only major Iranian poet who is also a major filmmaker, and she is the only major filmmaker who is also a major poet. Nobody else shares that singular distinction with her.[8] She is as seminal in the making of modern Persian poetry—the only women in the halls of its patristic generation—as she is constitutional to the making of modern Iranian cinema. Nothing visually significant happens between Shahla Riyahi's pioneering *Marjan* and Forough Farrokhzad's masterpiece *The House Is Black* (1962), and it is not until then that Iranian cinema fully recognized and dully celebrated the birth of its first woman filmmaker from the bosom of its most celebrated female poet. By 1962, Forough Farrokhzad (whom too the Persian patriarchal pathology still prefers to call simply "Forough") was already established as the single most important woman poet of her country and one of the most distinguished of her generation.[9] Three successive collections of her poetry—*The Captive* (1955), *The Wall* (1956), and *Rebellion* (1958)—had indisputably established Forough Farrokhzad as a major poetic voice of her time.

The House Is Black is a poetic ode to beauty in the heart of misery. Shot in 12 days at the Babadaghi leprosy colony in Tabriz, this film established Forough Farrokhzad as a major visual artist of her time. *The House Is Black* has valiantly survived its overpoliticization by a succession of malnourished film critics. It is only at the most artificial level that *The House Is Black* can be watched as a commentary on Iran under the Pahlavis, a society sick and afflicted with a disease and yet incapable of curing its ailment with reason and science. Left to its own magnificent devices, *The House Is Black* is a gem of a black-and-white movie, stealing beauty and teasing joy from the depth of despair and the heart of darkness. It is no Manichean bifurcation of good and evil; it is a prophetic call to purposeful prayer. Forough Farrokhzad moved through the lens of her camera and beyond just imagining herself inside the world she saw, and she kissed the world's wounds and cuddled its pains, casting a long cascade of love and affection on its most afflicted, toward its most forgotten. It is impossible to describe the fear and loathing that the mere mentioning of leprosy would invoke at the time the film was made—very similar to when AIDS had just emerged publicly in the 1980s in the United States. The horror and harassment to which the gay community in particular was subjected compares well with the experience of lepers in Iran. There was something mysteriously repugnant about leprosy, as if it were some sign of divine punishment. It was feared like a bubonic plague and believed to be deadly contagious.

In Forough Farrokhzad's time and location, leprosy was the absolute limit of the petrified imagination, a frightful frontier that no one would dare cross—no poet, no novelist, no photographer, and no filmmaker. A leprosy colony was a *terra incognita*. One never knew that they even existed, and then suddenly Forough Farrokhzad picked up a camera and went to look for life, beauty, and music smack in the middle of the most feared and forbidden disease. Leprosy is a progressive infectious disease caused by a bacterium (*Mycobacterium leprae*) that attacks skin, flesh, and nerves. It symptoms are nodules, ulcers, white scaly scabs, deformities, and the eventual loss of sensation. But what Forough Farrokhzad saw there was no pathetic colony of human rejects; instead she saw humanity at large, singing, dancing, falling in love, getting married, and thanking God for the beauty of nature and the place of humanity in it. She saw the quiet whispers of life in the midst of decay and death. She showed a woman holding a mirror in front of her ravaged face, applying cosmetics to make herself more beautiful. What did Abbas Kiarostami exactly do in his astonishingly effective *ABC, Africa* (2001) about victims of AIDS other than extend the narrative logic of Forough Farrokhzad's *The House Is Black*, shot about forty deuteronomical years earlier?

The House Is Black cast a long and enduring light on the Iranian cinema that followed it. It would not be an exaggeration to suggest that the entire texture and contour of Iranian cinema is indebted to Forough Farrokhzad's *The House Is Black*. In fact, one may very well argue that because of Forough Farrokhzad, there is something feminine and maternal about Iranian cinema. There is only one film, Farrokh Ghaffari's *Downtown* (1957), that predates Forough Farrokhzad's masterpiece and is worth mentioning as a pioneering effort in the current crescendo of Iranian cinema. But Ghaffari's *Downtown* comes nowhere near *The House Is Black* in terms of its impact and significance among the Iranian filmmakers themselves. Practically all major Iranian filmmakers, man or woman, trace the origin of their realism to Forough Farrokhzad's *The House Is Black* and Sohrab Shahid Sales's *One Simple Incident* (1973), which was made more than a decade after *The House Is Black* and was itself influenced by it. In numerous conversations and interviews, Mohsen Makhmalbaf has traced the origin of his cinema and much of note and significance among his peers' to *The House Is Black*. In an essay that Makhmalbaf wrote on Forough Farrokhzad, "Forough Was Our Sister" (1995), he confessed how he and his fellow Muslim revolutionaries, smack in the middle of their pious dedication to the causes and consequences of an *Islamic* revolution, confided in each other their devout dedication to Forough Farrokhzad: how they secretly paid visits to her grave and offered her the depth of their devotion, their sincerest signs of humility, treating her as if she were a saint. This was Forough Farrokhzad, shunned and scandalized throughout her life as a whore and officially cast into the depth of hell after her death as a harlot. And now here, in the most austere moral moment of an *Islamic* revolution, its rising artists, totally committed to their revolution, treated her like an angelic sign of divine mercy. In his critical assessment of *The House Is Black*, Makhmalbaf places it above Alain Resnais's *Night and Fog* (1955) and praises it in a language that is instrumental in understanding not only his own cinema but much of the best that the rest of Iranian cinema has to offer:

> When we see this film the least we learn is how—just like Christ—to look for white teeth in the carcass of a dog. With this film, Forough teaches us that the person who closes his eyes on darkness has committed two mistakes: First, she perpetuates that darkness, because unless we look at darkness we won't do something to make it bright; and second, by closing our eyes on darkness, we deny ourselves the sight of the amazing light that palpitates in the heart of that darkness and which is called life.[10]

There is scarcely any other description more apt and accurate than this in capturing the very soul of the best in Iranian cinema. Makhmalbaf's public confessions about his and his comrades' affection for Forough Farrokhzad, as well as his critical assessment of *The House Is Black*, are crucial in grasping the *matristic* origin of the entire cast of contemporary Iranian cinema. It would not be an exaggeration to suggest that that *maternal cast*, smack in the middle of a patriarchal monarchy that anticipated a theocratic mullarchy, subverted the medieval constitution of the Iranian political culture with such exacting precision and lasting impact that the rest of Iranian visual art, not just inside Iran but as far out as Shirin Neshat's work in New York, could never escape or surpass its whiplash sharpness and decisive intelligence. With the stroke of one gem of a short documentary, arisen from the heart of her *poetic vision* and at the height of her caring intellect, Forough Farrokhzad cast the definitive character of Iranian visual art. Both the patriarchal order constitutional to Forough Farrokhzad's culture and the colonial gaze integral to the modernity of her character wanted her *blind* and *invisible*. She turned the table around so mercilessly gracefully that no Iranian filmmaker can ever look through a camera without seeing the world through her eyes. She *is* their eyes.

THE NEXT MOVE

After Forough Farrokhzad's *The House Is Black*, the emerging Iranian cinema could not boast of any major women filmmakers for a very long time. As Dariush Mehrjui, Bahram Beizai, Abbas Kiarostami, Amir Naderi, and a host of other directors began to map out the contours of a spectacular national cinema, not a single woman was found among the leading directors.

Marva Nabili's quietly shot and secretly smuggled *The Sealed Soil* (1977) kept the hopes and aspirations of Iranian women filmmakers alive. Marva Nabili is so tangential to Iranian cinema that one must believe in miracles on observing how she appeared in the 1970s to establish a barely visible thread between Shahla Riyahi in the 1950s, Forough Farrokhzad in the 1960s, and the orchestral rise of a whole constellation of women filmmakers after the Iranian revolution of 1979 in the 1980s. While in Iran, Marva Nabili had worked with Fereydoun Rahnema on his pioneering *Seyavash in Persepolis* (1967). She subsequently studied cinema in London and New York and then returned to Iran to direct a television series based on Persian fairy tales. It was in the mid-1970s that she discretely shot *The Sealed Soil*, smuggled it out of Iran, and premiered it in San Remo film festival were she was awarded "The Best New Director" award. Marva Nabili's protagonist, Roybekheyr, is a young peasant woman, rebellious against her immediate surrounding, not particularly attracted to the promises of an urbanized life, and impatient with some inner palpitation she cannot quite articulate. She refuses to heed her family's advice to marry, and in a moment of frantic frustration she violently kills a chicken, which results in her being entrusted to a local soothsayer. The final shot of *The Sealed Soil* shows Roybekheyr yielding her body, almost like a planted tree, to the downpour of a bounteous rain, uniting her with the elemental forces of a nature she has been forced to repress.

Marva Nabili never returned to Iran after the revolution. She moved back to New York, where she made *Nightsongs* (1984), a critically significant feature film about a Chinese-Vietnamese woman who comes to New York and lives in Chinatown on the margin of an already marginalized community. Not deeply rooted in Iranian cinema like the other expatriate filmmaker Amir Naderi, Marva Nabili became the precursor of Shirin Neshat, who a generation later revolutionized what—because of its radically globalized aesthetic and political configurations—can no longer even be called an *Iranian* visual art. In Marva Nabili, we see the beginning of a globalized gaze that even in the depth of a remote village in Iran is fully cognizant of the multiplicity of sites in which it will be seen. Nabili is critical in facilitating that global gaze, opening one, however small, window from which the world could now peek into the otherwise closed circuits of a culture, as that culture was using the same window to cast a long and lasting look at the world at large. Nabili lent to the Iranian woman's camera her indispensable lens of a globalized gaze, in and of itself perhaps not so significant, but when planted in the right slot adds a universalizing momentum to the camera's apparatus. Nabili's singular achievement was that her camera remained native to Iranian sensibilities while decidedly perceptive in the wide angle of its global perspective.

Forough Farrokhzad's significance in the gradual mutation of her *poetic voice* and *prophetic vision* into an *agential memory* only grew more pronounced in time and became even stronger after her early and tragic death in an automobile accident in 1967. While the reach of *The House Is Black* was limited to a small but increasingly influential group of cineastes, the appeal of her poetry for Iranians at large was simply astonishing and entirely unprecedented. There is a visionary translucence to her poetry, a perceptive penetration into the nature and texture of things, which her readers inherited far beyond what she had given them in her single cinematic masterpiece. In her poetry, she planted a revelatory camera in their minds with which by virtue of *reading* her they *saw* themselves. Forough Farrokhzad's poetic voice is pronouncedly *visual*, seeing far beyond and above what is forbidden to see. In her poetry, generations of women (and men) could see the world and place and posit themselves in it. There is something almost sacred about being present at the moment of her poetic pronouncements:

> I come from the midst
> Of the roots of carnivorous plants
> And my brain still
> Resonates with the screams of a butterfly
> That was crucified with a pin in a booklet.[11]

In that voice hides a vision, and in that vision hides a defiance: a defiance of enforced veiling, of manufactured blindness, of engineered invisibility. In that poetic voice, women—as the primary target of totalitarian states that have lost the violent site of their very legitimacy—have found their vision, surpassed their mandated blindness, and defied their public invisibility. The history of Iranian women's liberation is written and registered by neither Reza Shah nor Khomeini but a whole different cast of characters.

What would later be called the "Islamic Revolution" was one of the most violent events in modern Iranian history, two years of sustained rebellious uprising culminating in a massive mobilization that destroyed the old regime and brutally executed its public officials and military officers before it faded into a bloody eight-year war with Iraq. But the same revolutionary disposition ushered in a period of unprecedented creative effervescences from which the Iranian cinema had the lion's share and in which women had an exceptional presence. Suddenly a whole panorama of women filmmakers picked up the camera and began to make one film after another. Kobra Sa'idi's *Maryam and Mani* (1980), Marziyeh Boroumand's *The City of the Mice* (1983), Pouran Derakhshandeh's *The Little Bird of Happiness* (1987), Tahmineh Ardakani's *Golbahar* (1986), Rakhshan Bani-Etemad's *The Foreign Currency* (1989), Faryal Behzad's *Kakoli* (1989), Tahmineh Milani's *Children of Divorce* (1989)—where were all these filmmakers before? *The Sealed Soil* was scarcely seen inside Iran, nor was Marva Nabili exactly a household name. Shahla Riyahi's *Marjan* was a mere matter of archival curiosity. Forough Farrokhzad's *The House Is Black* was still not a widely watched or extensively discussed film. There was no sustained record, no collective memory, of any woman filmmaker. But place Forough Farrokhzad's *poetry* where it was best preserved, in the minds and souls of the generations that came after her, and there remains no mystery. She saw for them in her *poetry* what they would later see for the entire world in their *camera*.

The story of Iranian woman filmmakers before and after the Islamic Revolution of 1979 cannot be told either chronologically or teleologically. What has ultimately happened is the gradual and mosaic assembly of a camera with a set of sustained and supportive lenses built into it one after the other, making every subsequent shot, if coordinated carefully, more focused than the shot before. After the revolution, the long and lasting history of women's emancipatory movements, from peasant and urban uprisings to literary and artistic achievements, could not be brought to an abrupt, tyrannical end—not after what they had endured under the two Pahlavis, not even under the brutalities of a theocracy. The banalities of an Islamic Republic were in fact bound to create an opposite effect. The political subject had invested too much in the making of a historical agent (and all through the caring camera of a few but furiously persistent band of visionaries) to allow it to dwindle into the domains of bureaucratic censorship and ideological fanaticism. The massive participation of Iranian women in the course of the 1979 Revolution and an illustrious record of women novelists, poets, painters, photographers, singers, and actresses had resulted in a critical mass and a creative core that could not but come to artistic fruition. Urbane, publicly educated for a generation, cultivated in the tumultuous torrents of their history, and in full public view, Iranian women joined the creative corps of the postrevolutionary artists in opposition to sustained institutional violence perpetrated against their vision and symbolized in their forced veiling.

One cannot point to the central significance of Forough Farrokhzad in the poetic vision at the heart of women filmmaking today without noting the erotic cast of her *bodily creative* character. Forough Farrokhzad was an exceptionally erotic poet. She dared to think, imagine, and write moments of sexual intimacy in a language and elegance never before done or dared in Persian poetry. Her poem "Lovingly" ("*Asheqaneh*"; 1964) has no match in the entire history of Persian poetry, and *there* we are in the presence of some mighty forces. In the simplicity, brilliance, and courageous imagination of its daring diction, "Lovingly" is a manifesto in praise of physical lovemaking, sublated to a joyous celebration of bodily life against a whole history of pathological mystification of love. Verses such as "O you! The palpitations of my burning body!," "My body smells of love-making," "You are the flood in the bed of my veins!," "My cheeks burning with the heat of desire," "Oh you stranger to my shirt / Familiar with the green pastures of my body," "Oh you! The tremors of pleasure in my body!," and "Oh You! The lines of your body the shape of my shirt!" had never been heard or uttered with such poetic elegance, such confident beauty in Persian poetry. And yet there is an innocence, a sudden and unexpected seriousness, about Forough Farrokhzad's eroticism. I know of no other poet among her contemporaries who so easily marks and distinguishes the difference between ennobling eroticism and degrading pornography. Later on, a whole spectrum of women filmmakers would master the art of visually projecting the poetic eroticism of Forough Farrokhzad. But already embedded in her poetry is an erotic energy that is at once ennobling and visionary, perceptive and eye opening. There is a rugged reality that informs her eroticism that makes of love(making) not a *futile escape* but a *fruitful inevitability*:

When my confidence was hanging
From the loose rope of justice,
And when all over the city
They were breaking to pieces the heart of my lights,
When they were blindfolding
The childish eyes of my love,
And from the anxious temples of my hopes
Blood was gushing forward,
And when my life was nothing,
Nothing but the tic-tocking of the clock on the wall,
I knew
I knew that I must, I must, I simply must
Love madly.[12]

That poetic eroticism—robust, physical, celebratory, confidant, joyous, and Dionysian—went piercingly against a whole history of bodily denial and moral duplicity constitutional to the character of the monarchical and clerical cultures. The patriarchal gaze wanted Forough Farrokhzad *visually blinded* and *physically invisible.* She taught that dead and deadening corpse two lessons: First, she placed a mirror in the hand of a woman to hold in front of her leprosy-ravaged face, gently to color and add luster to its persistent beauty; then she made a poetic point of her own body in moments of ecstatic bliss, and thus brought back to life and adorned, she sent it off to visit and be visited by the whole wide world. That *vision* could never be blinded; that *body* could never be invisible. That vision *was* the very sight of a whole emerging culture; that ecstasy *was* the very definition of the body.

In the course of postrevolutionary Iranian filmmaking, an entire generation of women filmmakers gradually emerged as the leading visionaries of their time. In achieving this vision, their caring hands were held in the capable palms of Forough Farrokhzad:

Just one window is enough for me,
One window open
Upon the moment
Of awareness and glance and silence.
Now the walnut tree has
Grown so tall that it can interpret the wall
For its young leaves.
You just ask the mirror the name of your savior.
Isn't the earth
Trembling under your feet—
More lonesome than you?
The prophets have brought
Their ruinous mission
To our century—

Are these endless explosions
And are these poisonous clouds
The echoes of their sacred verses?
O friend, o blood-brother, o comrade:
When you reach the moon remember
To write the history of the massacre of the flowers.[13]

At the conclusion of the Iran-Iraq war (1980–1988) and on the death of Ayatollah Khomeini in 1989, the reign of charismatic terror that had for a decade brutalized a nation subsided. The established filmmakers continued to thrive, and new names were added to them. Rakhshan Bani-Etemad's *Nargess* (1991), Tahmineh Milani's *The Legend of Sigh* (1990), Yasaman Malek Nasr's *The Common Pain* (1994), Zahra Mahasti Badi'i's *Hasanak the Fortunate* (1995), Faryal Behzad's *The Invisible Man* (1995), and Pouran Derakhshandeh's *My Homeland* (1998) were chief among a whole constellation of films made by women and addressing a host of issues domestic to their concerns and yet universal to their nation at large. By the end of 1980s, the feminine figure of modernity was squarely placed beyond the reaches of the colonial and patriarchal shadows in the universe of the Iranian creative imagination. No amount of veiling, no forceful banning of young women from soccer stadiums, and no systematic campaign of terror and intimidation or gender apartheid could compromise what in the realm of creative imagination these filmmakers had already achieved. Women could be juridically barred from having their bodies exposed to the public gaze and thus accumulating bodily memories, but through the camera of a succession of women filmmakers, in it already planted the supportive lenses from Shahla Riyahi to Forough Farrokhzad and Marva Nabili, they could already see and imagine themselves otherwise. That *otherwise* was *written on paper* long before it was *shot on camera:*

The dreams always fall
From the height of their simplicity
And die.
I smell a four-leafed clover
That has grown over the grave of old concepts:
Is the woman who is buried in the shroud
Of her expectations and innocence
My youth?
Will I ever again climb
The steps of my curiosity
To greet the good God
Who is walking on the roof?[14]

The election of President Mohammad Khatami in 1997 marked the beginning of a new era in modern Iranian history. When Samira Makhmalbaf premiered her *Apple* (1998) in Cannes, the whole world knew that her nation had entered a new phase in its long and embattled encounter with the prolonged predicament of colonial modernity. Soon she moved to make her second feature, *The Blackboard* (2000), and was joined by Marziyeh Meshkini and her stunning debut, *The Day I Became a Woman* (2000). Members of the previous generation were still equally active. Pouran Derakhshandeh made her *Love Without Frontier* (2000), and soon Maryam Shahryar joined forces with them with her first feature, *The Daughters of Sun* (2000), a fine film with very precise and measured movements toward the cultivation of a potentially promising career. Tahmineh Milani's *Two Women* (2000) and *The Hidden Half* (2001) registered her as one of the most socially conscientious and politically controversial filmmakers of her time. She is not a filmmaker of any enduring aesthetic significance or sustainable cultural insight, but she is a courageous rabble-rouser of uncommon dedication. Rakhshan Bani-Etemad's *Under the Skin of the City* (2001) and *Days of our Lives* (2002), meanwhile, took full advantage of the relative liberty that Khatami's presidency had made possible. When Niki Karimi, by far the most celebrated Iranian actress of her generation, made her first documentary, *To Have or Not to Have* (2001), the established significance of filmmakers as the authors of their national destiny had already led yet another woman to authorial position. Niki Karimi is the conclusion of Shahla Riyahi: Both celebrated in their chosen profession, *the bodiless face* of Niki Karimi now completes *the faceless body* of Shahla Riyahi to make up one complete human being integral to the fate of a nation, competent in their gaze, complete in their vision, jointly imagining a whole people in their place in history. To the future of that history, Forough Farrokhzad was a testimonial in her time:

> I feel that the time is over:
> I feel that only "the instance" is my share
> From the page of history.
> I feel that the desk is a false distance
> Between my hair and the hands of this sad stranger.
> Tell me something—
> What would a person who is giving you the kindness
> Of a living body
> Want in return
> Except to grasp the feeling of being alive?
> Tell me something—
> I am in the shadow of the window.
> I have a connection to the sun.[15]

GENDER APARTHEID

The banning of Iranian women from participating in soccer matches is only one, and by no means the most serious, aspect of a whole systematic program of gender apartheid that is constitutional to the Islamic Republic—or would be, if it were left to its own devices. In hospitals, for example, women are separated into an isolated section and limited to being treated by female staff, with sometimes criminal consequences. It seems paradoxical (or does it?) that a theocratic regime so medieval in its misogynist practices could be the republic of such visionary women with a global panorama of emancipatory vistas in their cinema. The numbingly cliché-ridden narratives of *modernization* and *Islamization* completely fail in the face of such apparent contradictions. How could these women see so much through those veils? What audacity placed them behind those cameras? The atrocities of the Islamic Republic against its women citizens, which only matches and mirrors the universal abuses of power it perpetrates against all its citizens, have now created a false assumption that women's status was far superior under the Pahlavis. This is not the case. Pathology of a different sort, a state-sponsored *modernization* with grotesque consequences, was the hallmark of women's status under the Pahlavis. The issues pertaining to women in Iran or any other so-called *Islamic society* should never be understood within dynastic periods or claims to republican reforms or revolutions. A far more reliable source of assessment is the sustained record of women's own creative imagination, critical thinking, and the torrent of their own crossfeeding on each other and nourishing the generations they thus hold together.

What is happening today in much of the Iranian cinema directed by women, and then beyond, is indebted to Forough Farrokhzad in ways and manners far beyond her single masterpiece, *The House Is Black*. In a brutally brief creative career that was tragically cut short by an automobile accident, Forough Farrokhzad generated and sustained a visionary recital beyond the habitual veiling of her gender and the limitations of her culture. She was born in 1935 and died in 1967. Her first collection of poetry, *The Captive*, appeared in 1955 and her last, *Let us Believe in the Commencement of the Cold Season!*, appeared soon after she died. She was still in high school when the CIA and the British Intelligence Service arranged for a coup to topple the democratically elected government of Mohammad Musaddiq and bring back the runaway monarch to power. She spent much of her adult and creative life under the reign of the second Pahlavi. When it comes to the status of women, the entire Pahlavi project of state-sponsored *modernization* becomes a grotesque joke in comparison to what Forough Farrokhzad was single-handedly able to achieve. The dignity of place that Forough Farrokhzad secured for her gender is embedded in a succession of poetic raptures that she discovered in five collections of poetry. If we are to speak of emancipation in terms domestic to a movement, Iranian women in their most recent history prior to the Islamic Revolution were liberated in a dream that Forough Farrokhzad saw for them in her poetry. It is by sheer historical serendipity that the most celebrated Iranian woman poet was also a pioneering filmmaker. But there is nothing accidental about the expansive vision of Forough Farrokhzad and the confident unveiling of her dream.

The dialectical link between vision and veiling is not exclusive to an Islamic Republic, though such a state carries it to atrocious ends. Under the state-sponsored *modernization* projects of patently secular monarchies, the power-basing operation of the modern state is constitutionally conducive to the blinding of the vision and the control of the body in an even more pernicious way. Visions are blinded and men and women alike are prohibited in seeing themselves in the collectivity of an emancipatory memory of themselves so that the panoptic operation of the state is made possible. The Pahlavi censorship of all sorts of artistic expression went far beyond a blatantly political control of any sign of protest. Literary, visual, and performing arts of any kind were under strict censorial control. The state's panoptic control of its subjects is always predicated on the blinding of their self-perceptions, the creative imagining of themselves in alternative universes. Veiling is coterminous with the blinding of the vision because body has emerged as the primary site of the violence that the state perpetrates on its subjects. With the rapid globalization of the capital and labor, the territorial claims of the state pale in comparison to the claims that the state lays on the physical bodies of its subjects, thus desubjecting them under the gaze of its panoptic observations. Beyond the jurisdiction of any Islamic state or the predicament of any colonial condition, the rules and regulations of any state in the very heart of capitalist modernity on abortion, control of reproductive organs, gay and lesbian relationships, capital punishment, and euthanasia are variations on the same theme.

States though are no match for the creative effervescence of their presumed subjects. The Pahlavi monarchy may have mobilized a brutal machinery of oppression, as the Islamic Republic now does even worse than the regime it toppled, but the blinding of the vision and the torturous control of the body to the point of veiling it is challenged and opposed in ways beyond the state's control. In Forough Farrokhzad's case, chief among a whole panorama of creative resistances to tyranny, vision becomes even more piercing by stealing its light from the heart of its surrounding darkness, and the body casts its veil and nakedly overflows into uncontrollable directions. Forough Farrokhzad's poetry reads like a beacon of light shining from the depth of darkness. Not only did she announce ex nihilio the necessity or inevitability of freedom; she actively and persistently sought, saw, and visualized it from the depth of moral and political bondage. Her five collections of poetry commence with a full, almost paralyzing awareness of the depth of moral impediment in which she and her contemporaries live (*Captive* and *The Wall*), continues with an almost insipid articulation of revolt (*Rebellion*), and then comes to full, fruitful, and emancipatory crescendo in her masterpiece, *Another Birth*. Her posthumous *Let Us Believe in the Commencement of the Cold Season!* is so sagacious that it seems it must have been her very last and necessarily postmortal work. The same logic of progression, the dialectical breaking of vision from the fact of veiling, is equally evident in the best of her poems: in the singularity of their poetic perception.

Forough Farrokhzad's poetic persona can be summoned in a vision that she best projected in "Swamp"—a poem from her most mature volume, *Another Birth*—a vision that dreamed of pouring into a sea while knowing the body that had engendered it is living in a swamp. Her vision in this poem is nocturnal, but her eyes are wide open:

The night darkened and
Sickened, the eye though revolted
To remain awake.
The eye cannot not see, alas!
Alas! The eye knows not
How to conceal.[16]

If there is one moment to name as the commencement of Forough Farrokhzad's visionary recitals, and with hers that of her nation at large, it is when this poetic eye, wide open in the depth of darkness and sick in and of itself, revolts against its blindness. The ocularcentricism of this poem is exemplary of Forough Farrokhzad's visionary recitals. Her eyes assume a cosmic sight, a vision beyond history and geography, a staring, a gaze set in motion, deep in the dark of the night, and then begin to see things undreamt before. What is it that they see?

It looked and saw
In me an old cemetery,
It saw my all existence
An ancient awaiting.
It saw that desert, and it saw
My loneliness in it,
It saw my sun and my moon, and it saw
Them both made of paper.

The astonishing aspect of this poem is that Forough Farrokhzad's poetic vision assumes a reality sui generis, almost independent of herself, as if autonomous in and of itself. The vision that she thus projects becomes a piercing perception that begins to look into the person who has engendered it. Forough Farrokhzad's body now becomes the focal point of the vision she has poetically projected. But this body is no longer just her own. There is a universality to this body in correspondence to the globality of the vision she has just generated. The corporeal body that this piercing eye now sees is dead and deadly, a cemetery of deceased bodies. Two opposing metaphors begin to face each other: a piercing vision seeing things beyond its veil and a dead body, flat and deflated, devoid of all signs of life—one hopeful, the other realistic. Forough Farrokhzad commences at the two opposing ends of vision and veiling: the vision extrasensually perceptive and the unveiling having just revealed a dead and deadening body. Beginning with these two opposing metaphors, the imageries she now unveils are the tearing seams of a paradox. Inside herself she sees birth and death at the one and the same time, and yet each is at odds with its own nature:

Like an old fetus fighting
With the uterus tearing
The walls of the womb
With its claws—

Alive and yet anxious
To be born,
Dead and yet longing
To die.

These miraculous verses are the gifts of that vision. Expressions such as "old fetus," "alive and yet anxious to be born," or "dead and yet longing to die" are peerless in the vast riches of Persian poetic imagination. What they do is poetically postulate a tension, a paradox, a pulling at the seams of reality where birth is no longer birth, death no longer death, and the whole universe is at the commencement of its own otherwise-than-being. The vision continues to be ever more perceptive, revealing the very dialectic moment of birth out of death, being out of nothingness, and the body begins to show signs of life beyond its veiling veneers. Forough Farrokhzad's paradoxes thrive on reality pregnant with its negated possibilities.

Selfish out of disliking herself,
Asleep with the dream
Of rising—
My laughter
An irrelevant sadness,
My shame
A pointless piety.

Halfway through the perception, Forough Farrokhzad changes the personal pronoun from *her* to *me*, completely collapsing into each other her own body and the generalized body of the entire nation of sentiments she now represents—a poetic premonition of Shirin Neshat's photographic self-portraits. On the site of that body, nothing is what we habitually take it to be. Arrogance is born out of despising oneself, sleep out of being awake; laughter is an irrelevant sadness, shame a pointless piety. This is the very alphabet of a whole new lexicon of moral sentiments, deliberately contrapuntal, pregnant and paradoxical, pulling as they push, asking as they answer, taxing as they ease, blinding as they show, like a twilight zone where things might go either way, as much toward a sunrise of hope as toward a sunset of despair, and yet things are miraculously clear, vision in and from the depth of veiling. The paradoxes unfold even further:

My lasting loneliness
Out of love,
The swift passion of death
In my lovemaking.
I never descended
From my own roof,
Stood on a mount and saw
My own execution.

Finding loneliness in the heart of having just fallen in love or seeing death at the very moment of lovemaking collapses habitual binary oppositions, and nothing any longer means what it was wont to mean. The master-verse of this poem is "the swift passion of death in my lovemaking" (*shur-e tond-e marg dar hamkhabegim*). The phrase *shur-e tond*, which I have had to translate as "swift passion," is impossible to convey in one single English phrase. *Shur* suggests "passion" and "excitement," adds to it a tasteful pinch of "salty," surmises a passionate, sweat-soaked lovemaking, mutates it to death, and then relays it back to the act of lovemaking—all at one and the same time. Death, as a result, becomes an act of lovemaking, full of passionately pregnant possibilities, while lovemaking is given a desperate, final, and yet indeterminate urgency. It is on that basis, on the premise of that convulsion of *the real*, that Forough Farrokhzad can manage to remain earthly but rising, realist but rebellious:

> An earth-worm and yet
> The earth is fragrant,
> Her balloons flying
> High in the heavens.

In the suggestion of that fragrance, her earthly disposition is at once realistic and yet rebellious. The same is true about the image of balloons that remain rooted on the ground and yet flying high. There is a nakedness to both the earthworm and the balloons that unveil and expose the body they implicate beyond any customary veiling. Veiling, in fact, is never just the customary habit of political cultures concealing the body. The very supposition of the body, the verticality of its hierarchical surveillance, is always-already culturally coded and thus veiled before any garment is added to it. It is only from the naked stripping of the body beyond its cultural codification that Forough Farrokhzad can begin to postulate an alternate agency for herself—strange but familiar, friendly but borne in hostile circumstances, a stranger to its own owner:

> Unknown to her hidden half,
> Ashamed of her human face,
> Neighborhood after neighborhood
> Running after and addicted to
> The smell of her mate.
> She finds her every once in a while and
> Yet incredulous—
> Her mate even lonelier than she.
> Both fearful of each other
> And trembling,
> Bitter and to each other ungrateful—
> Their love a doomed hope,
> Their unison a doubtful dream.

This vision has given birth to a split character, the breaking through of the singularity of her repressed vision and veiled body divided into two halves, gushing forth her sight and soon her body. The encounter is doubtful and dubious, but the spell is broken; the vision has given birth to its alternative—alterity, alter ego, a body double. She does not let go of her real foot on the ground and the historical fate of her generation:

Oh if I only had a way
To a sea,
When would I fear
Plunging?
If into a swamp a river
Bends, it will diminish
From stillness.
Its soul will become the abode
Of darkness,
Its depth the graveyard
Of the fish.

Her final cry is dreaming of an overflowing river, while she herself is trapped in a swamp. In this final crescendo of the poem, the vision that she sees and to which she entrusts her alternated body carries the hopes, aspirations, and enunciated future of her gender and with that her nation:

Deer, oh deer of the prairies!
If once in the passage of flowerbeds
You found a singing river
Running towards the blueness
Of the seas,
Laying upon the chariot
Of its own rebellion,
Gliding on the silk
Of its own flow,
The horsetail of the wind
In its claws,
The red soul of the moon
Behind it,
Opening the green thighs
Of the wet branches,
Stealing the virgin fragrance
Of the bushes,
Shining on its every bubble
The generous reflection
Of the sun—
Remember the dream of the one who could not sleep!
Remember the death in the swamp!

By the conclusion of the poem, the vision has unveiled her body and metamorphosed it into a thunderous river, gushing forth in all glory and force toward the seas. In her material realism, definitive of her poetry at large,

Forough Farrokhzad commences her vision with the primacy of her visual perception but ultimately mutates her body from "an old cemetery" into "a singing river / Running towards the blueness / Of the seas, / Laying upon the chariot / Of its own rebellion, / Gliding on the silk / Of its own flow." This is the texture of the creatively crafted *corpus amorphous*—defiant, anarchic, beyond the measure and means of any legislated semantics, signating with ferociously unfolding temptations, tumultuous, furious, determined, just like a voice giving birth to a vision, a vision beyond veiling.

BLINDING THE BODY TO ITSELF

The state has now moved to blind the body to itself so that it can rule it in the darkness of its self-amnesia, its virtual disappearance. The state does so by subjecting the feminine gender (*naming it weaker*) to a bodily blindness. This the state seeks to achieve not just by veiling the feminine body but also by preventing it from cultivating a visual memory of itself by watching, seeing, or observing things in and beyond its own corporeal horizons. This will result in both a muscular atrophy of the body (by not allowing it to be seen so that it can exercise and accumulate a *passive* visual vocabulary) and ultimately a total disappearance of the body (by not permitting it to see things and by seeing things placing itself in its own field of vision, in the world, and thus accumulating an *active* visual vocabulary).

To resist that total negation and annihilation of the body—a systemic project that will result in the state ruling ruthlessly on a mere *apparition* of a territorial simulacrum—women's visual art is a collective act of going out and seeing things and thus placing their bodies in the public domain. By thus placing their bodies, they call and claim them. Because women are the primary target of state violence, while men are the primary victims of opposing that violence, women tend to aestheticize the human body in order to restore its bodily memory and thus give it historical agency, while men tend to overpoliticize the human body by either turning it into the principal site of state violence or else resisting that violence by the self-explosion of the body—its sudden, radical, and spontaneous eradication from under the feet of the state—so that they make a public spectacle of the fact that the state has nowhere to stand and must fall on the ashes of the (once) human body, just like the figure of President Bush on the remains of the World Trade Center and all its inhabitants and assailants on September 11, 2001. That was no longer a president, because there was no state—there was nothing, no*body*, to rule.

Chapter 6

Corpus Amorphous

The explorer, on the other hand, felt greatly troubled; the machine was obviously going to pieces; its silent working was a delusion . . .

—Franz Kafka, *In the Penal Colony* (1914)

If in the previous chapter I have opted for a strategic gendering of *an aesthetics* and *a politics* that seeks to see how the body resists the state-sponsored depletion of its agential memory, it is to assay and navigate the body's modes and manners of resistance to the state and its constitutional tendency to eradicate the bodily memory of its subjects by covering and blinding them. In the following chapter, I want to trace the emerging contours of the body in its *posthuman* reconfiguration. I believe that since Martin Heidegger we have all been sent on a wild-goose chase of restoring agency to the subject in the advent of technological modernity, while globalized capital is running amuck in an entirely different, markedly *posthuman* direction where humanism is too busy being *secular* to be of any help in sustaining the physical boundaries of the body. My principal purpose in this chapter is to intercept the correspondence between the *amorphous capital* and the *amorphous body* that it has necessitated and manufactured.

Removing an Eye (for an Eye)

In August 2000, the Iranian press reported on a case in a Tehran court in which the presiding judge had ordered one of the eyes of Gholam Hossein Aryabakhshayesh to be removed in accordance with the law of retribution, which is part of the current Iranian (Islamic) penal code. For blinding a man named Mohammad Ali Qorbani in a traffic argument in April 1997, Mr. Aryabakhshayesh met his juridically articulated punishment.[1] In a separate incident, Amnesty International also reported that five Iranians, including sisters Tahereh and Sima Yaghubi, were publicly flogged on May 16, 2001, in the northern city of Tonekabon for allegedly having extramarital sexual relationships. The two sisters and two of the men received 91 lashes each, while the third man received 74 lashes.[2]

An alarming increase in the frequency of public torture in the Islamic Republic of Iran at the threshold of the twenty-first century alerted human rights activists inside and outside the country. The entrenched judiciary, in deadlocked opposition to the reformist aspirations of Iranians at large that were repeatedly recorded by the massive landslide victories of President Mohammad Khatami in 1997 and 2001 as well as the parliamentary election of 2000, was publicly flexing its muscles and defying both the executive and the legislative bodies of the government within which reformists were hard at work preventing such atrocities. When on August 1, 2001, a revolutionary court in Torbat-e Heydariyeh in northeastern Iran sentenced two political supporters of President Khatami to periods of imprisonment plus 40 lashes following arrests made in connection with celebration of the President's reelection, there remained no doubt that the borders between the political and the corporeal bodies had been publicly crossed.

THE POLITICAL BODY UNDER CONTROL

The public punishment of the *physical body* in a symbolic gesture to bring the *political body* under control is squarely rooted in its juridical regimentation. The judiciary branch of the Islamic Republic of Iran is now the full beneficiary of a sustained history of Islamic jurisprudence in which bodily torture in public, otherwise known as "just retribution" (*qisas*), is constitutional to its penal codes.[3] Within all scholastic divisions in Islamic law and throughout Islamic history, regimented bodily harm—up to and including capital punishment and public stoning to death—is juridically articulated and exactly executed. Public execution by stoning has been rampant in Iran since the Islamic Revolution. On July 11, 2001, Amnesty International reported that Maryam Ayoubi was stoned to death in Evin prison in Tehran. Another woman, identified only as Robabeh, was also reported on June 24, 2001, to have been first flogged and then stoned to death.[4] The charges usually brought against these victims are rape or murder in the case of men and adultery or murder in the case of women.[5]

The physical body is juridically regulated and publicly punished at the slightest violation of that regulation. The cultural control via juridical regimentation of the body is constitutional to the formation of the *body politic*. Naked, the body is the most dangerous site (and sight) of resistance to culture, particularly to its political constitution. To ascertain their successful operation, cultures control—as law legislates—the otherwise nakedly defiant body. As the mobile site (and sight) of the culture, body defies all attempts at regimenting its defiant presence. In and of itself, body is the signifying site (and sight) of resurrection against all repressive measures to control and acculturate its shapes, gestures, and movements. The tension between the body and the culture is the battleground for the political operation of jurisprudence. The culture commands covering and behaving. The body defies in its concealed nakedness and manifest misbehaving. The political apparatus of the state is far more endangered by a defiantly naked body than by an army of revolutionary uprising. All revolutionary uprisings replicate the power of the state they oppose. The naked body exposes the symbolic subterfuge (a.k.a. the ideological justification) of the naked violence of the state. Thus exposed, the state can scarcely conceal its naked violence under the subterfuge of the metaphysics of its presence, the claims of its ideology, or the teleology of its fabricated history. Naked, the body exposes that violence by mirroring it, stripping it of its metaphysics, ideology, and teleology.

The jurisprudence of bodily regimentation is the link between the politics and the metaphysics of denying and repressing the body. The political juridically regiments the body, as the metaphysical narratively represses it. The metaphysical denies the body via an unexamined privileging and celebrating of its Other, code-naming it the "Soul." There is a direct trajectory that connects the political claims of the state to legitimacy to the metaphysical denial of the body, culminating in its juridical regimentation. The political repression of the body manifests itself in public torture and other forms of corporeal punishment, including public execution of various forms. The juridical regimentation of the body legislates and codifies its public and even private behavior. The metaphysical denial of the body postulates a shadowy Other for it and celebrates this Other as its "Soul" by way of denouncing its material corporeality and bringing it under its juridical control.

The jurisprudence regulates, the metaphysical denies, and the political punishes the body. The metaphysical denial of the body is code-named the "Soul." The metaphysical constitution of the "Soul" is the most pernicious denial of the body at the most hidden hideout of a culture: its sacred certitude, its solemn claim to authenticity. Mulla Sadra Shirazi (1571–1640), one of the most seminal Muslim philosophers of all time and by far the most distinguished Shi'i philosopher ever, was acutely aware of the metaphysical privileging of the *soul* over the *body*. In Mulla Sadra's metaphysics, man consists of a *veiled aspect* (superior) and a *revealed aspect* (inferior). His *veiled aspect* is his soul (*nafs*), while his *revealed aspect* is manifested in his body (*badan*). To Mulla Sadra, all the sublime attributes of the human are invested in his soul. The soul is of "a Divine Substance, a Pure Essence, a Heavenly Delicacy, an Ethereal Flame, a Spiritual Word, A Godly Creation, a Spaceless and Timeless Act." The body, conversely, "is this corpus which has the shape of a ship and in which we sail through the sea of materialities towards the abode of spiritualities."[6] Mulla Sadra's metaphysical celebration of the *soul* at the expense of the *body* is constitutional to his epistemology. "Understanding is of two kinds," he believes. "The evident (*mashhur*) and the concealed (*mastur*). What is *evidently understood* is based on bodily sense-perception, while what is *innately understood* is spiritually Soul-based." What is understood via body-based sense perception is inferior to what is understood via soul-based intuition, because "when what is understood via bodily sense-perception increases so does its weakness and corruption, while when what is understood Spiritually increases in proportion and dimensionality so does its rationality and comportment."[7]

This philosophical denial of the body is tantamount to its metaphysical repression in the Qur'an. Mulla Sadra denounces the body philosophically with the same logic that the Qur'an represses it metaphysically. The Qur'anic descriptions of hell are particularly fearsome when it comes to bodily tortures. "But as for those who disbelieve, garments of fire will be cut out for them; boiling fluid will be poured down on their heads. When that which is in their bellies, and their skins too, will be melted; And for them are hooked rods of iron."[8] The jurists have been very particular that *bodily resurrection* on the Day of Judgment is to be taken quite literally. It is in this very body we live in this life that we will be resurrected and then rewarded or punished in the next. For centuries, theologians and philosophers have been at each other's throats over the possibility of *bodily resurrection* on the Day of Judgment. Jurists, however, have been particularly adamant about the principality of the body and quite unwavering that the Qur'anic injunction will have to be taken literally. Philosophers such as Mulla Sadra turn the body into a corporeal vessel to carry the soul and denounce the jurists for their literal-mindedness. "Woe unto those belligerent, literal-minded, jurists who believe that man is just this evident and palpable body, this corpus full-of-fissure, and nothing more. Among them there are those who actually believe that to God belongs no other world except that which is inhabited by these lowly bodies, and that He has created no other creatures save these wretched beasts and animals." Mulla Sadra, on the contrary, believes that "there is in existence another world in which dwell *Spiritual Beings* and *Divine Persons,* and towards which point the souls of people, once they are purified of pollutions and contaminations."[9]

Contrary to philosophers who have the luxury of speculating about the *soul* and its separation from the *body*, the jurists have no such concerns. They are too political to abandon the physical primacy of the body. The jurists insist on the principality of the body, bodily resurrection, and particularly hellish torture in the afterlife because of their immediate proximity to the political order. For the jurists, the resurrection will have to be bodily in order for them to regiment the body in this life and thus safeguard the *body politic.* In order to define and safeguard the state in Islamic terms, they must script and legislate the body, and in order to control, punish, and regulate the body, they have to insist on bodily resurrection on the Day of Judgment. But the philosophers' insistence on the separation of the body from the soul is not particularly emancipatory either. In fact, they are worse, because they deny the body altogether without rescuing it from either its metaphysical condemnation to hellish torture or its juridical mutation into the site of the *body politic.* A direct, logically consistent line links an Islamic metaphysics, theology, jurisprudence, and now the claim to a "republic" together. The focal point of convergence for the regulatory forces of these facets of the Sacred is the physical body, which the Qur'an metaphysically punishes, Islamic law juridically regulates, and Islamic government politically pinpoints as the principal site of its violence.

A Historic Battle

Never in Islamic history has the state, from its medieval metaphysics to its current claim on a "republic," been as thoroughly challenged as it is now in Iranian cinema. Today we are witnessing a historical battle: a constellation of bodily resurrections against the body's political punishment, its juridical regulation, and ultimately its metaphysical repression. Iranian cinema, at its best, is the visual return of the verbally repressed body.

The official censorship in Iranian cinema is integral to the politics and metaphysics of an "Islamic Republic." Veiling the body and denying its defiant sensuality is the central, most significant theme of the Islamic censorship. "Sex and violence" are said to be forbidden in an Islamic cinema. But what is forbidden is far more fundamental than accidental sex or structural violence. Both sex and violence are rampant in the best of Iranian cinema. Creatively sublated, sex and violence are now integral to the very cast of the Iranian cinematic cosmovision. The battleground between Iranian cinema and Islamic censorship is not sex and violence; it is the *site* of sex and the target of violence that is forbidden. It is the human body. It is not by virtue of a moral authority that states prohibit sex and forbid violence in works of art. It is by political necessity that states must appropriate the site of sex and target of violence as the exclusive territory on which they exact and exercise their power. But by an astonishing turn of the table, official censorship has now been transmuted in the best of Iranian cinema from a debilitating political imposition to an enabling aesthetic force. Official censorship is not as much imposed politically as it is grafted aesthetically onto the very texture of the Iranian creative imagination. Cinema has turned the scissors of censorship into the cutting edge of the creative excision of the bodily sign in unpredictable, expansive, flamboyant, Bakhtinian, and carnivalesque directions, and thus censorship is integral to its aesthetics. The cumulative result is a palliative, extenuating, and mitigating effect of the mutated signs of the body on the rectitude of their presumed signification. This in short is the mutiny of signs against the tyranny perpetrated on them by a violent metaphysics of signification, which is itself scared witless of misbehaving signs dismantling its reign of terror. Iranian cinema does not defy censorship so much as it subverts it, takes it in, and turns it around itself, taking it for a spin, as it were, and running it in its own opposite direction. To be sure, the custodians of the sacred *body politic* continue to impose and exact severely repressive measures on Iranian filmmakers, among other artists. But for the censorial policies of the Islamic Republic, this is a losing battle. They don't even know where they are being hit. The opening up of the symbolic into its suggestive signs is far more subversive, deeply more dangerous, to the custodians of the Sacred, from its metaphysicians to its politicians. Iranian cinema today has successfully turned the metaphysical inhibition of the body into its aesthetic celebration, its juridical closure into its symbolic exposé, its political censorship into its semiotic emancipation. In one word, Iranian cinema has creatively *disembodied* the symbolic body and desedimented it into suggestive signs that it has in turn let loose into wildly unpredictable, deeply dangerous, and far more subversive directions. The *corpus hierarchicus* of the culture, in short, is now turned into a creative *corpus amorphous*, visually mapped out and artistically celebrated, and there is no cop on the beat to even see, let alone seize, the perpetrators, who are all on the loose in film festivals around the world.

Body is culturally symbolized into an obedient verticality of behavior that it silently defies. Iranian cinema has given visual space to that verbal silence. If in the repressed verticality of an Islamicized body, sex is forbidden, Mohsen Makhmalbaf in *Gabbeh* (1995) redefines the body, breaks its symbolic obedience into emancipatory signs, expands it, spreads it out, and breaks it down to forms, shapes, colors, and suggestions. In *Gabbeh*, Makhmalbaf tells a love story in the weaving colors and shapes of a Persian carpet. If in the entire tapestry of classical Persian poetry the male lover has authorial agency to define what love is and whom he loves and we scarcely ever hear a feminine voice to balance the trade (until that glorious accident, Forough Farrokhzad), all Makhmalbaf has to do is cast the masculine lover entirely in long shots and the female lover in close-ups. We scarcely ever see the man of her affection in any close-up. She alone is in a position of addressing and imagining her love. When it comes to sexual intercourse, what if the Islamic censorship cannot stomach it? All Makhmalbaf has to do is come up with a creative mise-en-scène in which the female partner is sitting down on the ground next to a goat and milking her innocently. In comes into the frame the male partner, casually placing his groin next to the goat's mouth. In an innocent medium-shot, the body of the goat is now the intermediary *liaison* between the man and the woman, extending the suggestion of his genitalia to hers through an arch that runs through the goat's mouth, to its belly, to its udders, to the woman's fingers milking them, and into a bowl placed right in between her legs. Body is a supposition. It can be easily reconfigured visually, expanded into shapes, shades, and corporealities of different suggestions and subtleties.

Abbas Kiarostami is globally, and justly, celebrated for his gentle and caring camera. But his camera has a habit of getting occasionally nasty. Scenes of rape are of course absolutely forbidden in an Islamic cinema. But Kiarostami's *The Wind Will Carry Us Away* (2000) manages to weasel out one of the most brutal scenes of sexual violence in any film, reconfiguring the human body into Picasoesque disproportionalities. In *The Wind Will Carry Us Away* (2000), Kiarostami tells the story of a group of Tehrani filmmakers who go to the Siah Darreh village in the Kurdistan province to shoot the mourning ceremony of a local woman near her death. As they await the looming event, the lead character in charge of the crew roams through the village and gets to know the locals, among them a young woman he scouts on her way to visit her fiancé. In one scene he enters her house and goes into a stable where she is milking a cow. Kiarostami's camera here forgets all it had learned in that last, glorious shot of *Through the Olive Trees* (1994), where it knew how not to get close to the young lovers' private conversation. It follows the intruding man into the young woman's dark stable where she is sitting next to a cow and milking it. The camera's phallic intrusion into the young woman's dark stable completely takes over for the masculine gaze and frames her in the tight grip of a medium-shot from which she has no escape. The shot is grimly dark; the frame is tightly embracing. The woman is sitting next to a cow, right next to its genitalia, milking it into a bowl, while the man recites for her, at that very moment, one of Forough Farrokhzad's most beautiful poems, from which comes the title of the film. Farrokhzad's poem has never sounded so graceless, and there has scarcely been a woman shot so helpless, a camera so shameless, and a rape scene so violent. The body is here mutilated, disfigured to cubist contortions, simply to accommodate the sexual whims of a sinister camera.

Whether expanded gently by Makhmalbaf to breathe the air in *Gabbeh* or transfigured violently by Kiarostami to brace for an assault in *The Wind Will Carry Us Away*, the body is creatively extended into its surrounding shapes and shades, transgressing its metaphysical boundaries, semiotic limitations, and cultural habits. In Marziyeh Meshkini's *The Day I Became a Woman* (2001), this transfiguration becomes generational, where the body travels from one habitation into another. Havva, Ahu, and Hura are three characters in three episodes of Meshkini's stunning debut. In three apparently unrelated and yet narratively linked episodes, Havva is a young girl about to enter puberty, Ahu is a married young woman, and Hura is in the winter season of her life. Meshkini narrates and constitutes a collective memory for her three characters and spreads them among their three bodies—childish, young, and old. What is extraordinary about *The Day I Became a Woman* is the fact that each character remembers the one before herself via a bodily metempsychosis never before so beautifully articulated in visual terms. Ahu remembers Havva in her defiance, and Hura remembers them both in their compliance, except in the final twist of her bodily forgetfulness where she has tied a piece of cloth around her finger to remind herself of something she never can remember. Body is the trace of its memories. It can forget itself. The memory invested in the body by the tyranny of the metaphysics of its denial will have to be forgotten before it can first unlearn and then remember itself. Art is an agency of bodily anamnesis. Juridical censorship invests inhibitive memories in the body, while art divests that memory from the body by reminding it of its effusive suggestiveness.

In visually extending the physical memory of the body, Meshkini takes her imaginal clues from the poetic legacy of the by far most important contemporary theorist of the transubstantial body, Forough Farrokhzad:

> The end of all forces
> Is to unite
> With the enlightened principle
> Of Sun—and then to pour
> Into the consciousness of Light.
> Of course
> The windmills rot.
> But why should I stop?

I will place the young shafts of wheat
Under my breast
And I will breastfeed them.[10]

There has scarcely been a more magnificent moment in Persian poetic imagery. For a woman to breastfeed the budding shafts of wheat, much more than a poetic imagination is needed. The bodily metempsychosis that it intimates is no longer a suggestion of the *soul* migrating from one body to another but the body in and of itself mutating from one material configuration into another, suggesting a polygenesis of itself into other bodily forms. The body, in effect, escapes its own symbolic constitution, metaphysically conditioned and juridically censored, and runs away into its suggestive signs. To see how that transmutation of the body into things in its vicinity, organic and otherwise, visually operates, there is no better place than in Rakhshan Bani-Etemad's *The Blue-Veiled* (1994), in which she paints visual imageries of Titianesque precision and beauty to show how bodies move and mutate. A love story between a young woman and an older man, *The Blue-Veiled* exudes a bodily mutation to suggest sensuality and evoke eroticism. Rasul Rahmani's visit to his young bride Nobar Kordani occasions one of the most sensual sequences in contemporary Iranian cinema. Through a combination of light, mise-en-scène, camera movement, and a careful configuration of bodies and fruits, *The Blue-Veiled* manages to intimate sexual intercourse right in front of the censor's blinded eyes. In a dimly lit courtyard, the camera moves with Nobar as she puts together a trayful of fresh fruits and carries it to her husband Rasul Rahmani, who is sitting with his back against the wall and his wife's younger sister sleeping with her head on his lap. Nobar places the tray of fresh fruits on the floor right next to her younger sister, called Senobar (and thus vocally three times reminiscent of the fresh fruit, which is Nobar's own body). If the camera were to freeze at that moment, we would catch a glimpse of Nobar's body pulling out to touch the fruit, aided by her first name that means "fresh fruit" (suggesting her virginity); the fruit touching her younger sister, aided by her first name, Senobar, magnifying the virginity of Nobar's offer; and the young girl touching Rasul Rahmani's body as she is taking a nap on his lap. The moment is as innocently shot as it is erotically charged. In *The Blue-Veiled*, we see the visual echo of Farrokhzad's poetic detonation of the voice:

Voice, voice, only voice:
The translucently supplicant voice of water
To flow,
The flowing voice of the light of star
Pouring on the surface femininity of the earth,
The coagulating voice of the fetus
Of meaning, and of the expansion of the mutual memory
of love—
Yes voice, voice, voice,
It's only the voice that will remain.[11]

Generated in the innermost being of the body, channeled through the lungs, and emerging from the throat, the voice becomes the airborne carrier of the vibrant body it once animated, occupied, and vocalized. Airborne, the body becomes invisible, amorphous, and evanescent, its vertically repressive memories dismantled and miasmatic. Now no censorial bureaucracy can see, let alone censor, the body and its defiant effervescence. In *The May Lady* (1998), Bani Etemad picks up precisely on this vocal modulation of the body to suggest lovemaking between a man and a woman. How else can a woman director intimate sexual intercourse in an Islamic Republic? In *The May Lady*, Bani Etemad opts not to show the male character with whom Forough Kia, her lead protagonist, is in love. Forough Kia is a single mother with a teenage son, and she is in love with a man she is afraid to engage for fear of social disapproval. They communicate mostly through letters and telephone calls. When she reads his letters, initially we hear his voice-over reading his own words, but soon Forough's voice joins in and doubles an epistolary duet that orally (with tongue) and aurally (into ear) simulates sexual intercourse. Through this vocal intercourse, the two lead characters of *The May Lady*—one visible, the other invisible, both verbal—echo their respective bodies into their overlapping, underlying, and interlacing voices. Their voices, in the act, become the vibrant transmutation of their bodies into uncharted and unsignified territories. The words they exchange are not particularly romantic or even amorous. The Islamic Republic would not allow that. They are the vocal outlets of their breath, the hidden and invisible suspiration of their breathing bodies. These words mean the bodies that have produced them—the mouth, the throat, the vocal chords, the lungs, the language, the abdominal muscles, and the cultural intelligence that have collectively occasioned them. They are their bodies vocalized, stripped of all their corporeal clothing, and they are making love right there in the bright daylight of the screen in front of the censors' blinded eyes and deafened ears.

Bodies can be made to move miasmatically, infused with the material evidence of and in their surroundings. To see its evidence on the wide screen of Iranian cinema is also to trace its visual gestures back to their poetic environment. It is crucial to place the Iranian cinema in the larger frame of its cultural context. The miasmatic texture of the body, for example, comes as no revelation to those who may have heard of the idea of *wahdat al-wujud*, or "the unity of being." Rumi's poetry is the best source of it:

> I died to the inorganic and I grew,
> I died to the vegetal and I became an animal,
> I died to the animal and I became a human:
> Why should I fear, when did I lessen by dying?
> One more move and I will die to the human
> So that I may soar to the angels.
> I must jump though even from the angels—
> "Everything is perishing except His Face."
> Once more I shall be sacrificed among the angels,

I will become that which is yet to be imagined.
Then I become Nothing, absolutely Nothing
"Verily, unto Him shall we return," singeth the Organ.[12]

In Rumi's classical dissemination of the physical body back and forth into inorganic and angelic realms, the body breaks its customary habitation in one organic form and via an expansive diffusion of its corporeality becomes transubstantially mobile. Samira Makhmalbaf's *The Blackboard* (2000) has a wedding seen between a widow and a wandering teacher that visually attenuates the same opening of the symbolic constitution of the body into suggestive signs beyond any cultural or metaphysical control. The wedding ceremony consists of the bride sitting down on the ground and holding her son (from a previous marriage) between her arms and her lap, in a very familiar scene in the region, to pee. Meanwhile the man who presides over the ceremony hands her the end of a wooden stick (which he uses to walk), while extending his other arm to the groom sitting behind a blackboard he holds with his left hand. A circle is thus generated among the bride, the extended stick, the presiding elder, the groom, and the blackboard, alternating between organic and inorganic, living body and dead wood. The circle is altogether a fluctuating topography of corporeal body. The fact that the wood of the stick in the elder's hand and the wood of the blackboard in the groom's hand are dead objects means nothing in a culture in which inanimate objects like wood can actually sing (the praise of God). Referring to *Oston-e Hannaneh*, a legendary piece of dead wood on which the Prophet of Islam reclined and for the love of the Messenger of God it began to sing his praise, Rumi praises a drunkard man in a famous ghazal:

Such a beautiful drunkard man, how could he be less than a piece of wood?
Did the Column of Hannaneh not begin to sing?[13]
Or in *Mathnavi* he is quite emphatic that:
Man denies inanimate objects praising the Lord
While the inanimate objects are masters of praising the Lord![14]

Rumi's corporeal metempsychosis would have forever collected dust in bookshelves with no visual memory of itself had it not been for Dariush Mehrjui's *The Cow* (1969), an absolute masterpiece of Iranian cinema that made much of what came after it possible. Adapted from the work of Gholam Hossein Saedi (1935–1985), Mehrjui's *The Cow* was the first collaboration between the two masters of their respective fields. By the time Mehrjui joined forces with him, Saedi had already established himself as the undisputed master of modern Iranian psychotic realism, anchored ingeniously on an almost clinical psychopathology of the uncanny (and that long before Gabriel Garcia Marquez was globally celebrated). Mehrjui, on the other hand, was fresh from his college years, studying philosophy at UCLA in the early 1960s with the dubious distinction of having just made his first film, *Diamond 33* (1967), a thriller about the young niece of a professor of chemistry who has discovered a formula to make diamond from oil. She comes to Iran and gets involved with a local driver who saves her from the evil designs set against her. Although only five years his senior (Saedi was born in 1935, Mehrjui in 1940), Saedi had already succeeded in establishing himself as the leading dramatist and novelist of his generation. *The Cow* became the first collaboration between Saedi and Mehrjui, and it led to a close creative relationship that lasted until Saedi's tragic death in 1985 in Paris in the aftermath of the Islamic Revolution. Before that fateful tragedy (Saedi practically drank himself to death, in deep depression after the rapid Islamization of the Iranian Revolution of 1979), Mehrjui achieved for Saedi what he could have never attained on his own—a masterful visualization of his psychotic realism—while Saedi did for Mehrjui what he could have never imagined on his own—a direct, and laser-beam accurate, access into the collective *embodiment* of his culture.

Premiered two years after its production in the Cannes Film Festival, *The Cow* suffered from a mind-numbing overpoliticization by Iranian critics who insisted on reading it as a political allegory, yet another pathetic commentary on the state of poverty in Iranian villages of which no one needed to be reminded. The principal culprit in this impoverished reading of the masterpiece was of course the Shah's censorship that forced Mehrjui to predicate the film by a disclaimer that the story had taken place about forty years earlier. This became the opening shot of a whole history of relentlessly undertheorizing and overpoliticizing it at the expense of the narrative revolution it had occasioned in Iranian visual culture. A disastrous consequence of bureaucratic censorship in Iran (both before and after the Islamic Revolution) has been the creation of a jaundiced cultural criticism (film and literary in particular) in which nothing can be read except as a silly suggestion of the corruption of the Pahlavi monarchy or the state of destitution in Iranian society, neither of which is an earth-shattering revelation. Iranian cultural criticism has never recovered from this pathological malaise, as if perpetually arrested in an infantilized state. Meanwhile, in poetic, literary, visual, and performing arts, acts of ingenious creativity have been exploring uncharted territory in a critical reconstitution of the subject and of the real, which has remained almost entirely untapped in its theoretical implications. This, by far, is the most damaging consequence of bureaucratic censorship both during the Pahlavi monarchy and now under the Islamic theocracy.

Before his untimely death in exile in Paris, Saedi had established himself as a novelist and playwright of unrivalled mastery, with a force and a precision of insight not matched before or after him. By appealing to a *psychotic realism* of ingenious creative force that relentlessly desedimented itself into a psychopathology of unknown or inarticulate fears, Saedi at once addressed the most pathological maladies of his social surroundings and reached for a contraction of their proportions that would tease out their unreal realism. There is an almost complete absence of emotive inroad in Saedi's *psychotic realism*, an emotional paralysis that flattens the moral universe of imagination in order to tease out the hidden anxieties of the real. Saedi's *homo societas* becomes *homo psychosis* not by virtue of any clinical diagnosis but by the very fact of association, of being party to a collective community of anxieties. Tyranny is thus detected and revealed not in the concentration of power but in its dissipation. Saedi's medical education and psychoanalytic training were instrumental in helping his abnormative insights. But the same background resulted in his critics yet again reading his work too psychoanalytically and not enough as creative works of fiction. Read as works of art, Saedi's fiction does not as much psychoanalytically diagnose as psychotically expose. His penchant for the abnormal and the uncanny is far more effectively read as a fictive trope rather than a psychoanalytic inroad. There is absolutely nothing surreal about Saedi's *psychotic realism*. Everything is in its right place. Every gesture, every word, every event resonates with an air of matter-of-factness. And yet it is precisely this matter-of-factness that is so unreal.

Mehrjui's *The Cow* is based on a story from Saedi's *Azadaran-e Bayal* (*Bayal Mourners*; 1964), a masterpiece in modern Persian fiction. The great achievement of Saedi's *psychotic realism*,—throughout his work but particularly in *The Cow*, and as visualized and globalized beyond its verbal limitations by Mehrjui—is to trace a way back from a case of metempsychosis into psychosis and then from the psychosis back to a suspension of the signified real.[15] But in the received conception of metempsychosis as the passing of the soul at death into another body, human or animal, we have exactly the opposite direction in Saedi/Mehrjui's case. Here we witness a metempsychosis in which it is the evident disposition of an animal that passes at death into a human body and thus radically defies the fabricated boundary between the human and the animal. Through this oppositional constitution of metempsychosis, we do get to a particular case of psychosis. But Saedi suffered as much from a bad psychological reading of his profession as from a bad political reading of his fiction. *The Cow* is not simply a psychological case study of metempsychosis as psychosis, of a man who becomes mentally deranged, loses his connection to reality, and thinks himself his dead cow. *The Cow* narrows in on a case of psychosis as a creative literary event in order to designify and then resignify the real. For in psychosis, it is the nature and disposition of reality that is being pathologically reconstituted. Saedi creatively thrives on that pathology and puts it under a magnifying glass to examine not the psychotic but the reality that it evades and thus dismantles. It is not in the mirror but in the speculum of the psychotic Other that Saedi looks for the disposition of the real. Reality can no longer hide itself in that speculum. The broken mirror of psychosis is the best reflection of reality. It does not distort it. It restores it. Thus, in addition to Forough Farrokhzad's *The House Is Black* (1962) and Shahid-Sales's *One Simple Incident* (1973), Mehrjui's *The Cow* is equally critical in the making of Iranian realism, albeit deeply rooted in Saedi's *psychotic realism*. In Saedi/Mehrjui we witness an alternative creative strategy to work the *reality* out of the routinized *real* than the one we witness in, say, Kiarostami, who is deeply rooted in Sohrab Shahid-Sales's. In Farrokhzad/Shahid-Sales/Kiarostami's case, they hold the camera so intensely constant on the real until all its received *namings* ooze out of it and the sheer chaotic majesty of the unnamed reveals itself through its fictive transparency.

But that is only one mode of realism, which in Kiarostami's case we can call it *actual realism.* Mehrjui's realism is not rooted in Sohrab Shahid-Sales's; he traces his creative lineage to Saedi, arguably the most brilliant Iranian dramatist of the twentieth century.

What we see here is something far more exciting than a mere "subversion of the content by form," as Theodor Adorno once hurriedly called it. Of course the formal confrontation with the real jolts its claim to authenticity, but the mechanism of that confrontation is not a mindless, head-on collision between content and form. The formal presence of the work of art confronts the substantial claim of the ossified real with an alternative revelation of the real as the anxiety-provoking Other—sufficiently familiar but alarmingly different. In this way, works of art do not as much *point* to the aporias of a given society as *constitute* them. Even if we accept Karl Marx's diagnosis and Adorno's acknowledgement of the constitution of such aporias being a by-product of the division of labor between intellectual and physical labor, as an emancipatory strategy it remains indispensable in our lived experiences of *modernity.* But something that neither Marx nor Adorno considered are the conditions of artistic production at the colonial edges of the capital. On those edges, such a clear-cut division between intellectual and physical labor does not take place if for no other reason than the fact that, because of a maligned relations of production, artistic creativity stands for theoretical articulation. This can as much result in what Antonio Gramsci articulated as *inorganic intellectuals* as in a mode of critical creativity that blurs the demarcation between the theorist and the artist. Saedi/Mehrjui's *The Cow* is the content that blasts the form and the form that mocks the content, both, in opposite directions, dodging the Kantian articulation of an autonomous European subject at the expense of all other *nations*, offering the objective world as the pacified site of its colonial operation. Theoretically desubjected at the dawn of European modernity, the colonial subject turns the table by concealing its critical apparatus under the camouflage of its creative urges. The result is a mode of artistic creativity in which resistance is rooted in the material evidence of reality, not articulated in theoretical abstraction.

Loosening the metaphysical boundaries of the body, the kinds of creative collisions that *The Cow* represents cross the juridically drawn borders of meaning and smuggle their rambunctiously misbehaving signs—bursting out of the Bastille of their signification—into outlandish territories, where they begin to party and prance as bandits and outlaws, invisible to the naked eye. Animate or inanimate, organic or inorganic, vegetal or animal, *the body* as the material evidence of being thus moves and modulates into a vast, never-ending topography of physical signations that inform of its constituent signs defying their metaphysically tyrannical signification. Iranian cinema today is creating visual memories for the forgetfulness of the body almost exactly the same way that generations of poetic legacy did against the charge of the juridical casting of the *corpus hierarchicus.* Against the very letter and spirit of Islamic law—in which bodily resurrection was tyrannically scripted to erect a vertical body, punish it corporeally in this world, and subject it to torture in the next—Rumi posited a theory of the body revolutionary in the outcasting of its legalized signification. Rumi sought single-handedly to create a memory for the forgetfulness of the body in the vast topography of its animate and inanimate existence, thus spreading it across a wide landscape of existence beyond any juridical or metaphysical control:

> First having come into inorganic being,
> He moved from the lifeless towards the vegetal.
> For years he lived in the vegetal,
> Never remembering the inorganic, so self-alienated he was.
> Once he moved from the vegetal to the animal,
> He could not remember his vegetal state,
> Except the attraction he has to the vegetal,
> Particularly during the Spring and the season of sweet herbs.
> Just like the attraction of infants towards their mothers,
> Not knowing the secret of the pull in their lips,
> Just like the extreme affection of a novice
> Towards his blissful and joyous master.[16]

In this linear progression, *time is untimely*, *space is amorphous*, and *movement is spontaneous*. From inorganic to vegetal, from vegetal to animal, and from animal to human, the body meanders into shapes and shades of its corporeal memory, though never remembering itself otherwise. If we like flowers and greeneries, particularly during the Spring, we are vaguely *re-membering* our own body in its former states and for Rumi anticipating its future forms. The constitution of this amorphous memory is miasmatic. It moves from light to opacity, from objects to their shadows, from ipseity to alterity.

> His particular intelligence is from his master's universal intellect,
> The movement of this shadow is from that stem of rose.
> The shadow of the rose will finally disappear
> Back into the rose and it will know the secret of its attraction.
> How would the shadow of any other branch
> Move, my friend, were it not for the movement of the tree?[17]

This is the fading of the body into its alternating suppositions. Rumi navigates the *theocentricity* of his culture and cultivation into a *theo-eroticism* of bodily movements. Reason itself collapses and evaporates into stages and shapes, modes and moods, impossible to limit into one or another argument:

> Yet again from animality to humanity
> Will draw him that creator whom you know.
> He would thus move from clime to clime
> To appear now so intelligent and sharp.
> He cannot remember his earliest intellects and
> Yet from this very intellect he will again surpass:

So when rescued from this avaricious Reason,
He will see one hundred thousand intellects in wonders.[18]

The dream world and the real world are interchanged; the real is fantasy, the fantasy real, and in between the body is invested with new memories of its own, cleansed of its cultural heritage. Rumi forces the body to remember its own innate, fleshly reminiscences. Once thus divested of its metaphysical heritage and reinvested with its own corporeal memory, the body can reverse every term of dead certainty stored and sanctified in its vertical obedience:

Though he slept and forgot the past,
He would never be left alone in his forgetfulness.
He will be awakened from his sleep
To laugh at his own assumptions:
"What a senseless sorrow I suffered while asleep,
Having all forgotten the reality.
How could I not know that such sadness and misery
Was all a dream, an illusion, a fantasy?"
Same as the world which is like a dream
where the dreamer thinks it's permanent.
Until the Mourning of Judgment is dawned
And he is rescued from the darkness of suspicion and deceit.
He will then laugh at his sorrow,
Once he sees where he really resides and where he is.[19]

The two worlds collapse and the body that inhabits one widens and swells to occupy a vastly variegated topography. Rumi takes the phenomenological traces of the body—tears, moaning, laughter, pains, and so on—and expands them from one to another world, thus deleting their categorical separations. Death means nothing to Rumi's body. The body that emerges as the embodiment of those affects is nebulous, tenuous, contingent, amorphous, pre-eternal (*azali*), posteternal (*abadi*), expansive, and never-ending, dodging death and with death all political powers that bank on the fear of death and thus perpetrate terror in the world.

Whatever of good and evil you see in a dream
Will all appear to you on the Day of Judgment.
Whatever you have done in this worldly dream
Will appear to you when you are awake.
Lest you think these evil acts
In your dream have no interpretation,
Beware, you who tyrannize your victims, that these laughters
Are tears and moanings on the Day of Interpretation,
While your tears, pains, sadness and sorrows
Will turn into happiness when you awake.
You who have torn the cloak of Joseph!
Beware that you will awake a wolf from this deep slumber.
Your evil habits have all turned into wolves

> Savagely tearing your limbs to pieces.
> Thy blood will not rest from revenge,
> Don't you assume that you will die and it's all over with.
> This earthly retribution is but a joke,
> Next to the one to come it's like a playful thing.
> God called this world a "playful thing"
> Precisely because next to that punishment this is but a joke.
> This retribution is to prevent war and sedition,
> That one is like emasculation, this like circumcision![20]

All these amorphous memories of the body have been poetically sublated and culturally repressed. Iranian cinema is the return of the Islamic repressed. By the time we get to see Rakhshan Bani-Etemad's *Nargess* (1991), something far more serious than the fluid boundaries of the body are renegotiated. Narrating the story of a volatile ménage-a-trois, *Nargess* shakes up the received inhibitions of the body by leading them to transgress their most fearful taboos, forcing the regulated body to run away from itself in fear (and anticipation). An older woman in love with a younger man, oscillating between his lover and his mother, Afagh defies the limitations of aging and culture on her regimented body. Afagh and her lover Adel are the walking embodiment of a transgressive love affair, accentuated by the fact that they are both thieves living on the peripheral margins of the moralizing society. The supreme transgression is ultimately in the body of Afagh, which in an earlier version of the film Bani Etemad had intended to set on fire in a defiant act of self-immolation before she repressed her own creative truth and opted for having Afagh run over by a truck instead. To Adel, Afagh is both a mother and the lover, in her body transgressing the supremely incestuous boundaries of the two. Afagh is old enough to be Adel's mother, young enough to be his lover, and ambiguous enough to be both *at one and the same time*. In moving fluidly from mother to lover and back, Afagh's body does more than transgress its metaphysical boundaries and regimented texture; it defies its own metaphorical tyranny. Her body refuses to choose, opts to be both, and moves from maternal to erotic with the vaginal center of her metaphoric definition at once ejective and receptive. Afagh's body turns less out and about than around and against itself. Her body is circulatory, spiral, substitutional, and conjectural on its own contingency, forgetting its own memory and remembering its own forgetfulness. No censorship can catch a body so furiously dodging itself, chasing after its own tail, and evading its own reach. Afagh's body is contravening itself, searching for its own emancipated memory in the shadow of its regimented verticality, and teasing that memory from its own juridically mandated amnesia, as will against nature, nature against culture, and the Eros against the Sacred.

Such twisting and tossing of the erotic body does not always land on all fours. It can and does mutate a fortiori into the political. The move from the erotic body to the political body is metamorphic. To detect and read it, we can start from any number of places and see the cinematic seizure of the political body. But nowhere would be as critical and poignant as one of the most atrocious examples of Pahlavi censorship paving the way for the even sharper scissors of the Islamic Republic. It is impossible to exaggerate the brilliance of Amir Naderi's *Requiem* (1975), a masterpiece of Iranian cinema that very few people have actually seen and that has now been forever lost except for a poor video copy made from the destroyed original print.[21] With the tradition of early Italian neorealism squarely behind it, *Requiem* is a black-and-white tour de force with a now entirely disappeared Tehran as its background. Narrated around the routine life of three street entertainers, *Requiem* takes its title from a famous line of a poem of Mehdi Akhavan-e Sales (d. 1990), one of the most prominent Iranian poets of Naderi's generation: *Marsiyeh-khan-e vatan-e mordeh-ye khisham* ("I sing the requiem of my dead homeland"). When screened by the selection committee of Tehran Film Festival, its members were so scared witless of even being known to have seen this film that they all left the screening room assuring each other that they had *not* just seen this film! The story of *Requiem*, like that of all the other Naderi films, is a nonstory. The lead character Nasrollah is released from prison to go back to the wild metropolis of the Pahlavi period Tehran in the early 1970s, when the Shah of Shahs had just celebrated the twenty-five-hundreth anniversary of the Persian monarchy. The paralyzing power of the poverty and destitution that Naderi's *Requiem* quietly chronicles in deceptively simple shots does not hit its target until we find out the work that Nasrollah does to make a meager living.

Straight out of the urban poverty of the Iran of the Pahlavi monarchy, Nasrollah roams around the metropolis with a shotgun and a board, offering entertainment to passersby by way of shooting practices. This is in the Tehran of the early 1970s, when the imperial hubris of the Pahlavi monarchy could not stomach the slightest challenge to its autocracy. With a daring imagination unparalleled by his contemporaries, Naderi suggests the possibility and indeed the necessity of an armed struggle by simply and suggestively placing a (fake) gun in the hand of a desperate man, carrying also his own target around. When idle men, young and old, target the gun at suggestive spots on the half-naked bodies of models cut from newspapers and magazines and pasted on the target board and then shoot, Naderi leaves very little room for imagination as to what is soon about to happen. When he defied the authorities and with a creative audacity matched by none of his peers actually depicted an urban guerilla shot in the leg and surrounded by police, the SAVAK (The Shah's secret police), and an idle crowd, he knew, as he told his producer, that "this is a film that we will make for posterity." The act was simply beyond belief. "It was like being pregnant with a baby," Naderi said once in January 2002, "and then hoping desperately for the delivery date, just to hurry up and burry your newly-born baby!"

Naderi crosses the border between erotic and political bodies so smoothly that the two become figuratively metamorphic. The voluptuous bodies of naked women, ostensibly "foreign" in their figurative representations and so blindingly out of reach for those desperate gazes that target them with their phony but fully loaded guns, are the erotic sites of the political impotence they uselessly excite. Everything in this erotic act of pathological paralysis is fake. The gun is fake, the men are forlorn, the women are made of paper and pasted on a board; the site is tiresome and tasteless. They are all in the make-believe world of masturbating excitement, pathetic and pitiful, in the jaundiced space of political impotence. Men with their elongated guns rise for no cause, women are the paper-pasted pictures of a body they are denied, and yet from the jaded gestures of these very men and the emptied sensuality of these very naked bodies exudes the pictorial suggestion of a political uprising.

Nasrollah gradually befriends two other public entertainers: a Luti and a Morshed. A Luti is a character who roams the urban scene with a chimpanzee and provides entertainment in neighborhoods, much to the amusement of kids, singing and playing on his handheld shallow drum (*dayereh*) for the feeble creature to dance. He is proverbially an opium addict, and so is his chimpanzee. The Morshed's business is to mourn the lives and deaths of Shi'i saints in the classical Persian art of *Pardeh-dari*, or storytelling in front of an unfurled canvas on which is depicted scenes of their saintly sufferings. Add to that scene a woman who sells lottery tickets while mothering her two young children and then a whole slew of pimps and prostitutes, drug addicts and idle bystanders, maddening traffic and a dilapidated urbanity, and there you have Naderi's cast of characters in one of the most brilliant Iranian films that today stands as the unacknowledged masterpiece of Iranian realism, scarcely seen anywhere beyond the very limited film festival crowds. The brilliance of *Requiem* is not just in the depleted eroticism of a jaundiced culture of masturbating futility. It is far more effectively evident in its creative splitting of the body of the artist himself. The erotic body of Naderi's characters' object of desire is matched and modulated by the split bodies of his protagonists: three male artists, repeating each other as the split persona of Naderi himself—homeless entertainers and storytellers, centrifugal in their splitting personalities. The three characters—Nasrollah, the Morshed, and the Luti—are metamorphic, repeating each other, and circumambulating around one another's bodies, and thus as one dies, the other rises, while the third moves away. Naderi's bodies are split and repetitive, recurring in their cyclical remembrances of each other, inveterate as they transmute. Bodies dodge and artists mutate as the creative space meanders to escape the culture of its metaphysical domination. There is magic in this realism.

If Naderi's bodies are split to pieces, Bahram Beizai's are vaporized into thin air in the full view of the censorial scissors and wandering audience. Beizai's *Stranger and the Fog* (1974) is miasmatic. Shot at the coastal shores of the Caspian Sea, *Stranger and the Fog* might as well have been shot in a dreamland, where bodies melt into the environmental vicinity of their corporeal presences, absenting themselves from their significant proportions and dissipating themselves into the misty suggestiveness of their repressed signs. Just like Naderi's *Requiem*, shot at the height of Pahlavi censorial power, Beizai's *Stranger and the Fog* is the visual rendition of an inarticulate fear, of the invasion of unknown sea monsters attacking an unsuspecting coastal village deep in its fog-forest of misty uncertainty. Is this a dream or a nightmare where bodies melt into their own shadowy apparitions? Ayat comes from the seaside suggestion of a foggy dream to marry Ra'na, the widowed loneliness of a bewildered land lost in the sea-forest side of a territorial uncertainty, where a village full of ghosts has no conception of time or assumption of space. Fog, nothing but fog, is the defining unmoment of Beizai's miraculous assignation of shapes, shadows, and semiassurances. Bodies have dissolved in *Stranger and the Fog*. They are nowhere to be seen because they are everywhere to be seen. They are in the full view of their opacity, hidden in the veil of their transparency. *Stranger and the Fog* is the postmetaphysics of the body, the dissolving of its spiritual pretensions (assumptions) sublated into the semiotics of its material celebration. In that semiotics of ultraviolet vision, the censorial sight is blinded by insight.

From bodies disseminated to bodies hidden—Jafar Panahi's *The White Balloon* (1995) centers around the subterranean voice of a father and surfaces about the meandering fate of his children. Watching *The White Balloon*, much of the world's attention is drawn to Razieh, the chief protagonist, a feisty little girl in search of a goldfish. Neglected is the tangential fate of her brutalized brother and his extended shadow in a lonesome Afghan child laborer. Panahi's first feature film is a masterpiece precisely in the manner that he has taught his camera to look at things slightly off-center and by suggestion. The abusive character of the father is kept entirely in the dungeon-deep of a subterranean bathroom where he is taking a bath and relentlessly harassing his wife and children with one obnoxious demand or another. We never see the father, but his underground voice haunts his household, his son in particular. At one climactic scene, we see Razieh's teenage brother coming to help him, and on his face and his shirt we notice the unmistakable signs of physical abuse. Panahi, in a moment of creative genius, decides never to articulate what exactly the circumstances are in which the child is brutalized, and yet he leaves ample evidence for speculation that the source of violence perpetrated on him is his father. On the brutalized body of the young teenager is marked the abusive relation of power that an unseen but domineering father exercises over his wife and children. The fact that we are never absolutely sure that it is actually the unseen father who has perpetrated this violence effectively adds to the atmosphere of fear and intimidation generic to the film. In an inarticulate and thus deeply anxiety-provoking way, that violence burdens the visual weight of the film.

We feel anxious after noticing the first sign of violence on the young boy's body and person, and then though we do not see him for a long time we continue to worry, less about him than about the barely suggested but impossible to ignore evidence of violence in and about our own visual domain. This is an astonishing moment of creative brilliance because, through a very simple narrative strategy, Panahi manages to cast a long and lasting shadow of inarticulate violence on his otherwise perfectly innocent-looking film about a young girl determined to get hold of a voluptuous goldfish. That shadow of violence hovers about the film for the entirety of its duration and then at the end materializes in the person of an Afghan child laborer who as a solitary figure—fatherless, nameless, and homeless—becomes the visual evidence of that fear, up until this moment scattered around and about our conscious encounter with the film. As Iranians across the nation are then depicted at the end of the film to be sitting at home with their families, celebrating their New Year, the solitary figure of this Afghan child emerges as the visual summation and the climactic resolution of all the fear and anxiety generated and sustained by the suggestion of violence perpetrated on Razieh's brother. The character of the young Afghan refugee laborer, a solitary balloon vendor at the very last shot of the film, is the very picture of absolute solitude with which Panahi concludes his film. Standing erect on the earth is now this sentinel figure of defiant solitude; screaming beneath him in the subterranean dungeon of the culture is the voice of a father, buried alive, crying from his open grave, his voice loud and audible, his meaning mute though demanding: faceless, bodiless, disturbing, but impotent.

What censorship, both official and internalized into the very fabric of creative imagination, is doing in Iranian cinema is in fact inadvertently forcing a relentless mutation of the body, as the site of cultural contestation, into unimagined directions. If what Panahi does in *The White Balloon* is the creation of a bodily shadow, emanated from the signs of violence on the body of the young boy and materialized in the body of his Afghan counterpart, what Samira Makhmalbaf does in her debut feature *Apple* (1998) is positively palindromic. If body were a word, its movements a phrase, its suggestions a verse, and its life a sentence, a work of fiction could read it the same way but backward, the same as it is read forward. Fiction borrows the body from reality. Suppose reality were to borrow the body from fiction. The twin bodies of Samira Makhmalbaf's twin sisters in *Apple* are visibly palindromic. They do not just resemble and repeat each other one way or another. They replicate that palindromic paradigm in the relation between fiction and reality they intimate. Reversing Jafar Panahi's deadly panopticon in *The White Balloon* and unearthing two twin sisters who were practically buried alive, Samira Makhmalbaf's *Apple* suggests a mode of narrative reversal unprecedented in film or fiction. This is how it works: In late July 1997, the Tehran police reported that two twin sisters about 11 years old were found in a dimly lit cubical, incarcerated by their father. Samira Makhmalbaf took that actual story and turned it into the most damning condemnation of her patriarchal culture.

The power of *Apple* is in its reversing the very logic of an allegory, switching the reference and the referent. If an allegory is a narrative in which abstract ideas are personified, *Apple* is a counterallegory in which real people move into fiction and take abstracted ideas to task. Samira Makhmalbaf does not use professional actors to represent the twin sisters. She uses the twin sisters themselves "to act" and thus take the whole cultural universe of their imprisonment to task. Their contorted bodies and muffled speech counterrepresent the fictionalization of their characters. Zahra and Ma'sumeh Naderi are not fictive characters who come out of the pages of a script or a screen and walk into the streets and alleys of Tehran—quite the contrary. They are real people who walk out of the street and enter the fictive universe of imagination. Their bodies are not substitutional for reality. They are incremental to fiction. They are the fictive mutations of themselves. By virtue of reversing themselves as counterallegories, their bodies become palindromic in the bidirectionality of their movement. They can be read both ways: from fiction to reality and from reality to fiction. We never know which is which, and we are made more resolute in that indecision.

When made visually pliable, bodies can be as much matrixical as palindromic. Jafar Panahi's *Circle* (2001) is the best example of matrixical bodies, where bodily shapes and identities are the accidental articulations of a material universe, easily transmuting into each other and colliding ipseity and alterity into a circular remembrance of each other. The very first sequence of the film is a masterpiece of cyclic transmutation in which the announcement of the birth of a female infant by a female nurse to the infant's grandmother is then aided by the miraculously meandering camera, which accompanies the grandmother down a spiral, is interrupted by another woman climbing up with a bouquet of flowers, continues to go down the spiral, exits the hospital, enters into the street, and witnesses two young women whose story then picks up the bodily transmutation for the rest of the film. The matrixical bodies in Panahi's *Circle* become like incidental projections from the worldly surface of the matter: pointed intrusions; accidental, entirely interchangeable, corporeal bumps; asperities. He carries this circuitous transmutation of bodies into each other, from one character to another, as if they were part of a more universal predicament, and at the end he brings them all together inside a prison cell. Here the camera navigates their bodily asperities and points of commencement and departure into a circular dodging of their particularities and makes them intimate a universal truth without committing a metaphysical dishonesty. It is a simulation of matrixical bodies, true and committed to the matter-of-factness of their corporeal evidence, that sustains a suggestion of universal truth without committing the violence of implicating them to a metaphysical claim on their ephemerality. This is what Gianni Vattimo meant to say by *il pensiero debole* ("the weak thought"): a claim to truth without resorting to metaphysical violence.[22]

From the subterranean dungeons of Tehran to the desolate landscape of Kurdistan—Bahman Qobadi's *A Time for Drunken Horses* (2000) takes the censored body to the extremities of its politically denied destitute. Three orphaned Kurdish children—fleeting moments of life charged against the vast, desolate, snow-covered mountains of Kurdistan—narrate the background story of how the horses of smugglers trafficking between Iran and Iraq need to be fooled into drinking vodka to make it through the unforgiving cold of this arctic brutality. A teenage boy, his younger sister, and their crippled brother need to raise some money to have a surgical operation performed on the afflicted younger brother's body so that he *may* live a few more months. The crippled brother is a midget, a dwarf, his growth arrested, his body twisted into the bundled brutality of an incarcerated hope. A disproportionately huge head hangs patiently over a body too tired to have a claim to rectitude. The body is about to give in. Some godforsaken surgical procedure is said to be able to prolong his agony. But life is life. The able-bodied teenager works like a drunken horse and the younger sister is sold as a child bride—all under the frozen gaze of the crippled brother, too tired to raise an eyebrow, too sullen to hope, and yet too caring to turn the other way.

Who are these children? What abandonment of hope in humanity are they the offspring of? Drunken horses and children are cast into the bestial brutality of a world too cold to care, the indifferent adulthood of people in positions of power: Qobadi's landscape is *bitter cold and sick at heart*—brutal, honest, arid, desolate, and factual. This is no fancy footwork "neorealism." This is not *new*. This is the dawn of history. This is no *realism*; this is real—like the stone-covered heart of a teenage girl about to be sold into bridal slavery, like a snow-covered land too barren even to dream of any seed. What can censorship do to prevent or punish a brutality too evident to detect, too obvious to see, and too atrocious to fight? Twisted to turn the pain, drunken to bear the cold, and sold into bridal bondage, Qobadi's bodies are too cruel to censor. They put the censor to shame. From the Kurdish corner of a people's pain, untold for centuries and denied forever, now through the ice-cold camera of Qobadi emerge the scattered bodies of a nation brutalized equally by the thuggish militarism of Saddam Hussein in Iraq, the NATO-naturalized tribalism of generals in Turkey, and the medieval Islamism of the Mullahs in Iran. None of these political atrocities have the moral authority to censor Qobadi's camera or contradict the cruelty of these honest revelations of his bodies.

The Body Is Dangerous

Censorship is the denial of the body and the negation of the danger it poses to any republic, *Islamic* or otherwise. The body is dangerous. The body is the repository of the repressed. Its feeling intellect is subversive. *Corpus amorphous* is the site of all tyrannical signifiers melting into signs that signate joyously against and now beyond any legislative control, the result of which is the desedimentation of the subject on which all acts of signification are contingent. The desedimented subject is now freed to meet the globalized world. The desedimented world needs a decentralized subject. The only subject that can face the globalized world is the one occupying the *amorphous body*, the site of the etherized subject, which is put together by mutant signs having successfully rebelled against the violent metaphysics of their forceful signification and now jubilantly on the loose.

The world desedimented, the subject decentered, and the body amorphous, and the supposition of a superpower thinks itself in control! Here is the Trojan horse: the *USA TODAY* on Tuesday, 29 January, 2002, reported that the attorney general of the United States, John Ashcroft, had decided that he would no longer be photographed in front of two partly nude statues in the Great Hall of the Department of Justice.[23] The report adds that the department had spent eight thousand dollars on blue drapes to cover the two giant aluminum art deco statues because the attorney general did not like being pictured in front of them. The blue drapes were initially rented according to Shane Hix, a spokesman, but were subsequently purchased. Since 9/11, Ashcroft had been pictured several times in front of the female statue that represents the Spirit of Justice, on which one breast is exposed. The other statue, a man with a cloth covering his midsection, is called the Majesty of Law. Both statues were installed in the 1930s when the building was finished. The same issue of the *International Herald Tribune* also reported that the New York Police Department was planning to strictly enforce an 1845 state law during the World Economic Forum in New York City, a law that bans groups of demonstrators from wearing masks. Protest organizers had said that many marchers were planning to wear costumes and carry giant puppets to emphasize their antiglobalization messages. Some of the puppets were to be worn over their heads. Between the mandatory veiling of two statues in the US Department of Justice in Washington, DC, and the mandatory unmasking of faces of antiglobalization demonstrators in New York City, unveiling bodies and defiant gazes were troubling people in positions of power far beyond the boundaries of a mere Islamic Republic. The world at large was well in danger.

Chapter 7

Corpus Anarchicum

Once the machine is set in position, this steel cable tightens up immediately into a rod. And now the performance begins.

—Franz Kafka, *In the Penal Colony* (1914)

The captured corpse of the living Saddam Hossein, paraded and publicized by the US viceroy, Paul Bremer, in Iraq on December 14, 2003, is the fear of the dead body of Arab *nationalism* and the exhumed cadaver of now a globalized *Islamism*. His heavily bearded face, disheveled hair, ignoble demeanor, demeaning oral examination, and photographic *ihanah* (insult)—as a Moroccan political scientist put it—is the nightmare of the body that for the fear of being thus buried alive opts to blow itself up. "Why could he not just put a bullet to his own stupid head," was the question in the crowded streets and back alleys around the Central Train Station in Rabat the following day. That *ihanah* haunts and humiliates the colonially desubjected body that can only restore its own agency by blowing the corpse of the captured Saddam Hossein out of the bone and flesh of the suicidal bomber. Literarily disinterred out of a tight grave, the dead body of the living Saddam Hossein cuts a frightful figure, the disturbing nightmare of a people that must (but do not) choose between a monstrous empire and a tyrannical grotesquery. Neither of those two choices are acceptable, and thus in this concluding chapter, I will look closely at the self-explosive body of the suicide bomber who has eradicated the final platform of political violence by a violence equal in its intensity, once and for all denying the state its sole surviving site of legitimacy. In this final reflection, I propose the exploded body of the suicide bomber as the excavated territory of the state where it has categorically crumbled.

Uprising

With the commencement of the Oslo Peace Process in September 1993, the Palestinian popular uprising, the *Intifada*, against the interminable military occupation of their homeland by the state of Israel was intensified and led to a crescendo in the frequency of suicidal violence. Beginning in

1994, Hamas assumed responsibility for a series of devastating attacks against Israeli military and civilian targets carried out by Palestinians who exploded themselves in public. The crescendo of suicidal bombing increasingly intensified between 1994 and 2001. In 2001, a record number of 12 cases were reported. By June 19, 2002, however, Palestinians had launched some 23 suicidal attacks only halfway through that year. Although they targeted both military personnel and civilians, the crowded Mahane Yehuda Market in Jerusalem was their chief target. For the Palestinians, suicidal attacks were integral to their war of liberation from military occupation, the same way that the Algerians had fought against their French occupiers. For the Israelis, this was an orchestrated campaign of terrorism targeting their civilians and had to be crushed by all means necessary. A brutal reoccupation of the occupied territories ensued, with massive civilian casualties reported by Palestinians. The collapse of the Oslo Peace Process was marked by the Palestinians and the Israelis being deadlocked in a vicious cycle of suicidal attacks and massive military retaliation.

On September 11, 2001, the phenomenon of suicidal violence was lifted from an isolated corner of the world and made massively global when the symbolic sites of globalization—the World Trade Center in New York—and the military might behind it—the Pentagon in Washington, DC—were targeted. On that day, a succession of civilian airliners were hijacked by Arab suicidal assailants and crashed into the Twin Towers of the World Trade Center in New York City, the Pentagon in Washington, DC, and a suburb of Pennsylvania. All the suicidal assailants and a massive number of military personnel and civilians were killed in this attack. On October 7 of the same year, President Bush led a devastating military operation against Afghanistan, where a man named Osama bin Laden and an organization called al-Qaeda were reported to be in hiding and chiefly responsible for the attacks against the United States. The US invasion of Afghanistan resulted in massive military and civilian casualties in a land already devastated by years of Soviet military occupation and the subsequent civil war. Afghanistan had been pacified by a mediaeval theocracy led by a fanatic religious sect called the Taliban, which had been trained and armed by the Pakistanis under the direct supervision and on the behest of the US military.

The Military and the Militant

The massive military retaliation by Israel against the Palestinians and by the United States against the Afghanis and then the Iraqis buried the phenomenon of suicidal bombing under the rubble of their respective propaganda and categorically dismissed it as yet more evidence of the barbarity and religious fanaticism rampant among Muslims. While a *suicidal* culture of martyrdom and sacrifice seemed on ascendancy among militant Muslims, a *homicidal* culture of self-victimization and retribution was rampant among the Israeli and US militaries. An army of latter-day Orientalists (area specialists and their contingency of native informers) entered the scene, and once again a ghostly apparition called "Islam" was summoned to explain the phenomenon of suicidal violence. Repeated examples of suicidal violence among Jews, Christians, Hindus, Buddhists, Sikhs, as well as plain old agnostics and devout atheists suddenly disappeared from collective memories, as did the horrific remains of two teenagers named Eric Harris and Dylan Klebold—typical Muslim names—who in April 1999 went on a killing spree and massacred their classmates and teachers at Columbine High School in Littleton, Colorado—the hotbed of militant Muslims—before committing suicide.

The problem with dismissive assessments of the phenomenon of suicidal violence as exclusive to a religion, a culture, or a people is not that it is factually flawed but that it prevents a more global understanding of the phenomenon beyond the propaganda purposes of both parties. Today, the phenomenon of suicidal bombing has become the cruel subject of the propaganda war waged between two groups of militants: those who are in power and those who are resisting power. It is as much a piece of propaganda nonsense to dismiss suicidal violence as the barbaric sign of a fanatical faith or a lost cause as it is criminal to celebrate it as religiously or ideologically sanctioned because it will lead to the liberation of a nation from colonial tyranny. The dead bodies of the Palestinian suicide bombers will come back to haunt the legitimate aspirations of Palestinians to a free and democratic homeland when the specter of an "Islamic Republic of Palestine" will emerge in a post-*Intifada* culture of martyrdom. To this day, thousands of the dead bodies of the victims of the Iran-Iraq war (1980–1988) are kept refrigerated by the custodians of sacred terror in Tehran and summarily produced as "new" martyrs of the revolution and the "Imposed War" every time there is a democratic movement to curtail the atrocities of the Islamic Republic of Iran. The catastrophe called the Islamic Republic of Iran will have to remain a paramount warning in the noble aspirations of Palestinians for their liberated and democratic homeland in order to prevent the equal nightmare of an Islamic Republic of Palestine—and the time to warn and worry about that specter is not later; it is exactly now. But, on the other hand, the overwhelming demonization of Palestinian (and now Iraqi or Afghan) Muslims at large, driven to desperate and drastic measures by a shameless occupation of their homeland, has equally prevented their middle-classed, white-identified, globalized civil society yuppiedom from acknowledging their extraordinary sacrifices for the liberation of their homeland. Middle-class Palestinians are by and large Christian and secular; suicidal bombers are by and large Muslim and poor.

Neither their *demonization* by a propaganda machinery nor their *glorification* by a deadly subculture of martyrdom will offer an iota of insight into the circumstances when a teenager wraps deadly explosives around his thin waist and blows himself up in an instantaneous act of suicidal homicide. Discredited are both the propaganda apparatus that abuses the paralyzing horror of suicidal violence in order to justify the unleashing of an infinitely more destructive military machinery and the militant celebration of martyrdom in order to radically Islamize a national liberation movement. The only legitimate site of reading suicidal violence is on the exploded bodies of the assailants/victims themselves: the blood, bone, and lacerated flesh of their *corpus delicti*.

Today the self-exploding body of the suicidal assailant is the singular sign of a violent denial of the state the first and final site of its violence with a violence equal in its force and ferocity. Suicidal violence is the last proclamation of the death of state and its monopoly of physical force. Suicidal violence is the physical removal of the principal target of violence—the human body—constitutional to the very definition of the state. In the immediate aftermath of 9/11, US Deputy Secretary of Defense Paul D. Wolfowitz said, "It's not just simply a matter of capturing people and holding them accountable, but removing the sanctuaries, removing the support system, *ending states* who support terrorism."[1] The commencement of this moment in the history of the very idea of the state, when one aggressively globalized conception of the state is ending all others, is coterminous with the phenomenon of suicidal violence. To see the correlation, we need to go back and revisit the classic definition of the state as an institution with a monopoly on the use of violence.

"Every State is founded on force," exclaimed Trotsky at Brest Litovsk, and Max Weber built his entire theory of state, the most perceptively accurate and enduring in the course of capitalist modernity, on that prophetic proposition.[2] At the gunpoint of the fear of "anarchy," Weber proposed that the state is the only social institution with a claim to the legitimate use of violence. "Today," Weber proposed in his classic essay "Politics as Vocation," first delivered as a speech at University of Munich in 1918 at the conclusion of the First World War, "the relation between the state and violence is an especially intimate one."[3] That intimacy has a definitive character to it before and beyond that particularly violent phase in its European history. As Weber noted, "in the past, the most varied institutions—beginning with the sib—have known the use of physical force as quite normal. Today, however, we have to say that a state is a human community that (successfully) claims the monopoly of the legitimate use of physical force."[4] The "today" of Weber's time is the time of capitalist modernity and its constitution of the state as having a "monopoly of the legitimate use of physical force." In the postmodernity of our condition, under a globality in the operation of capital that no longer allows the use or abuse of the nation-state, both that legitimacy and that monopoly are epistemically outdated and violently opposed.

As the only surviving superpower, the United States is no longer a nation-state. It is a postmodern empire—that is, the operation and range of its violence is beyond its territorial sovereignty and extends well into an amorphous global site and thus surpasses the very idea of the nation-state as it was codified in the course of capitalist modernity. As the chief military base of the Unites States at the service of its global grip, Israel has never been a legitimate nation-state. It is a postmodern colonial outpost, built on the broken back of Palestinians and the dream of their homeland. Suicidal violence against this empire and its colony denies them the principal surviving site of their violence: the human body. With the effacement of territorial sovereignty as the defining site of state legitimacy, the physical bodies of its citizens have emerged as the sole locus of its violence. Without systematically exercising that violence, the globalized state will have no anchoring claim to legitimacy. Suicidal violence, the self-exploding body, is as a result a *corpus anarchicum* denying the state its sole site of self-legitimizing violence. We must visit the three adjacent sites of *corpus politicus*, *corpus particularis*, and *corpus universalis* in order to map out the specific contours of this argument.

Weber took for granted, and thus left entirely undertheorized, the fact that every state is founded on (the presumption of legitimate) violence *on the human body*. In his definition of the state, he was entirely derailed by a superfluous, though in his time necessary, attention to the *geographical* territory at the disposal of the state, and he paid no attention to the *bodily* territory it primarily targets for its self-legitimizing violence. "Today, however, we have to say that a state is a human community that (successfully) claims the *monopoly of the legitimate use of physical force* within a given territory." That territoriality is secondary to the primacy of the physical presence of the citizens who populate it. The authority of the state is sought to be legitimated by the violence it perpetrates on the physical bodies of its citizens. There is one other factor that Weber equally misread in his theorization of the state. What the states do is *not* an exercise of "legitimate" violence, of which Weber himself was so unsure that he always qualified it by parenthetically adding "(i.e., considered to be legitimate)."[5] States exercise violence on the body of their citizens *by way of* legitimizing themselves. This violence is considered legitimate *not* by those who are at its receiving end but by the state itself that thus seeks, exacts, secures, proves, and demonstrates its "legitimacy." Eradicate the physical site of exacting that legitimacy, and the state will lack any claim to such legitimacy because it no longer has a site to exercise and demonstrate it. This exercise of violence on the body of the citizens may assume a range of manifestations, from as innocent an exercise as a simple traffic light that dictates and exacts the motion or stillness of a body on a street corner, to public torture and ceremonious execution. The public life of a society, in war and in peace, is inundated with a continuum of violence perpetrated on the bodies of its inhabitants by the governing state *in order to* ensure the necessity of that violence. The role of the state in legislating laws for or against abortion, drafting military conscription, waging war, condoning slavery, codifying imprisonment, institutionalizing marriage, exacting taxes, and determining gay and lesbian rights are chief among the innumerable instances in which the state targets the site of the physical body as the principal locus of exercising its definitive violence and thus seeks to legitimize itself.

Given the theater of this operation within the boundary of the nation-state, Weber thought that "territory is one of the characteristics of the state."[6] That territoriality has never been the primary site of a state apparatus, however, and today it has long since been overshadowed by the rise of the globalized capital to which the national economy is as superfluous as the national polity. Today the World Bank, the International Monetary Fund, and the World

Trade Organization see to it that no national economy or national polity stands in the way of the global operation of capital, and as a result no territorial claim of a nation-state is constitutional to its definition and operation. The very idea and thus the practice of the nation-state are now completely outdated and rendered obsolete by the globalized capital, which has in turn generated a postmodern empire (the United States and all its attempted simulacra such as the European Union) and its postmodern colonial outposts (Israel and all its attempted simulacra such as Pakistan). Today, the amorphous body more than ever is the principal site of attempted legitimacy on the part of the globalized state and the definitive *territory* of its monopoly on violence.

Had he not been distracted by his almost obsessive preoccupation with the predicament of capitalist modernity, Weber would have noted the primacy of the body as the principal site of the state violence in his immediate European and Christian context. As the principal site of political violence, the human body of first the medieval subjects and now the modern citizens of the state have their roots deep in the bodily supposition of royalty, "the king's two bodies," as Ernst H. Kantorowicz theorized it some half a century ago. The physical body of the king stood as the signal sight of his authority by virtue of his representation of the political body at large. There was of course a period of political resistance by the Christian Church to yielding its empowering claim on the body of Christ. As early as 1302, Pope Boniface VIII articulated the corporeal doctrine of the Roman Church in the lapidary sentences of the bull *Unam sanctam* that Kantorowicz quotes: "Urged by faith we are bound to believe in one holy Church, Catholic and also Apostolic . . . without which there is neither salvation nor remission of sins . . . which represents one mystical body, the head of which is Christ, and the head of Christ is God."[7] Kantorowicz then adds that this passage "betrays the supreme effort on the part of the spiritual power to answer and, if possible, to overcome the challenge of the nascent self-sufficiency of the secular bodies politic." Pope Boniface was obviously interested in "putting political entities in what he considered their proper place, and therefore stressed, and overstressed, the hierarchical view that the political bodies had a purely functional character *within* the world community of the *corpus mysticum Christi,* which was the Church, whose head was Christ, and whose visible head was the vicar of Christ, the Roman pontiff."[8] But the secular state had already molded itself precisely on the corporeal conception of the body politic and sought to exercise the range of its power and authority on the corporeal body of its subjects as much as on the territorial realm of its sovereignty.

The medieval conception of the corporeal state was in no way changed by the further "secularization" of it all the way to Thomas Hobbes (1588–1679) and his writing of *Leviathan* (1651), which in fact further corporealized the texture of the body politic. Hobbes was chiefly responsible for radically de-Christianizing the corporeality of the state by casting radical doubt on the corporeality of God.[9] Far more significantly, the conscious and deliberate association of the state with the human body in *Leviathan* is positively uncanny, particularly in the mechanized conception of the body that Hobbes so succinctly puts forward:

> Nature (the Art whereby God hath made and governes the World) is by the Art of man, as in many other things, so in this also imitated, that it can make an Artificial Animal. For seeing life is but a motion of Limbs, the beginning whereof is in some principall part within; why may we not say, that all Automata (Engine that move themselves by springs and wheels as doth a watch) have an artificial life? For what is the Heart, but a Spring; and the Nerves, but so many Strings; and the Joynts, but so many Wheels, giving motion to the whole Body, such as was intended by the Artificer? Art goes yet further, imitating that Rationall and most excellent worke of Nature, Man. For by Art is created that great LEVIATHAN called a COMMON-WEALTH, or STATE, (in latine CIVITAS) which is but an Artificial Man; though of greater stature and strength than the Naturall, for whose protection and defence it was intended; and in which, the Soveraignty is an Artificial Soul, as giving life and motion to the whole body. The Magistrate, and other Officers of Judicature and Execution, artificial Joynts; Reward and Punishment (by which fastened to the seate of the Soveraignty, every joynte and member is moved to perform his duty) are the Nerves, that do the same in the Body Naturall: The Wealth and Riches of all the particular members, are the Strength; Salus Populi (the peoples safety) its Business; Counsellors, by whom all things needful for it to know, are suggested unto it, are the Memory; Equity and Lawes, an artificial Reason and Will; Concord, Health; Sedition, Sickness; and Civil war, Death.[10]

Hobbes's identification of the state with the physical body goes so far as calling his leviathan or commonwealth an "Artificiall man." He then proceeds to devote the first part of *Leviathan* to a discussion of "Man," and then he builds his argument on the nature of the commonwealth in the second part entirely on a metamorphic expostulation of the body and soul of man into the organs and functions of the state. Hobbes's metaphor of man for state is crossmetamorphic, assimilating one into the other and vice versa.

About a century after the composition of *Leviathan*, the public torture and execution of the would-be regicide Robert-François Damiens in 1757 documented, as Michel Foucault would later theorize, the body of the subject as the principal site of state violence.[11] As Foucault has demonstrated, cases such as Damiens's mark not just the precision of juridical execution of "justice" but the political demonstration of power. In what Foucault calls the "classical age," crimes were considered as offenses against the person of the monarch. The physical body of the monarch is the simulacrum of his political body and by extension the moral sublation of the body of his subjects. That assumption, embedded in Foucault's argument but left dormant, implicates the body of the subject as the principal and primary site of the political sovereignty of the monarch. Territorial sovereignty becomes entirely secondary and tangential to political authority of the state. As Foucault notes in passing, "If torture was so strongly embedded in legal practice, it was because it revealed truth and showed the operation of power . . . it made it possible to reproduce the crime on the visible body of the criminal. It also made the body of the condemned man the place where the vengeance of the sovereign was applied, the anchoring point for a manifestation of power, an opportunity of affirming the dissymmetry of forces."[12] To almost a century after the public torture and execution of Damiens, Foucault dates the commencement of a systematized penal system, when "in Europe and in the United States, the entire economy of punishment was redistributed." Thus by the late eighteenth and early nineteenth centuries, representational and analogical punishment emerged as the normative mutation of public torture and execution and paved the legal way toward the political mutation of the body into a machinery of what Foucault calls "docility-utility," or "discipline." The body, Foucault thoroughly documents, is now controlled in such disciplinary detail, with such economy and efficiency, and along the lines of such uninterrupted and constant military coercion that it is aggressively mechanized beyond anything witnessed in monasteries, armies, or workshops before.[13] In making this assertion, however, Foucault pays exclusive attention to the legislated mechanics of the body in such public institutions as factories and hospitals. Surprisingly, Foucault disregards the metaphoric origin of such a precise mechanization of the body in political thinkers like Hobbes who about two centuries before the institutional regimentation of the body in the early nineteenth century had already given a thoroughly mechanical assessment of it.

Be that as it may, Foucault's documentation of the increased systematization of the disciplinary control of the body in schools, factories, hospitals, armies, and prisons corresponds to two simultaneous developments in the *economy* and *polity* of the emerging nation-state. *Economically*, the aggressive instrumentalization of the body into the assembly line of the productive machinery, the critical subject of Martin Heidegger's essay "The Question Concerning Technology," corresponded to the political abstraction of the state from its medieval origins in the Christian conception of *corpus mysticum Christi* and the monarchical conception of "*the King's Two Bodies*."[14] Jeremy Bentham's idea of the *Panopticon* for a prison system becomes the model of social control of the body beyond the prison walls, anticipates George Orwell's *1984*, and regiments and legislates the human body as the primary site of state violence: actual as in capital punishment and conscription, representational as in slavery and imprisonment, or symbolic as in the innocent look of a traffic light that regulates the actions of the citizens' bodily movements. Thus, with the birth of the nation-state as the political realm of the capitalist modernity, its territorial sovereignty became tantamount to its political legitimacy, while its medieval roots in Christianity and its secularization in the body of the king were both routinized and mutated into the body of the abstracted state and thus even more emphatically into the physical bodies of its citizens. The colonial shadow of Enlightenment modernity extended the corporeal site of citizens' bodies into the four corners of the world. Coming at a moment of critical self-awareness of capitalist modernity, Weber's poignant theorization of the state as the sole claimant to violence put undue emphasis on the *territoriality* of its sovereignty at the expense of an awareness of the primary and principal site of that violence: the bodies of its subjects.

If we begin with the bodies of citizens as the principal site of state violence, then we have an entirely different conception of bodily resistances to that violence. But first and foremost, suicidal violence needs to be taken out of its fabricated religious context. Suicidal violence may assume the cultural color of its locality. Jewish, Christian, Islamic, Hindu, and even Buddhist and Shinto self-sacrificing violence has been rampant throughout history. In more secular terms, there is scarcely a revolutionary or anticolonial movement in distant or recent memory that has not resulted in a communal sense of momentary *pseudo-Gemeinschaft*—to extrapolate from Ferdinand Tönnies' famous typology—or ideologically articulated "organic solidarity"—to borrow Emile Durkheim's—in which the physical body of one comes to represent the organic totality of the whole, which in moments of insurrectionary frenzy conclude in epidemics of suicidal violence.[15] What Durkheim also categorized as "altruistic" suicide, as opposed to other verities of suicide he typologized as based on "egoism" or "anomie," has been endemic to a whole variety of societies and cultures to the point of sustaining legitimate crosscultural typologies.[16] Thus historically evident, religiously or ideologically motivated self-sacrificial violence should not prevent us today from seeing the rise of a whole new countermetaphysics of the body and its reconfiguration into a *disposable machinery*. It is foolhardy to assume that religious justification is the cause, reason, or even the condition of self-sacrificial violence. Most religions, Islam included, forbid suicide and categorically prohibit the mass murder of innocent people. Yet all religions, Islam included, have been implicated in the most atrocious forms of murderous behavior. Understanding suicidal violence today requires an entirely different conception of the *human body* than any wild-goose chase after religious justification can provide.

Suicidal violence targets two, not one, sites for its execution. The violence that the suicidal assailant perpetrates only *secondarily* damages its target: the enemy's body and/or property. The *primary* site of its violence—when the explosives detonate, the plane is crashed into a building, or the boat is rammed through a warship—is the body of the one who committed the violence. In a fanatical and racist rush to condemn the suicide bombers, commentators on its *secondary* targets categorically dismiss its first and foremost victim, the very body of the suicide bomber himself or herself. The damage that bellicose ideologues have done in summarily dismissing the Palestinian, the Arab, and the Muslim suicidal assailants as rabid fanatics and lunatic barbarians is incalculable. There is a suffocating air of Stalinist density in the United States today. Responsible intellectuals scarcely dare to oppose the dominant atmosphere of fear and intimidation that can only accept a total and absolute surrender to the inanity of the dominant discourse and the criminal actions of both the United States and Israel. Any opposition to the racist and fanatical discourses by illiterate columnists and their accompanied actions is considered an act of treason or a justification of suicidal violence. Two, not one, sets of belligerent and intimidating courses of action and accompanying ideologies of justification are today preventing the formation of a critical discourse that can address such dangerous developments as suicidal violence: one represented by Osama bin Laden, the other ignored in George W. Bush. For reasons far beyond a simple countering of this fascist environment, we must begin any serious understanding of the phenomenon of suicidal violence with the very site of its *primary* target: the broken bones, the shed blood, and the lacerated flesh of the suicidal bomber himself or herself. So far as its *secondary* target is concerned, suicide bombing is squarely rooted in a politics of despair, a revolutionary protest against an inordinately more powerful enemy, such as Israel to the Palestinians or the United States to the Afghans and Iraqis. The *primary* target of suicidal violence is the body of the suicide bomber himself or herself. The destruction of that site—the very first constellation of bones, flesh, and blood that goes up in smoke—points to a whole different set of issues and demands a radical readjustment of the dominant moral prerogatives.

The site of reading a suicidal bombing is *not* the body of its innocent victims; and yet it is precisely the site of its innocent victims. In that palindromic paradox rests the heart and the crux of the matter. There are two, *not one*, sets of innocent lives lost to suicide bombing, and any understanding of the nature and disposition of the horror must begin with the absolutely irreversible fact that the two sets of victims are irrevocably the same. The aggressive criminalization of the suicide bomber has impeded the reading of his or her self-exploded body as the archeological site of an innocence that indicts the world that refuses to bear witness to it. The body is the physical site of the violence that seeks to legitimize the state that perpetrates it. Not its territorial expanse in an imaginative geography, nor indeed its expansion into the four corners of the world, but the physical bodies of its citizens and subjects, is where the state sets its normative claims to political legitimacy, with a helping hand from the reigning metaphysics of its sacred suppositions: Christianity in the United States, Judaism in Israel, Islam in the Islamic Republic of Iran, Hinduism in India, and so on. The exploded body of the suicide bomber—the Tamil Tigers in Sri Lanka, the Palestinian Hamas in Palestine—eradicates the site of political violence by a violence equal in its intensity, once and for all denying the state its principle site of self-legitimizing operation. The body is the most visible, most decidedly social site of the political violence of the state. The exploded body of the suicide bomber is the excavated territory of the state where it has been categorically rendered obsolete. The suicidal subject is the noncitizen of the discredited republic that is now denied the principal site of its self-legitimizing violence. What now will have to be called *the disposable body* has violently exploded in the face of the illegitimate state by denying it its first and foremost site of violence. The self-exploding body has liberated the sign of the body from the legislated semantics of its categorical signification in the tyrannical state. The body is legislated into a semantics of signification so constitutional to the legitimacy of the state that it no longer even recognizes itself as an autonomous, anarchic, and rebellious sign. The self-exploded body of the suicide bomber is the anamnesis of the self-forgetful body, now remembering its freedom of explosion and defying the state by denying it the principal site of its violence. The body has been wrongly fighting the state in the streets. The body now fights the state in its first and final symbolic site, its material relevance: the flesh, blood, and bone of its *condito sine qua non.*

The self-exploding body is now quintessential to the miasmatic mutation of the state, in correspondence with the amorphous globalization of the capital that the state seeks to serve, in unforeseen directions, now marked by an open-ended war on "terrorism." The globalization of capital is now fully beyond the principle and the parameters of the nation-state and the modernity of its primogeniture. The outdated state is now waging a war on *global terrorism* as the phantasmagoric blueprint of its own remodulation to correspond to the operation of globalized capital. The absurdity of the state trying to catch up with the self-exploding body was nowhere as pronounced as when George W. Bush stood on the rubble of the World Trade Center and proclaimed that he was going to punish those responsible for that carnage. He was too late. The remains of those responsible for that carnage were under his feet, under the tons of steel, concrete, flesh, and bone they had just exploded. They were beyond paying for anything. The subsequent wars in Afghanistan and Iraq and the murdering of innocent people there had nothing to subtract or add either from those self-exploded bodies or to Bush's delegitimated presidency and the state his presidency presumed to represent.

Halfway around the globe, the most backward state on the face of the earth, Taliban-ruled Afghanistan, simply echoed and reflected the obsolete legitimacy of the crowning achievement of Enlightenment modernity, the United States of America. The Taliban destruction of the two statues of Buddha in Bamiyan mirrors and reflects in diametrically opposed yet paradoxically complementary ways the destruction of the Twin Towers of the World Trade Center. The Taliban blew up the two statues of Buddha as a signal of their strict Wahabi dogmatism, believing that the figural, bodily representation was forbidden in Islam. Only God Almighty, demands the absolute Islamic monotheism deeply rooted in its Judaic antecedent, can create human figures. Man should not pretend to do so, thus imitating the singular creativity of God Almighty. The Twin Towers of the World Trade Center in New York were blown up as the supreme signs of global capitalism. These three words, "*World Trade Center*," ought to be read and pronounced not simply as the names of two buildings in downtown Manhattan but for what they actually mean: two buildings that were the center of global trading. It does not matter that globalization has no center. What matters is that these two buildings advertised and symbolized themselves as the *center* of *world trade.* The destruction of these four icons was the knocking down of a set of totem poles, the tribal prides of the enemy, on both sides of the imaginary geography of an outmaneuvered faith. The two Buddha statues were seen as the intrusion of *kofr* (blasphemy) and *shirk* (constituting rivals for God Almighty) from the East of that belligerent geography, and the Twin Towers were seen as the arrogant confidence of denying it legitimacy from its West.

In between the two statues of Buddha and the Twin Towers—the two giant totem poles at the two ends of a timetable that spans an eternity from the pre- to the postmodernity of a *present* to which the Taliban had no claim—the captive imagination of a faith mutated itself into a bellicose ideology of resistance first to colonialism and then to a predatory empire.

The destruction of the two statues of Buddha was a belated act of pious fanaticism in the heart of the most colonially deprived shadow of a nation-state, called Afghanistan. The destruction of the Twin Towers was the cutting down of two totem poles at the tribal square of a post-nation-state. Afghanistan was literally invented by colonialism not long after the United States was invented by the capitalist modernity. The same British colonialism that was defeated in order to invent the United States was victorious in inventing Afghanistan to protect its Indian territories against the Russians. The United States was invented in 1776, more than three decades before the closing of the eighteenth century, as the crowning achievement of capitalist modernity. Afghanistan was invented in 1837, more than three decades after the opening of the nineteenth century, as a prime example of a colonially manufactured nation-state. As a manufactured state at the colonial edges of capitalist modernity, Afghanistan could never have a completely territorial claim to its sovereignty. The British in the south and the Russians to the north saw to that. As a result of this colonial predicament, the bodies of its potential citizens were the principal sites of the violence that any state of Afghanistan had to exercise in order to legitimize itself. The maimed and massacred bodies of the Afghans in successive wars waged on their territories and mounted by their own regimes are the evidence to that effect. The destruction of the two statues of Buddha was nothing but a simple extension of the violence that any Afghani state, Taliban ruled or otherwise, has historically perpetrated on the physical bodies of its would-be citizens. All Wahabism has done here is add a fanatical doctrinal justification for an entirely colonial absence of territorial sovereignty translated into bodily violence. The destruction of the Twin Towers of the World Trade Center, on the other side of the colonial divide, was the elimination of the last symbolic site of any *territorial* claim to any conception of a nation-state, the explosive evidence that globalization has no center. We have now all been ushered into the vastly amorphous operation of capital, with the absolute and final eradication of all nation-states and the simultaneous rise of one global claim to an empire with a singular mission "to end states" that oppose its imperial hubris.

The destruction of the two statues of Buddha and the Twin Towers complement and mirror each other: one as the atrocious evidence of the bodily brutality perpetrated in colonially manufactured states like Afghanistan and the other as the definitive elimination of the last symbolic site of any *territorial* claim to sovereignty, the death of the nation-state, the final proclamation of the birth of the amorphous Empire, now registered with an open-ended war on "terrorism." At the end of the game of capitalist modernity, we have neither a sovereign Afghanistan nor a hermetically sealed United States. All boundaries and protections are now down and erased. What we have is one gigantic military machinery code-named "the United States" on one side and a vastly amorphous globe on the other. The worst elements of the colonial subjugation of the body have now finally come together to create a world in which the fragile bodies of the individual citizens of an amorphous globe are the single surviving site of a phantasmagoric violence at the disposal of the Empire. Suicidal bombing is the body eliminating the last surviving site of violence for the globalized Empire, without which it lacks all legitimacy.

THE PALESTINIAN, THE ARAB, AND THE MUSLIM

Three figurative markers have now assumed categorical characters in response to suicidal bombing: the Palestinian, the Arab, and the Muslim. They each correspond to a different dismantling of the state, as they all constitute a *corpus particularis* integral to a more universal mutation of the human body. There is a physical disembodiment that separates the self-exploding body of the suicidal assailant from the territorial body of the nation he or she thus seeks to represent. The dismembered body corresponds to the deterritorialized nation. The dialectics of this reciprocity is at the core of the *corpus particularis* of the Palestinian, the Arab, and the Muslim. The self-exploding body of the suicide bomber dismembers itself at the intersection of three paradoxical denials. Not all Muslims are Arabs, and not all Arabs are Palestinians, but *Palestinians*, *Arabs*, and *Muslims* (as categorical markers) are all their own paradoxical denials. The *Palestinian* was born at the moment of his death; the *Arab* is the multinational denial of the very idea of the nation; and the *Muslim* is the supranational rejection of the nation-state, the multicultural negation of the national culture. These three markers collide and dismantle the very idea and the prolonged practice of the nation-state on its colonial edges.

It is only too obvious that the self-exploding body of the Palestinian suicidal bomber should come from a *stateless subject* revolting against a *colonial state* occupying his or her land, denying his or her nation-state. The Palestinians are the last remnant of a stateless nation right at the end of the practice, purpose, and the very idea of the nation-state. The preposterous end of Yasser Arafat, having sold the dreams and aspirations of a nation for the ludicrous trappings of being called "the President," is a telling index of the last gasps of colonial nationalism. For more than half a century denied their claim to a nation-state, the Palestinians came to the half-closed gates of colonial modernity as a nation with no state. The ultimate tragedy of Palestine is that today the Palestinian nationalist fights for a nation-state at a time when the very idea and certainly the practice of it are categorically outdated. While the United States is the single superpower succeeding all other states and presiding over the practice of *ending states*, and while Israel is the last colonial settlement at a time of postcoloniality, the lacerated body of the Palestinian is the denial of the United States (as the global Empire) and Israel (as a colonial settlement and an illegitimate nation-state) their first and final site of violence. The pointer *Palestinian* thus marks the *corpus particularis* of the self-exploding body denying Israel its colonial and the United States its imperial claim to state legitimacy. This denial perforce comes from the stateless body of the Palestinian, bought into the idea but never delivered into the practice of the nation-state.

The self-exploding, stateless body of the Palestinian flies in the face of the atrocious promises of colonial nationalism. The idea and practice of the nation-state served the rising provenance of the capital with an optimum level of economy and polity and a corresponding culture at the commencement of its nationalization of economic production. The colonial shadow of the capital extended the idea and practice of nationalism into the four corners of the world. Whether opposed by such indigenous communitarianism as Islamism or else by the borrowed idea of nationalism, colonialism delivered and ossified the very notion of the nation-state over and against a federative tapestry of local webs of social and communal affiliations. The colonial production of nationalism the world over mutated the human bodies of citizens into the primary site of the violence of the states it engendered. The Palestinian mind was issued a nation-state check that the Palestinian body could not cash. The stateless body of the Palestinian self-explodes at the seams of its tension between that discursive expectation and that bodily denial. Their ideal of nationhood deterritorialized, the dismembered bodies of the Palestinians repeat on the site of their *corpus* now *anarchicus* their promised but denied territory. The shelled out and bombed headquarters of the Palestinian Authority in the course of the second *Intifada* is the physical simulacrum of the self-exploded body of the Palestinian suicidal bomber. The world is indifferent to the bombed and shelled out building of the Palestinian Authority headquarters but indignant to the suicide bomber. The two, however, mirror and reflect each other. The body of the Palestinian suicide bomber is already dismembered, long before it self-explodes. It is dismembered by the (absence of the) virtue of being a stateless national of a yet-to-be-born Republic of Palestine, belonging ipso facto to a dismembered and deterritorialized promise of a nation. The Palestinian national was born at the moment of his death: the birth of the state of Israel in 1948. *The Palestinian national* is always-already a dead man walking, a contradiction in terms.

The marker *Arab* now points to the *corpus particularis* of a divided and dissembled body—*divided* by the colonial nationalism that carved out the modern Arab nation-states and *dissembled* by a communal solidarity that defies the concocted artificiality of those borders. As the forced formation of colonial nationalism, "the Arabs" are a walking contradiction in terms: their communal affinity pulling them together across colonial nationalism and their concocted nations pushing them apart. The modern Arab was born a divided self, his colonially construed nation-state pulling him one way, her communal self-awareness pushing her another. The self-exploding body of the Arab suicidal assailant blows up into the fragments of its originary formation at the colonial periphery of capitalist modernity and its political propensity toward the nation-state. Within its own historical memory, the assignation *Arab* carries layers of its multiple mutations. From its originary *tribal* configuration, it mutated in the seventh century into first a *dynastic* and then an *imperial* designation that kept itself *culturally* dominant all the way to the thirteenth century when the Mongol invasion put an abrupt puncture into it. Soon after, under the Seljuqid and then the Ottoman empires, the cultural ascendancy of the signifier *Arab* was eclipsed by the Turkish *domination* and let loose only by the *colonial* dismantling of the Ottoman Empire. From its Seljuqid and then Ottoman eclipse, the designation *Arab* emerged in the colonial carving of the Ottoman Empire into fabricated nation-states, conscious and proud of its distant imperial heritage, angry and bitter with its recent colonial domination. Arab nationalism emerged as the pale shadow of colonial domination, fighting back first European and then American imperialism with an ideology at the root of Enlightenment modernity. Islamism and socialism soon joined forces with Arab nationalism to divide and conquer the political loyalty of the *Arab*, while in North Africa the incessant Amazighe (Berber) nationalism reminded it of its own colonial proclivities. Fragmented into so many momentous memories, the assignment the *Arab* makes for a defiant body, impossible to delimit to one symbolic mode of assignment. The self-exploding body of the *Arab* is the final denial of the very assumption of a state its first and final site of violence. The blown-up body of the Arab, thus designated and denied at one and the same time, denies the globalized Empire—the United States beyond the limits of a nation-state—and the last surviving colonial outpost—the Israeli occupation of Palestine—their singular site of violence.

Finally, the attribution *Muslim* is the already hollowed shell of a dispossessed agency that by self-exploding forever erases the specular reflection of *the West* in itself. As fabricated by an army of mercenary Orientalists and corroborated by a band of self-serving sheikhs and mullahs, *Islam* today is the supreme supposition of an Other for the fictitious symbolics of power code-named *the West*. As reimagined by militant Muslims who mutated their ancestral faith into the site of ideological resistance to colonialism, *Islam* reflected back *the West* and by opposing ossified it. As the civilizational Other of *the West*, *Islam* became the breeding pool of *Muslims* who were nonsubjects in default of agency. The self-explosion of the Muslim body is the final denial of the *Western* Self its supreme Other. The West became *the West* by looking at itself in the speculum of its *Islamic* Other. The self-exploding body of the Muslim is the erasure of that specular intermediary, the shattering of the mirror that raised *the West* and lowered all its Others, *Muslims* in particular. If they assimilate into *the West*, they have joined a nonentity. If they oppose *the West*, they ossify it and their Otherness even further. The blown up body of the Muslim is the erasure of one side of this binary opposition, once and for all breaking the dialectical nexus of their own denial. By self-exploding, Muslims are wiping out the shadow of *the West* in the colonial mirror of their historical subjugation. Erasing the *Islamic* reflection of *the West* erases *the West* itself. Now the world—Muslims, Jews, and Christians included—can find and place itself in nondenominational terms domestic to its worldly dispossessions.

In its highest Hebraic moment, the body of thought that has painted itself into the corner of *Western philosophy* sought to place Otherness at the heart of its presumed epistemological ipseity. The suicidal bombing is the explosion of that very heart, denying what Emmanuel Levinas sought to give it: its moment of supreme ethical superiority, to accommodate with Christian charity an Hebraic Other in the heart of its darkness. Vigilance, Levinas thought, should jolt the consciousness the same way that insomnia suspends the sleep, thus accommodating the Hebraic Other at the heart of the European Christianity. Completely Othered, with no Levinas to accommodate their central assimilation into the dominant Same, the Oriental Other self-explodes, denying the European Self the physical evidence of its claim to authenticity, originality, and Sameness. In Levinas, a dialogical intersubjectivity was meant to replace the immanent consciousness at the center of what has benefited from calling itself *European philosophy*. Out of his Hebraic Otherness in the midst of the European Same, Levinas sought to plant a generalized Other smack in the heart of the European Same. That was very Christian of him. The self-destructive body of the Palestinian, the Arab, and the Muslim is denying the *Western* Self the physical site of its Other. The charred body of the Muslim/Arab/Palestinian is the undoing of the Levinasian move to make the Other the site of the Same consciousness, as it is the denial of the state the site of its violence by a violence equal in its ferocity.

In Husserlian epistemology, summing up what Levinas read as the entirety of the Platonic (or what he called "Western") tradition, the movement of intentionality that was generated within the omniscient subject traveled toward transcendence and returned to the seat of its cognitive faculties to constitute agential knowing. That sort of subjective immanence did not sit well with the Hebraic sensibilities of Levinas. The Husserlian intentionality ultimately fails for Levinas, whose primary interest is in articulating an intersubjective consciousness, placing his Hebraic Other next to the generalized *European Self* by forcing it to *face* a generic non-European Other. Levinas's groundbreaking ambition was to plant the inscrutable *face* of a generalized, fictive, disturbing Other smack in the middle of the European confidant Same and thus transplant an insomniac *alterity* for the Husserlian *Ich* that claimed the whole European history of being. He then sought to siphon out the entire Heideggerian project of Dasein by seeking a mode of consciousness "beyond being," reading Martin Buber's "I-Thou" relationship as a mode of consciousness beyond the Husserlian *return* and thus outside the provenance of transcendental immanence. Levinas's concern with radically altering the Husserlian subject was not only limited to articulating a Jewish archeology for it. He was as much interested in Martin Buber (minus his Hasidism) as he was in Gabriel Marcel (minus his Christian Existentialism). In Marcel's treatment of incarnation and bodily resurrection, Levinas detected a Buberian "I-Thou" relationship, and in both he perceived two modes of intersubjective nexus that postponed and suspended the European proclivity toward Identity, Sameness, I-based consciousness, and ultimately transcendental immanence.

Levinas made it his lifelong task to examine in what particular way the *alterity* of the Other could be incorporated into the critical formation of the consciousness as a philosophical project. His epistemology of *alterity* thus soon lends itself to an ethics of heteronomy. The task of that ethics was fully to honor, and thus realize that it can never understand, the absolute otherness of the Other. Despite his principal concern with Edmund Husserl and occasional interest in Marcel, it was from a Jewish perspective that he sought to bring Martin Buber and Frantz Rosenzweig together and launch his ethical critique of European epistemology. His attempt to have a conception of *infinity* shot through and suspend the Husserlian (European) predilection toward immanence was in part indebted to Rosenzweig and his triumvirate reconceptualization of *creation* (the past relation of God to the world), *revelation* (his present relation to man), and *redemption* (his future relation to both). In the hands of Levinas and in the service of his Herculean task to alter the European consciousness, Buber, Marcel, and Rosenzweig were all moments in postulating a persistent dialogue (between God and man) that enabled and informed a dialogical substitute for the soliloquial predilection in the European philosophy toward absolutist immanence.[17] "The Other remains infinitely transcendent, infinitely foreign; his face in which his epiphany is produced and which appeals to me breaks with the world that can be common to us, whose virtualities are inscribed in our *nature* and developed by our existence."[18] The charred body and the wiped out face of the suicidal bomber—of the Palestinian, the Arab, and the Muslim—is the denial of the European Self its supreme transcendentalized Other at its sublimest Hebraic moment when *the* philosopher of European Jewry *par excellence*, Emmanuel Levinas, sought finally to implicate the face of the Other in the European ethical imagination, its ever-cosmogonic ontology that does not leave even ethics alone.

What Michael Tausig grapples with in what he calls "public secrecy," in *Defacement: Public Secrecy and the Labor of the Negative*—namely, the *surfacing* of the repressed in acts of public *defacement*—goes a long way in explaining the *effacement* of the Palestinian in both the collective conscience of the Israelis and the critical ethics of Levinas. The sort of knowledge that Tausig calls "knowing what not to know" is precisely the form of social knowledge at the root of the Israeli collective dismissal of the Palestinian. Tausig's critical attention to the paradoxical roots of the conception of the "sacred" as both "accursed" and "holy" is at the heart of Levinas's ambiguous relationship to the Palestinian face: at once the very site of testing his ethical philosophy and yet the very sight of his horror.[19] Levinas remained loudly silent on Rosenzweig's hatred of Islam, and except for his admiration for Anwar Sadat (because he visited Israel), he had nothing to say about that faith, the *face* of its alterity, its *altered* face, the altered faith *of* Judaism. Was it the very author of the *face* of the Other who in the aftermath of the Sabra and Shatila massacre in 1982 persistently spoke of "the lack of guilt here—and probably there, too," and who could only speak of "responsibility" in a Biblical sense, that is to say, "a responsibility which has nothing to do with any act one may really have committed," or even more atrociously "the responsibility of those who have done nothing."[20] Had the Israeli's under Begin and Sharon "done nothing" in Sabra and Shatila? Is this what Levinas meant by the ethical responsibility of one toward the Other, on the basis of which he then provided a theological justification, based on the Bible and the Talmud, for Zionism?[21] What exactly is the ethical basis of the outrage at the face of the defaced suicidal bomber who eliminates—with a violence equal in its ferocity to the violence of the state that thus denies him faith, face, and body—the site of not just that violence but the location of a self-raising, Other-lowering ontological ethics that thinks it has now actually looked at the face of the Other? What face of the Other? The late Palestinian poet Mahmoud Darwish is the face of Levinas's Other. Can he look at him?

> No one understands anyone.
> And no one understands anyone.
> No one understands.
> No one . . .
> No one.[22]

FORCING THE FACE

In the wake of President Jacques Chirac's announcement that Muslim French women will be barred from wearing their scarves in public places, Christopher Caldwell detected a major difference and pointed to a principal paradox between the French conception of *laïcité* and the US separation of church and state in an exceptionally insightful piece in the *International Herald Tribune*. In France, he observed, "Church and state were separated by means of '*laïcité*,' which is difficult to translate. It differs from the American tradition in that it seeks less to neutralize the public authorities in matters of religion than to neutralize religion in matters of public life." This verbal bit of a fancy footwork results in a noteworthy conclusion: "A paradox results: Since the Iraq war much of the world views France as the symbol of Western reluctance to provoke a civilizational clash with Islam. The United States has been assailed for willingness to run that risk. Yet France aims to curtail the religious expression of its Muslims in ways no prominent American has suggested."[23]

There are a couple of minor technicalities worth considering here that may perhaps result in the paradox resolving itself. First, Caldwell writes "the United States has been assailed" in the passive voice, as though all the criticism of its risking a civilizational confrontation was external. However, we must remember a little bit of an essay later turned into a sizeable book called "*The Clash of Civilizations*," which was written not exactly by "much of the world" as Caldwell says but by major US foreign policy strategist Samuel Huntington. It was he, not "much of the world," who proposed that what we are facing—here at what his like-minded state department functionary Francis Fukuyama had decided was "the end of history"—is a civilizational clash between "Islam and the West."[24] Long before *9/11* (2001), Fukuyama in "The End of History" (1989) and Huntington in "The Clash of Civilizations" (1993)—both first published in the US journal *Foreign Affairs*—had posited a civilizational battle between the Western side of their captured imagination and their Islamic nightmares. So it was not exactly a mere journalist invention code-named "much of the world" that abruptly assailed an innocent US bystander. The story was actually the other way around.

Once we keep that minor technicality in mind, then it is easy to go for the Achilles's heel of the argument and point to the other equally minor matter that it is the United States that is now poised as a major global empire, not France—and *that* not by something defective in the US DNA and healthy in the French but by virtue of the United States' accumulated gargantuan capital that flexes its imperial muscles where it matters most. France has long since passed the limits of its imperial power and the measures of colonial imagination and thus has no tolerance for the cultural diversity of its former colonies now coming home to roost. French Muslims are the return of the French colonial repressed, a cause of embarrassment, a bad faith coming home to haunt. Those former colonies ought to be wiped out of textbook maps and histories, never to be publicly mentioned and officially acknowledged. It is quite embarrassing for the selfsame logic of capital that once sent French colonialists and French Christian missionaries all over the globe to plunder people's wealth and deliver them to everlasting peace in Jesus Christ now to bring these veiled Muslims to Paris—the "Bride of all Cities," no less—and confuse the charm and shake the illusion. White and white-identified Parisians have an image of France that does not and cannot quite accommodate either veiled women or dark men speaking French better than the Parisians and then on top of it have young and rambunctious Algerians Gangsta rap it to shake out its hidden energies. *Non—ce n'est pas possible; nous avons le laïcité ici!*

As for the United States, it can perfectly afford the magnanimity of allowing Muslim women to veil themselves because as an always aspiring empire with no hegemony it could not care less what headscarf or yarmulke or crosses its people wear as long as they wear and tear their Nike shoes and Gap trousers at regular and repeated intervals. The imperial tolerance has a very long tradition that goes all the way back to Achaemenid kings who did not mind freeing the enslaved Jews of Babylon and having themselves coroneted in Jerusalem in Jewish, in Egypt in Egyptian, and in Persepolis in Zoroastrian terms—all the same cotton candies puffed around different sticks, as it were. The reason that Muslim scarves are tolerated in the United States is rooted in a much more hopeful paradox, which has scarcely anything to do with the innocent, but alas self-Orientalizing, assumption of a certain Hussain Haqqani who in an Op-Ed in the same issue of the *International Herald Tribune* Caldwell's piece appeared in believes "American secularism is far more palatable to ordinary Muslims."[25] The root of that momentary and fragile tolerance—which may indeed turn around any second after another terrorist attack on the mainland United States and in the blink of an eye result in across the board Muslim internment camps *à la* the Japanese during the Second World War—points to a much more hopeful battle: one worth fighting for. What the United States faces today is something of an ethical civil war, a historic choice between the *moral logic* of its own anticolonial past and the *economic logic* of its predatory capital. The two constitutionally negate and have historically contradicted each other on every turn of events. As the promised land of refugees and the persecuted from the four corners of the globe, the United States has a *moral logic* to its anticolonial history consistently challenged and overturned by the grotesque *economic logic* of its predatory capital, which has neither a dream of mercy for others nor a measure of memory for itself.

But there is a critical lesson about the battle over veiling currently raging in Europe. The globalized body no longer has a territorial or cultural limit to its contestations. What has happened to the Palestinian, the Arab, and the Muslim body, as *corpus particularis*, is integral to the predicament of the *posthuman body*, as *corpus universalis* at large. Severing the reading of that *particular* from the fate of this *universal* is the most pernicious legacy of Orientalism. The enduring Orientalization of the "Islamic World" has categorically cut it off from critical consideration in the global configuration of the human body. We are now beyond the limits of that mercenary mission. When the particulars of the suicidal assailant are linked to the universals of the posthuman body, it becomes evident that today there is something constitutionally different about suicidal violence than its antecedents in history. The suicidal violence we have witnessed in the case of the World Trade Center and the Pentagon or the Palestinian struggle for statehood is integral to a whole different conception of the human body: the makeup of the disposable, dispensable, emendable, mutable, *posthuman body.*

The current—politically fabricated, ideologically sustained—assumption that suicidal bombing is the result and consequence of Islamic fanaticism is entirely false and deeply rooted in the continued influence of an Orientalist imagination. Contrary to the sustained suggestion of that imagination, suicidal bombings have scarcely anything to do with religious fanaticism. Fanaticism of all sorts has always been constitutional to suicidal violence. Islam has had its share of the phenomenon, as has Christianity, Judaism, Buddhism, Shintoism, Sikhism, and any number of other religions, sects, and ideologies, as in fact has plain old madness. If ancient Jewish zealots at Masada, medieval Muslim assassins under the Seljuqs, modern Japanese kamikazes, and recent Christians at Waco, Texas, have all been prone to suicidal violence, then they implicate a larger frame of reference to explain them in their specific moral and historical circumstances. Contrary to all these modes of suicidal violence, the suicidal assailants today are in fact integral to a generic decline in the belief in metaphysics and afterlife. The ancient, medieval, and even modern suicidal violence may indeed have reflected a belief in an afterlife that the sacrificial death may have blissfully guaranteed. Jews on the top of Masada, Muslims in the gardens of Hasan Sabbah, and Christians listening to David Koresh in Waco, Texas, or Jim Jones in Guyana may have heard, seen, and been promised things entirely different from those informing and animating the suicidal assailants in the United States and Israel today.

The kinds of suicidal violence that we witness today require an entirely different mode of understanding, a mode much thwarted and delayed by the Orientalist fabrication of the so-called *Orient* and its moral and imaginal separation from the global condition of our *corpus universalis*. The suicide note of Eric Harris, who along with Dylan Klebold massacred his fellow students and teachers at Columbine High School in Littleton, Colorado, before committing suicide, is a clear testimony to the necessity of reading these desperate acts in terms beyond the parochial reach of *Western* triumphalism.[26] Even on the now iconic day of 9/11, the Arab assailants were not the only ones with a suicidal mission. According to a BBC program, *Clear the Air*, quoting Colonel Robert Marr, the US Air Force commanders were considering crashing their fighter jets into the hijacked planes. "It was very possible," Colonel Marr told BBC News, "that they [US pilots] would have been asked to give their lives themselves."[27]

Today, suicidal violence will have to be considered along the lines of deconstructive and desedimenting reconfigurations of the *posthuman body*, in which outdated national cultures and civilizational divides no longer play any role. The *posthuman*, disposable body now corresponds to the postmodern state, where the optimum limit of the nation-state, the principal polity favored by capitalist modernity, no longer holds or sustains the legitimacy of the state apparatus. Today, states have tenuous claims over their national boundaries as they are metamorphosed into the planetary mutations of themselves, crumbling under the forces of ever-expansive markets, labor migration, and the military thuggery of once two but now only one superpower. It is not just states like Pakistan, Afghanistan, Iraq, Iran, North Korea, Venezuela, Somalia, or any other so-called postcolonial state that are at the mercy of the one remaining superpower. The United States itself is mutating into an amorphous state beyond its national boundaries. While its national boundaries are corroding under tremendous pressure from global labor migration and the chronic collapse of the stock market, the United States as a superstate is expanding its territorial domain of operation in a phantasmagoric planetary direction. By posturing to fight against the ghostly apparition of an international terrorist conspiracy, the United States is militarily remodulating itself into a planetary power with extraterrestrial command and control of the planet Earth. The magnitude of the destructive power that this madness can unleash is unfathomable. The suicidal violence now aimed at the United Sates both inside and outside its territorial boundaries indicates its planetary mutation as well as its excessive vulnerability to defining and sustaining itself. As states are losing their territorial control of themselves, and as the United States (and potentially the European Union in competition with it) is mutating into a global reconfiguration of itself, they correspond to a posthuman body no longer compatible with the Enlightenment origin of both their inventions.

As we have known it so far, the modern state is the direct invention of the Enlightenment, in political correspondence with a secular humanism at the center of which stood the celebrated human body. The postmodern state no longer corresponds to its early creation in the course and at the service of Enlightenment (capitalist) modernity, squarely solid on territorial integrity and the bodily control of its subjects and citizens. The outdated state now corresponds to the disembodied simulacrum of its citizens, the bodies that can be genetically engineered, artificially inseminated, organically transplanted, plastically sculpted, medically assisted in suicide, or else self-exploded in violent service to a cause. Today, two states in particular are the specific targets of suicide bombing: the United States and Israel; one as the last claim on a global empire and the other as the last colonial settlement; both created ex nihilio in the span of some two hundred years from each other; one the crowning achievement of Enlightenment (capitalist) modernity and the other the colonial extension of its globalizing logic. Palestinian suicide bombing is now the most violent expression of a national liberation movement at a time when the very idea of the nation-state is obsolete. Thus the last surviving empire is now assisting the last colonial settlement in robbing a nation of its dream of a homeland at a time when that dream is long since irrelevant. We are in a bizarre moment in history. At the peak of one particularly nasty instance in the structural violence at the heart of capitalist modernity, the European Holocaust almost exterminated an entire people, and then those very people turned around to become the last colonial officers at the service of the strategic interest of the last empire.

Over the course of the last half century, from the end of the second European war (the so-called World War II) to the emergence of first two and then just one superpower, the gradual mutation of the modern state into an amorphous conglomerate of power has corresponded with a major reconfiguration of the very idea of the human body, from its conception to its death. The technologies of birth and death now at the disposal of the body are the very instruments of making the body *disposable*. Beginning with the variety of birth control techniques, the very commencement of the human body is now made entirely contingent and programmed to serve the changing patterns of marriage and reproduction, making it more compatible with a maximum correspondence to the labor force necessary and available in the market. The same determining factors of the market and an optimum level of labor at the disposal of the globalized capital have ushered an unprecedented number of women into the labor force and thus postponed or thwarted their childbearing age. Radical discoveries in artificial insemination have not only helped couples with a variety of infertility problems but also catered to women who decide to get pregnant later in their lives. The commencement of the life of the human body has lost all its incidental spontaneity and is manufactured by the instrumental reason serving the generic forces of the market and the labor force that it can as easily generate as discard.

Technological advancements in artificial insemination have now produced generations of test-tube babies. Milestone advancements in IVF (In Vitro Fertilization) techniques have now taken the very conception of a human being outside the human body and into the transparent matter-of-factness of a medical test tube. Since the birth of Louise Browne, the first test-tube baby, in 1978, hundreds of thousands of babies have been conceived in test tubes from the sperms and eggs of any number of parental combinations, in and out of wedlock. The very inception of the human being is no longer contingent on our received conceptions of marital, conjugal, or even sexual intercourse. The physical contact of two human beings in order to make a third possible is now an outdated prerequisite. There is an artificiality, a mechanic configuration, about the human body (and what used to be called its "soul") that makes of the mysteries of the very idea of humanity and the commencement of organic life with a conscience pieces of antiquarian curiosity. We can now actually see, with our own naked eyes, the tubal moment of the conception of a human being, with all its chances and probabilities, placed right in between two other tubes, imaginatively multiplied to the whole humanity, the entirety of our history and geography of emotions, the cosmic configuration of who we are and what we are meant to do. One tube is as good as any other. We don't seem to be the parents of our own children anymore. Those tubes are their (potential and actual) parents, with all their mechanical fragility, medical cleanliness, and scientific accuracy. We can no longer look at a human body as the repertoire of the madness and civility that defines any received conception of heritage, culture, inheritance, memory, pride, shame, fear, or hope.

During the last three decades, scientists have started mixing and matching genes from one creature to another, a "genetic engineering" with unfathomable consequences for the very definition of the human body, the very foundation of its soul, the very core of its imagination. Genetic engineers are now moving genes around among plants, animals, bacteria, and human beings regularly. In cloning, scientists are using the DNA of an existing individual to create a new individual, which will inevitably forever change the very conception of what we understand by an individual human being. In somatic cell manipulation, those cells in the human body that do not pass DNA on to the next generation are now regularly manipulated in order to *correct* the genetic component of certain diseases. In germline manipulation, the DNA that is passed on is changed in the germ cells, enabling it to be inherited by successive generations. This will forever change the very notion of heritage and inheritance, character and culture, identity and memory. Some scientists are now completely fascinated by the idea of germline engineering as a way to "take evolution into our own hands" by redesigning the genetic information in our children's cells. A barrage of tests, examinations, and genetic manipulations, including gender determination, is now facilitated by amniocentesis and other related tests like sonograms and ultrasounds. The immediate purpose of such tests is to ascertain the health of the fetus and the added knowledge of its gender. But a whole slew of less innocent consequences are contingent on amniocentesis and other similar observations and manipulations of the embryo. Corporations are already banking heavily on organ repair technologies and the whole range of human cell engineering. Through embryo cloning new human parts can be created, and through reproductive cloning complete cloned individuals, like Dolly the sheep, can be manufactured. If today genetic engineers are able to clone mice, cattle, and sheep, it is only a matter of time before human cloning will be able to produce a new person who is a near genetic copy of another person. A team of American and Italian scientists is reported to be working on that project.[28] The repercussions of these scientific developments and the commercial and corporate interests they serve are not limited to a number of so-called ethicists getting together once in a while with a band of rabbis, priests, pundits, and maybe even some mullahs, reflecting on the religious and ethical implications. The commencement of life, the conception of the body, the formation of memory, the constitution of heritage, and the disposition of identity are all in a mutant state of flux. The suicidal bombers did not fall from the sky or come from another planet. They are neither deranged nor on their way to paradise. Their *disposable bodies* are integral to the unfathomable changes that have happened to the very seed of our material being.

Issues and circumstances around the conception of the human body are ultimately interrupted by debates and controversies about the fact and practice of abortion. The conception and growth of the human body is now more than ever at the mercy of cultural and economic factors affecting the possibility of aborting it at the very moment of its prenatal formation. Today the normative consequences of the vastly facilitated possibilities of abortion (now possible with a simple taking of a Mifepristone pill) far exceed the limits of religious objections or medical indifference. Abortion today is one among a succession of moments that from birth to death render the human body, and with it the commencement of the human life, utterly dispensable. This does not have anything to do with medically, morally, or culturally necessary abortions that have always existed, nor indeed has it anything to do with the whole slew of moral or religious objections one might have with abortion. The current techniques and applications of abortion are integral to the gradual mutation of the human body to a *contingent machinery* that can be assembled and dissembled at will, nurtured or aborted by way of facilitating an optimum level of efficiency in the overall operation of a life cycle modulated to serve the labor force at the disposal of the capital best. The momentous instance of the human birth is no longer a matter of *natural* (vaginal) birth. A C-section is not a rare medical emergency to save a mother and child anymore. It has become yet another instance in the radical instrumentalization of the human body, mother *and* child, at the moment of its birth, with the scheduled surgery of an abdominal birth and all the pain of giving birth numbed and eradicated with a simple epidural injection.

The variety of ways in which the conception of a human being can be manipulated is now extended to the moment of the actual, potential, or aborted birth, vaginal or C-sectioned. From inception to birth, the human body has long since lost the integrity of its Enlightenment conception borrowed with nostalgic remembrance from medieval Christianity and Platonic philosophy. The path of the posthuman body continues well beyond its conception and birth and extends into its life span. The posthuman body is no longer limited to its innate and received organs and the natural course of their organic life. Vast and miraculous improvements in the technologies and medicine of organ transplants have given the posthuman body an entirely disposable character, wherein humans might one day change any number of their bodily organs as easily as changing a tire or the battery of a car. If the cost of exchanging one particular part—a heart, a liver, a kidney, or a leg—may prove to be prohibitive by organ transplant, cloning can make it possible to exchange the whole malfunctioning body for a brand new one, while the new eugenics has made it even better by allowing us to genetically engineer our children to play basketball like Michael Jordan, compose music like Mozart, play the violin like Yehudi Menuhin, and gaze at the stars like Einstein while looking like Nicole Kidman and Tom Cruise, speaking like Jeremy Irons, and singing like Ella Fitzgerald. Furthermore, they will live forever, because at the slight suggestion of a common cold (which will remain oblivious to all these medical miracles and continue to plague the earth) such a magnificently manufactured posthuman will be immediately cloned anew, not just in one or two replicas, but in millions of them, to populate the planet and roam the universe for an eternity.[29]

But before that eternity commences, and while we are here on planet Earth, where do the living organs that are to be transplanted into the post-human bodies come from? When poor children from Asia, Africa, or Latin America are kidnapped for their organs, or they just plain *donate* them for a pittance to live on, not much moral uproar is made of the travesty. But if the same kid attaches explosives to his or her belly and blows himself or herself up in the middle of a market, the whole world is up in arms against the immorality of the act. Yet it is the same logic of the *dispensable body* of the humanoid that is at work here. It is the totality of the body, in all its frailty and dignity, that has forever lost its integrity. The simple application for a driving license now entails the option of donating our organs to potential users. Interchangeable organs, scavenger bodies, human spare-part banks, premature death, prolonged vegetal living—the *posthuman body* is an always-already transitional machine, assembled and dissembled at will. In the aftermath of 9/11, the proponents of something that belligerent US anti-intellectuals in their nightmares call *postmodernism* were on the defensive, so much so that Stanley Fish had to go on a rampage exposing the attackers' illiteracy.[30] The astonishing thing is that the phantasmagoric condition of the *posthuman body*, the real *postmodernism*, does not give a moment of pause to anyone. But the fictive guilt of a simple suggestion of ideas does.

The approximation of machines to humans is now adding momentum to the aggressive mechanization of the human body, complementing the persistent formation of the posthuman from the other way around. Hobbes would have never dreamt that the world would take his metaphor so seriously when he referred to his *Leviathan* as an "Artificiall man." Recently at an event sponsored by the Center for the Study of Science and Religion at Columbia University in New York, Professor Manuela Veloso, a computer scientist at Carnegie Mellon University, offered the example of a robotic soccer competition to demonstrate that robots can creatively collaborate and spontaneously learn. The participating robots in Professor Veloso's experiment were fully autonomous with their own respective perception, autonomous cognition, and capability to initiate actions that enable them to handle a much more complicated set of situations than those for which they are specifically programmed. Today automatic teller machines (ATMs) join RoboCops, Terminators, and the Matrix to modulate the posthuman body on a continuum between machine and human with utterly erasable borderlines. In their preface to the brilliant collection of essays they have edited, *Posthuman Bodies*, Judith Halberstam and Ira Livingston propose that "a posthuman condition is upon us, and . . . nostalgia for a humanist philosophy of self and other, human and alien, normal and queer is merely the echo of a battle that has already taken place."[31] Artificial hearts, dialysis machines, vibrators that replace people's vocal chords, staples that hold the cut and pasted veins in open heart surgery, the disfigured vista of the distinguished physicist Stephen Hawking—half-human, half-machine—are only samples and indices of a far more regenerative condition in which computers have mutated into the semiconsciousness of their users. Smart bombs with built-in cameras and computer chips are launched from submarines, airplanes, or warships; dispatched toward a target; and halfway through their flight they can detect the site already being destroyed and then change their course to go and wreak havoc on another wedding party or Red Cross depot in Afghanistan. What is a bomb and who is a human? What is a human and who is a bomb? Smart bombs think like criminal humans. Desperate humans explode like smart bombs.

In the movie adaptation of a Marvel comic character, Sam Raimi's *Spider-Man* (2002), there is an even gloomier and more ominous vision of the moral psychology that popularly informs the crossings of the animal, the human, and the machine. Peter Parker here becomes the epitome of an animal/human/machine that begins and ends in itself, with an astonishing mix of patricide and castration commencing and concluding his/its life in and of himself/itself. Peter Parker lives with his Aunt May and Uncle Ben. Where are his parents? Who was his father? We are to believe that he lost his parents when he was an infant. Thus he surfaces like a machine, assembled *ex nihilio*, with no visual or moral identification with a set of biological parents. He is a "Peter" like Peter Pan, "the boy who refuses to grow up," the chief champion of "all the lost boys" gathered in the Neverland. He is a "Parker," just parking here momentarily like a car. As a stepson for Aunt May and Uncle Ben, he has already preempted them from having their own natural offspring. He is *like* a son to them, forfeiting their own biological son. But as soon as he is mutated into the Spider-Man, the first thing he does is "inadvertently" kill his Uncle Ben, the only father-figure with which we can identify him, by letting go of a thief who ends up killing the poor uncle moments after Uncle Ben just told the Spider-Man that "with great power comes great responsibility." The next father-figure the Spider-Man is identified with is in fact his arch nemesis, the Green Goblin, the mutant form of Norman Osborn. The mad scientist has an odd but persistent paternal attitude toward Peter Parker at the expense of his own son, Harry Osborn, who happens to be Peter Parker's high school pal, college roommate, and rival in love for Mary Jane Watson. Desperate to win his father's love, Harry Osborn is bitter and hurt by his father's blatant affection for Peter Parker. But what ultimately happens to Norman Osborn? Obviously the Spider-Man kills him. But how he kills him is the critical factor here. He dodges a weapon that the Green Goblin had targeted toward him and lets the sharp gadget go straight to his father-figure's groin, killing and castrating him at the same time. What does he do to Norman Osborn's son, Harry, his own friend and buddy? He steals Mary Jane Watson from him by courting her affection. That done, the possibility of Mary Jane Watson and Harry Osborn marrying and having offspring aborted, does he marry Mary Jane? No. He abandons her barren, in a cemetery, in love with the Spider-Man, and unable to marry anyone else. Thus ends the course of procreation, the universe commencing and concluding with an animal/human/machine that enchants the world with a worldwide web of affiliations but with no point of origin, no redeeming hope, and no saving destination. Why and whence such dark, deadly, castrating, and patricidal energy in an extremely successful popular movie?

The death of the body today laughs in the face of the postmetaphysical question that Derrida puts to it: "My death—is it possible?"[32] Consider the fact and the phenomenon of euthanasia, the self-willed termination of otherwise perfectly ordinary bodies, not of suicidal bombers, but of the neighbor next door with a living will signed and sealed with his lawyer. Euthanasia today has its varieties and modalities. In what is called "passive euthanasia," physicians withdraw the medical support they have initially provided for their patients and simply let the breathing organism exhaust itself and thus hasten the death of the person. Varieties of "passive euthanasia" include the removal of life support equipment such as turning off a respirator, stopping medical procedures and medications, or even stopping food and water and allowing the person to dehydrate or starve to death. The most common form of "passive euthanasia" is to give the patient large doses of morphine to control pain, despite the likelihood that the painkiller will suppress respiration and cause death earlier than it would otherwise have happened. Such doses of painkillers have a dual effect of relieving pain and hastening death at the same time. Today the administering of such medications is regarded as perfectly legal, ethical, and even humanitarian. In "active euthanasia," meanwhile, the death of a person is caused through a direct action, in putative response to a request from that person. A well-known example was the mercy killing in 1998 of a patient with Lou Gehrig's Disease by Dr. Jack Kevorkian, a Michigan physician. The patient is said to have been frightened that the advancing disease would cause him to die a painful death. He is said to have wanted a quick, painless exit from life. Dr. Kevorkian subsequently injected controlled substances into the patient, causing his death. In yet another variation, "physician assisted suicide," a physician supplies information and/or the means of committing suicide, such as a prescription for a lethal dose of sleeping pills or a supply of carbon monoxide gas, so that the patient can easily terminate his or her own life. The term *voluntary passive euthanasia* (VPE) is now added to the pejorative verb *to kevork* to indicate the range of possibilities in willfully ending one's life. The verb *to kevork* is derived from the name of Dr.

Kevorkian, who has promoted VPE and assisted at the deaths of hundreds of patients. Originally he hooked his patients up to a machine that delivered measured doses of medications, but only after the patient pushed a button to initiate the sequence. Later, he provided carbon monoxide and a facemask so that his patient could initiate the flow of gas themselves. There is even an "involuntary euthanasia," in which a person is killed without even asking to be aided in dying. This is most often done to patients who are in what is called a "persistent vegetative state" and will probably never regain consciousness. When exactly is the moment of death? When is the body terminated? And far more important, what happens to the very conception of the body when it can be willfully, cold-bloodedly, and with calculated calmness, terminated? It is as if *death* itself has lost all its mysterious anonymity, eliminated from the moral spectrum of imagination and assimilated backward into the instrumental reason that has mechanized and programmed it into the work-span of a humanoid machinery and its usefulness.

The precursor of euthanasia was the institutionalization of what is euphemistically called the "retirement home," where aging people are regularly deposited by their (grand)children who are unwilling to take care of their elders. Parents and grandparents used to live with or at least in the immediate orbit of their children and grandchildren. But aged beyond their bodily labor and active usefulness, they became a nuisance and a burden. They were then systematically and summarily collected and deposited in "retirement homes," and babysitters and daycare centers were recruited and set up to perform the function that the (grand)parents used to perform for their (grand)children lovingly and caringly. Aging people, as the signs and symbols of approaching death, of the frailty of the body, of the *decay* that is contingent on the *generation* and *corruption* of any living organism, have been collected and institutionalized in secluded homes, under the care of a professional staff, to be visited on weekends perhaps and per chance brought home to visit their grandchildren on a Thanksgiving, a Christmas, or a Chanukah. The removal of the aging (grand)parents from daily sight was the removal of the daily sight of "death," its denial and rejection. Children assumed center stage in daily life to provide regular encounters with rejuvenation: a deliberate, almost infantile, denial of mortality. But even the physical removal of the (grand) parents from daily sight was not enough. It was not cost effective. As working machines, they had done their services and were now beyond their useful years. What was the point of keeping them alive, "in a vegetal condition," in nursery homes, in the salvage yards? "Let's get rid of them altogether," mandated the dictum of instrumental reason. Isn't that more humane, not seeing them in frailty, letting them die in dignity? Aging, mortality, and the frailty of the body became indignant—thus the Greek root of *euthanasia*: *eu* for *good* and *thanatos* for *death*; the *good death*. But the "good death" is the pathological denial of death, the public disappearance of death, the death of death—the fear of mortality bending forward to meet the logic of instrumental reason at the service of the carnivorous capital. Cemeteries disappeared from public space and receded to remote and outlandish locations, scarcely visited by living bodies. Earthly burials gave way to cremation: the burning and final disappearance of the dead body, a holocaust testimonial to the Holocaust. The configuration of the *posthuman body* is coterminous with a universal denial of death, a fear of mortality put at the service of the mad logic of capital, the body made disposable, dispensable, and expendable, like any old Chevy with untenable retail value, unworthy of the valuable time of a used car salesman.

The visual vanishing of death from collective view corroborated and corresponded with the public disappearance of labor. The astonishingly popular television series *The Honeymooners*—featuring a New York City bus driver (Ralph Kramden/Jackie Gleason); his best buddy (Ed Norton/Art Carney), who is a manual laborer in New York sewer system; and their respective housewives (Alice/Audrey Meadows and Trixie/Joyce Randolph)—soon disappeared from popular imagination and were replaced by *Dallas* and the misadventures of the oil tycoon J. R. Ewing and his Texan clan of billionaires. The quadruple characters of Ralph, Alice, Ed, and Trixie from *The Honeymooners*, meanwhile, were catapulted into the Stone Age and reinvented in *The Flintstones*, where the characters of Fred and Wilma replicate Ralph and Alice, while Barney and Betty echo Ed and Trixie. The popular celebration of a bus driver and a sewer system worker in Brooklyn between 1960 and 1966, when the original series initially ran, were no longer compatible with the Ronald Reagan image of unfathomable wealth, which in turn gave rise to the obscenely rich J. R. Ewing's escapades in *Dallas*, which ran between 1978 and 1991 to a worldwide audience of some three-hundred-million people. It then gave rise to its offspring *Knotts Landing*, which ran for yet another 14 years, based on the *Dallas* characters of Gary and Valene Ewing. As workers disappeared from public scenes and were dispatched to the Stone Age, while rich millionaires in Dallas and yuppies in Philadelphia (the *Thirtysomething* show that ran from 1987 to 1991) came to the fore, the phenomenon of the suburbanization of American society intensified, which in turn gave rise to megasized shopping malls that categorically cut the production line of commercial goods off from public view. Shopping malls are spick-and-span marketing Meccas—clean and cool in summer, warm and cozy in winter—where consumer goods are staged for sale with not a trace of the manufacturing process about them. If Marx in the nineteenth century thought capitalism is conducive to commodity fetishism, this fetishization of consumer goods has to have a far more phantasmagoric term for itself. Ever-newer brands, shiny and glossy in shopping mall windows, became the simulacra of everlasting youth, visibly and symbolically cut off from the manufacturing labor that had given birth to them. Ever-newer products eradicated the signs of aging in commodities. Repair shops disappeared from public view with the same logic that health care systems and HMOs mechanized the human body, made it disposable, and thus forever eradicated the actual human body as the site of its medical diagnosis, replacing it with a barrage of mechanical records of its tests, trials, and tribulations.

Thus neither the commencement nor the duration, neither the term nor the termination of the bodily life has been left to anything remotely resembling what used to be called "the natural course" of a lifetime. People change their sex back and forth from one gender to another, implant genitalia and breasts or else surgically remove and change what they have. Plastic surgery now sculpts the body of fat people into supermodels' figures, planting new breasts, enlarging their penises, downsizing their noses, pulling up their facial skin, and tucking in their bellies. Human bodies in the hands of plastic surgeons are like the Biblical clay in the hands of what used to be called *God*; surgeons reform and reshape them before breathing life back into them. The whole world is inundated with disposable bodies, from birth to death subject to a whole industry of fabrication, engineering, assemblage, dissembling, salvaging, storing, revamping, improving, renovating, cloning, exchanging, and mutating from one assemblage to another. The hearts, livers, and kidneys of African, Latino, and Asian kids are now in the bodies of investment bankers, corporate executives, certified public accountants, litigation lawyers, Washington lobbyists, secretaries of defense, undersecretaries of intelligence, ministers of information, and vice presidents of arts and sciences in major Ivy League universities.

The State Control of the Posthuman Body

The posthuman body has become amorphous in correspondence with the amorphous texture of the globalized capital and the postmodern state that now claims the body as the sole site of its self-legitimizing violence. The principal role of the state in the battle over abortion, gay and lesbian rights, and the death penalty is far less about the (im)morality of the acts, as Christian fundamentalists in the United States like to think, than about the state control of the posthuman body, from birth to death. The physician-assisted suicide has put the Oath of Hypocrites to test but has tested far more seriously the power of the state to allow or prevent a body's entrance and exit into the political site of power. The self-exploding body, the *corpus anarchicum*, is in defiance of the postmodern state that draws its legitimacy from the legislated regimentation of the posthuman body as its principal site of violence. *Corpus anarchicum* is one rhetorical moment in the logic and lunacy of the *corpus amorphous*, when the body self-explodes in its defiance of its state of being. The suicidal bomber is the ultimate, very last sign of a whole new countermetaphysics of the posthuman body: the end of Enlightenment modernity and its glorification of the human body. Had the suicidal bomber not been so radically demonized, exoticized, Islamicized, Orientalized, and dismissed by an army of mercenary Orientalists, illiterate experts, and embedded journalists, we would have sooner seen it as the supreme sign, the very last indication, of the radically instrumentalized reason corrupted into necessity, concluded in the making of the *disposable body*.

The resistances of the *posthuman body* to its mutation into the singular site of state violence now assumes an *amorphous* disposition in art and an *anarchic* character in politics—thus the connection between the aesthetics of our defiance and the politics of our despair.

As for hope, let me conclude with a voice above mine: a poet mourning the suicidal death of another; Mahmoud Darwish remembering Khalil Hawi—the poet of a homeless people honoring the poet of a disembodied land; a Palestinian embracing a Lebanese:

> Where shall I go this sunset? I'm weary of this staircase here. I'm weary of that chatter there. Over there is the balcony of the poet who foresaw the fall of everything and fixed a date for his own end. Khalil Hawi took a hunting rifle and hunted himself, not only because he wanted not to give evidence for or against anything but also because he wanted not to be a witness for or against anything. He was weary of the state of decay, weary of looking over a bottomless abyss. What's poetry? Poetry is to write this cosmic silence, final and total. He was alone, without an idea, a woman, a poem, or a promise. Was there anything left after Beirut fell under siege? Any horizon? Any song?[33]

Conclusion

A Postmortem

People demand the overthrow of the regime!

—The chief slogan of the Arab Spring

Mahmoud Darwish (1941–2008) did not live to see the Arab Spring. Is the Arab Spring the opening horizon toward which his emancipatory poetry always looked—with hope, and in desperation?

The death by suicide of the young Tunisian man Mohamed Bouazizi reassembles the bodies of the Arab and the Muslim for a renewed pact with history. In less than a year after the suicide of Mohamed Bouazizi, in late October 2011, hundreds of Yemeni women burned their veils in angry defiance against their government's suppression of their democratic uprising. "The women, among the most conservatively dressed in the Arab world," reports indicated, "hurled their black, full-body garments into a pile in the capital Sanaa, doused them with oil and set them ablaze, crying: 'Who protects Yemeni women from the crimes of thugs?'"[1] By that time the Yemenis had been actively pursuing their democratic aspirations for some ten months, having suffered many casualties and much hardship, but their ruling regime, headed by Ali Abdullah Saleh, was unrelenting. "It was a highly symbolic act," the reports said of the burning of the veils, "that reflected the fury of many Yemenis at President Ali Abdullah Saleh's harsh handling of anti-regime protests that have escalated from peaceful street demonstrations calling for reform into bloody clashes for dominance between rival elites and the government."

The public spectacle of burning veils had far more serious implications than just calling attention to a particular tyranny. The act was not in defiance of voluntary veiling as such, when and if people had opted to wear it voluntarily. Tawakkol Karman, a leading revolutionary woman challenging the power of the regime in Yemen, was arrested in Paris and fined because of her veiling. (The fact that the Norwegians had given her the Nobel Peace Prize was more to their credit than to hers.) The symbolic burning of the veils signaled not a gesture against veiling as such but the liberation of the *corpus anarchicum* from a politics of despair, flexing its muscles in the inaugural moments of a global uprising.

Between the suicide of Mohammad Bouazizi and the burning of the Yemeni women's veils, the bodies of the Arab and Muslim had been liberated from domestic tyranny and foreign domination alike. The *corpus anarchicum* had remained the same, but instead of just *resisting* the ruling regime, denying it a site of legitimacy, it was now dismantling it. At the writing of this conclusion late in 2011, the Arab Spring has challenged the status quo, dismantled the ruling regimes of three Arab states (Tunisia, Egypt, and Libya), and endangered the survival of the rest. The globalized condition of the *posthuman body* remains amorphous in correspondence with the amorphous capital and the postmodern state that continues to claim it as the sole site of its self-legitimizing violence. But the Arab Spring had announced the end of the condition of postcoloniality as far as the production of ideologies of resistance was concerned. The self-exploding body, the *corpus anarchicum*, had remained in defiance of the postmodern state and yet (and here is the rub) it had been liberated from its delusion of postcoloniality. The body of Bouazizi self-immolated in defiance of its state of being, still the ultimate, very last, sign of a whole new countermetaphysics of the *posthuman body*, the end of Enlightenment modernity and its glorification of the human body as the site of its imagined liberations.

In the span of a decade, between 2001 and 2011, as Mohamed Atta was denounced, Mohammad Bouazizi was valorized, credited with an emancipatory moment of a world on the verge of a global uprising. This was not just the year of the Arab Spring. It also brought the European Summer and an American Fall—season after season of revolt against the status quo, whereby the Tahrir Square in Cairo had assumed iconic significance for what was now called the "Occupy Wall Street" movement, echoed around the globe. Though happening in multiple contexts, something about these uprisings resonated globally. "Dear young man who died on the fourth day of this turbulent 2011, dear Mohammed Bouazizi," began a letter by Rebecca Solnit, an American Occupy Wall Street activist, addressing the diseased Tunisian peddler, "I want to write you about an astonishing year—with three months yet to run. I want to tell you about the power of despair and the margins of hope and the bonds of civil society." From a politics of despair to a politics of hope, the *corpus anarchicum* had transmigrated from a site of resistance to a site of defiance—now seeking to dismantle the ruling regime altogether. From the ashes of Mohamed Atta's politics of despair had come memorabilia for Japanese tourists, but from the ashes of Mohamed Bouazizi's defiant politics of hope sprouted the Arab Spring, which branched out around the globe. Hope had come home to roost; *corpus anarchicum* was at home in the world.

> I wish you could see the way that your small life and large death became a catalyst for the fall of so many dictators in what is known as the Arab Spring. We are now in some sort of an American Fall. Civil society here has suddenly hit the ground running, and we are all headed toward a future no one imagined when you, a young Tunisian vegetable seller capable of giving so much, who instead had so much taken from you, burned yourself to death to protest your

impoverished and humiliated state. You lit yourself on fire on December 17, 2010, exactly nine months before Occupy Wall Street began. Your death two weeks later would be the beginning of so much . . . Who could have imagined a Middle East without Ben Ali of Tunisia, without Mubarak, without Gaddafi? And yet here we are, in the unimaginable world . . . If the Arab Spring was the decade-later antithesis of 9/11, a largely nonviolent, publicly inclusive revolt that forced the Western world to get over its fearful fantasy that all young Muslims are terrorists, jihadis, and suicide bombers, then Occupy Wall Street, which began six days after the 10th anniversary of that nightmarish day in September, is the other half of 9/11 in New York.[2]

NOTES

INTRODUCTION

1. Omar Khayyam, *Ruba'iyat of Omar Khayyam*, trans. Edward FitzGerald. introduction by Dick Davis (London: Penguin, 1995).

CHAPTER 1

1. See Frantz Fanon, *A Dying Colonialism* (New York: Grove Press, 1965), 35–67.
2. Ibid., 42. Emphasis added.
3. For a groundbreaking essay on the identification of the feminine body with body politic that predates Fanon's and reverses the gaze toward the French woman, see Lynn Hunt's "The Many Bodies of Marie Antoinette: Political Pornography and the Problem of the Feminine in the French Revolution," in her edited volume *Eroticism and the Body Politic* (Baltimore: Johns Hopkins University Press, 1991), 108–30.
4. Fanon 1965: 27–30.
5. Ibid., 40.
6. Ibid., 36.
7. Ibid., 37.
8. As persuasively argued by Nicholas Dirks in *Castes of Mind* (Princeton: Princeton University Press, 2001).
9. As a case in point, see Karin Andriolo's "Murder by Suicide: Episodes from Muslim History," *American Anthropologist* 104, no. 3 (2002): 736–42 for an examination of three examples of suicidal violence in Islamic history by way of explaining the events of 9/11.
10. Andriolo 2002: 741. Frankly, I do not see much of a difference between this anthropological study and a CRS (Congressional Research Services) report for the US Congress, titled "Terrorists and Suicide Attack" (August 28, 2003; available through CRS Web, Order Code RL 32058) prepared by a certain Audrey Kurth Cronin, "Specialist in Terrorism" in the "Foreign Affairs, Defense, and Trade Division." Though equally centered on Islamic cases of suicidal violence, Cronin's study is, in fact, far more open-minded—even neutral—in its findings than Andriolo's essay.
11. Edward W. Said, *After the Last Sky: Palestinian Lives*, with photographs by Jean Mohr (New York: Pantheon Books, 1985), 79.
12. Ibid., 80–81.
13. Ibid., 82–83.
14. Ibid., 83–84.

15. Mahmoud Darwish, *Memory for Forgetfulness: August, Beirut, 1982*, trans. Ibrahim Muhawi (Berkeley: University of California Press, 1995).
16. I was the intermediary between the UNESCO officials in New York and Makhmalbaf in Tehran.
17. For a detailed reading of Forough Farrokhzad's *The House Is Black*, see the first chapter in my *Masters and Masterpieces of Iranian Cinema* (Washington, DC: Mage Publishers, 2007).
18. See Richard Warry, "Conjoined Twin Surgery Highly Risky," *BBC News*, July 8, 2003, http://news.bbc.co.uk/2/hi/health/3053862.stm.
19. Ramin Ahmadi's essay was published on the Gooya website (http://www.gooya.com) in July 2003. Ahmadi's legitimate criticism of the Islamic Republic later degenerated into his active collaboration with US authorities to document human rights abuses in the Islamic Republic. No attention was paid to similar, if not worse, abuses by Americans in Iraq, Afghanistan, and elsewhere. He is now an entirely discredited collaborator and native informer jeopardizing the cause of human rights in Iran.
20. On the rise of the Holocaust industry, see the extraordinary work of Norman Finkelstein, *The Holocaust Industry: Reflections on the Exploitation of Jewish Suffering* (London: Verso, 2001).

CHAPTER 2

1. Chapter "The Story," The Qur'an.
2. Sixth/Twelfth century Qur'anic commentator *Kashf al-Asrar wa 'Uddat al-'Abrar*, explaining the Nocturnal Journey (*Mi'raj*) of the Prophet to the Heavens to visit God the Unseen.
3. Sixth/Twelfth century Qur'anic commentator *Ruh al-Jinan wa Ruh al-Janan*, explaining why Joseph smashed the idols in his prison.
4. Qur'an 1:1. I use Marmaduke Pickthall's translation in *The Glorious Koran: A Bi-Lingual Edition with English Translation, Introduction and Notes* (London: George Allen & Unwin Fine Books, 1976).
5. Qur'an 2:1–4.
6. Such as the sixth/twelfth century Qur'anic commentator Shaykh Abu al-Futuh al-Razi in his *Ruh al-Jinan wa Ruh al-Janan* (Qom: Ayatollah al-Uzma Mar'ashi Najafi Library, 1404/1983), vol. 1, 39.
7. Al-Razi 1404/1983: vol. 1, 41.
8. On the anxiety of not being able to see ourselves, see Jean-Paul Sartre, *Being and Nothingness* (New York: Gramercy Books, 1956), 339–51; 351–59.
9. See the Qur'an 2:87; 2:136; 2:253; among many other verses.
10. Qur'an 3:59.
11. Qur'an 4:171.
12. Kevin Hart, *The Trespass of the Sign: Deconstruction, Theology and Philosophy* (Cambridge: Cambridge University Press, 1989), 7.
13. Ibid., 8.
14. Ibid.
15. Qur'an 2:2.
16. Qur'an 68:2.
17. Qur'an 96:1–4.
18. Hart 1989: 5. Emphasis added.

19. Jacques Derrida, *Of Grammatology*, trans. Gayatri Chakravorty Spivak (Baltimore: Johns Hopkins University Press, 1976), 49.
20. Ibid., 50.
21. Qur'an 2:115.
22. Qur'an 2:272.
23. Qur'an 28:88.
24. Compare, for example, the Naqsh-e Jahan Square in Isfahan to what, during the Shah's time, was called Shahyad Square in Tehran. At the center of the square in Isfahan stood nothing but a shallow pool. At the center of Shahyad Square was a resurrectionary monument. The Isfahan square is Islamic because it is a visual reminder of the Presence of the Absent (God); the Shahyad Square is imperial because it reminds of the Absence of the Present (the monarch—and thus its name, Shahyad, the royal memorial). The Islamic Revolution toppled the monarchy but was already too imperialized in its Persian imagination to notice the paradox of Shahyad Square and thought by renaming it the Azadi (Freedom) Square, it could Islamize it. It did not. The sign of the square defeats the signifier of its name.
25. Qur'an 12:1.
26. Qur'an 12:2.
27. Qur'an 12:3.
28. Qur'an 45:23.
29. Qur'an 45:24.
30. Qur'an 12:7.
31. Qur'an 12:6.
32. Qur'an 12:17.
33. Qur'an 12:21.
34. Qur'an 12:22.
35. In this reading of Joseph's story, I have deliberately avoided biblical scholarship on its Hebrew version because the Qur'anic version should be read independently. But I cannot refrain from expressing my astonishment when I see that the leitmotif of "Face" is identified as the key thematic element in the Hebrew Yaakov cycle that comes immediately before Yosef and then the story of Yosef itself being identified as follows: "Even 'face,' the key word of the Yaakov cycle that often meant something negative, is here given a kinder meaning, as the resolution to Yaakov's life." Everett Fox, *The Five Books of Moses: The Schocken Bible, Volume 1* (New York: Schocken Books, 1983), 173.
36. Qur'an 12:23.
37. Qur'an 12:24.
38. Qur'an 12:24.
39. Al-Razi 1404/1983: vol. 3, 126.
40. Qur'an 12:2.
41. Qur'an 12:30.
42. Qur'an 12:31.
43. For an account of the Kharijite subsect of the Maymuniyya excluding the Joseph chapter from their version of the Qur'an, see Richard Bell and W. Montgomery Watt, *Introduction to the Qur'an* (Edinburgh: Edinburgh University Press, 1970), 46.
44. See al-Razi 1404/1983: vol. 3, 128.

45. For al-Maybudi's account, see Abu al-Fadl Rashid al-Din al-Maybudi, *Kashf al-Asrar wa 'Uddat al-'Abrar*, ed. Ali Asghar Hekmat (Tehran: Amir Kabir, 1339/1960), vol. 5, 61.
46. There are wonderful folkloric accounts of how we have the "cuts" in the palm of our hands precisely where our ancestral mothers cut their hands. When they saw Joseph and were so distracted by his beauty, instead of cutting the orange they held in their hands, they cut their hands. In such accounts, every time we look at our own hands, we are, in effect, reminded of the beauty of Joseph, that one time Truth manifested Itself in its beautiful Face and then had to hide Itself.
47. Hart 1989: 12. Emphasis added.
48. See Husserl's *Logical Investigations*, trans. J. N. Findlay (London: Routledge and Kegan Paul, 1970): investigation 1, chapter 1, §1.
49. Jaques Derrida, *Speech and Phenomena and Other Essays on Husserl's Theory of Signs* (Evanston: Northwestern University Press, 1973), 17.
50. Qur'an 12:35.
51. Qur'an 12:40.
52. Al-Razi 1404/1983: vol. 3, 134.
53. Ibid., 147.
54. Ibid. The reference to the meaning of the name Nu'man is missing in al-Razi's account.
55. Qur'an 12:84.
56. Qur'an 12:87.
57. Hart 1989: 12.
58. Jacques Derrida, *Positions*, trans. Alan Bass (Chicago: University of Chicago Press, 1981), 19.
59. Ibid.
60. Derrida 1973: 18.
61. Derrida 1981: 19.
62. Qur'an 12:93. Pickthall adds a parenthetical "(again)" before "a seer." This does not appear in the original *ya'ti basiran*. It is important that we see Jacob as gaining a new kind of (in)sight.
63. Qur'an 12:94–95.
64. Qur'an 12:96. I have kept Pickthall's "he became a seer once more," but *fa-artadda basiran* is better translated as "he returned to being a seer." Again, the point is that there is a constitutional difference between the way Jacob sees now and the way he used to see. Joseph's Face, the Sign of the Unseen, is at stake.
65. Qur'an 12:102.
66. Qur'an 12:105–6. I have kept Pickthall's "How many a portent," but *ka-ayyin min 'ayatin* is far more accurately translated "How many a sign."
67. Qur'an 12:108.
68. James Hoopes, ed., *Writings on Semiotics by Charles Sanders Peirce: Peirce on Signs* (Chapel Hill: University of North Carolina Press, 1991), 141.
69. Hoopes 1991: 141.
70. Quoted by Derrida in *Margins of Philosophy*, trans. Alan Bass, with additional notes (Chicago: University of Chicago Press, 1982), 83–84. Emphasis added.
71. Ibid., 84.
72. Quoted in ibid.
73. Al-Maybudi 1339/1960: 58.

74. Ibid. Zoleikha's description of Joseph's facial beauty precedes a particularly erotic moment in the scene of seduction that from Ibn Abbas forward most commentators have reported. In such mystical commentaries as that of al-Maybudi, Zoleikha, in fact, gradually assumes a very positive character.
75. Al-Razi 1404/1983: vol. 3, 134.
76. Qur'an 12:106.
77. The most extensive examination of the pagan practice of worshipping *Allah* as one among many deities can be found in W. Montgomery Watt's "Belief in a 'High God' in Pre-Islamic Arabia," *Journal of Semitic Studies* 16 (1971): 35–40, and "The Qur'an and Belief in a 'High God,'" *Proceedings of the Ninth Congress of the Union Européenne des Arabisants et Islamisants* (Leiden: E. J. Brill, 1981), 327–33, and finally in his *Mohammed's Mecca: History in the Qur'an* (Edinburgh: Edinburgh University Press, 1988).
78. Qur'an 29:61–65.
79. Qur'an 39:38.
80. Qur'an 12:40.
81. Qur'an 23:84–90.
82. Qur'an 53:1.
83. Shaykh Abu Ali al-Fadl ibn al-Hasan al-Tabarsi, *Majma' al-Bayan fî Tafsir al-Qur'ân* (Beirut: Dar al-Ma'rifah, 1406/1986), vols. 9–10, 260.
84. Al-Maybudi 1339/1960: vol. 9, 353. The prophet reportedly became angry and cursed "Atbah Abi Lahab and asked God to let loose a beast upon him." Atbah was soon killed by a lion on a business trip with his father Abu Lahab in Syria.
85. Qur'an 53:2–3.
86. Qur'an 53:4.
87. Qur'an 53:5–6.
88. Al-Maybudi 1339/1960: vol. 9, 355; al-Tabarsi 1406/1986: vols. 9–10, 261.
89. In correspondence with the very famous incidence with Adam in the Qur'an "And He taught Adam all the names . . ." (2:31).
90. Qur'an 53:6–10.
91. Al-Tabarsi 1406/1986: vols. 9–10, 262. Emphasis added.
92. Qur'an 32:9.
93. Qur'an 53:11–12.
94. Qur'an 3:154; 5:50; 33:33; 48:26.
95. Qur'an 53:13–18.
96. Al-Tabarsi 1406/1986: vols. 9–10, 264.
97. Al-Maybudi 1339/1960: vol. 9, 376–78.
98. Al-Maybudi 1339/1960: vol. 5, 482. Original emphasis.
99. Al-Maybudi 1339/1960: vol. 5, 483.
100. Qur'an 53:19–22.
101. For an example, see Watt 1988: 30, 87.
102. Qur'an 4:171.
103. Qur'an 112:1–4.
104. See Bell and Watt 1970: 55; and Watt 1988: 86.
105. See Muhammad Reza Jalali Na'ini's introduction to Abu Mundhir Hisham ibn Muhammad Kalbî's *Kitab al-Asnam or Tankis al-Asnam*, trans. Muhammad Reza Jalali Na'ini (Tehran: Nashr-e No, 1364/1985), 21–24.
106. Quoted in Bell and Watt 1970: 55, these verses are "Satanic Verses" because, according to some accounts, the Prophet first uttered and then retracted them, explaining that he subsequently realized that Satan had revealed them to him. A

slightly different version is in Watt 1988: 86: "These are the *gharaniq* exalted; their intercession is to be hoped for; such as they forget not." *Gharânîq*, meaning "high-flying cranes," is an apparent reference to these three deities.

107. Watt 1988: 86.
108. Na'ini's introduction to Kalbî 1364/1985*:* 22.
109. For an account of the economic changes predicating the rise of Islam, see W. Montgomery Watt's *Muhammad at Mecca* (Oxford: Oxford University Press, 1953); and *Muhammad at Medina* (Oxford: Oxford University Press, 1956). Equally insightful is Watt's *Islam and the Integration of Society* (London: Northwestern University Press, 1961), especially 4–42.
110. Watt 1988: 30, 87.
111. See W. Montgomery Watt 1988 for an account of Arabia at the time of the Prophet. One of the earliest and most authoritative primary sources about the history of Mecca prior to the rise of Islam is Abu al-Walid al-Azraqi, *Akhbar Mecca*, ed. Rûshdî Salih Malhas, trans. Mahmud Mahdavi Damghani (Tehran: Nashr-e Bonyad, 1368/1989).
112. Ibn Khaldun realized this phenomenon and treated it in his *al-Muqaddimah*. See Ibn Khaldun, *The Muqaddimah: An Introduction to History*, trans. Frantz Rosenthal (Princeton: Princeton University Press, 1958); vol. 1, 264ff.; vol. 2, 302ff.
113. Qur'an 96:1–3.
114. Derrida 1974: 11.
115. Qur'an 17:13–14.
116. Derrida 1974: 11.
117. Qur'an 96:3–5.
118. Al-Maybudi, 1339/1960: vol. 5, 482. Original emphasis.
119. See Mawlana Jalal al-Din Rumi, *Mathnavi*, ed. R. A. Nicholson (Tehran: Amir Kabir, 1363/1984), vol. 1, bk. 1: 194–99, vv. 3157–227.
120. Rumi 1363/1984: 194–99, vv. 3200–202.

CHAPTER 3

1. Afsaneh Najmabadi's "Veiled Discourse—Unveiled Bodies," *Feminist Studies* 19, no. 3 (Fall 1993): 487–518, is a pioneering study of the disciplinary modification of the female body in the course of modernization in Iran and the corresponding veiling of the language women spoke. Najmabadi's central insight in this essay is the disciplinary modulation of the unveiled body that began to be compensated by the equally disciplinary modification of the language the women spoke. As the body becomes relatively unveiled, the language becomes metaphorically veiled. A more comprehensive study of the disciplinary modulations of the Iranian body in modernity is Darius M. Rejali's brilliant study *Torture and Modernity: Self, Society, and State in Modern Iran* (Boulder, CO: Westview Press, 1994), 43–61.
2. Friedrich Nietzsche, *Beyond Good and Evil: Prelude to a Philosophy of the Future*, trans. R. J. Hollingdale, with an introduction and commentary (London: Penguin, 1973), 13.
3. See Frithjof Schuon, *Sufism: Veil and Quintessence* (Bloomington: World Wisdom Books, 1979), 6–7.
4. Schuon 1979: 12.

5. Hamideh Sedghi in her *Women and Politics in Iran: Veiling, Unveiling, and Reveiling* (Cambridge: Cambridge University Press, 2007) has examined these alternating developments in detail.
6. For a preliminary assessment of this assumption at the heart of the European Union, see Etienne Balibar's *We, the People of Europe? Reflections on Transnational Citizenship* (Princeton: Princeton University Press, 2004), 225ff.
7. Ibid., 225.
8. See Paolo Fabbri, "Deformities of the Face," in *Identity and Alterity: Figures of the Body 1895–1995: La Biennale di Venezia, 46—esposizione internazionale d'Arte* (Venice: La Biennale di Venezia Marsilo, 1995), 29.
9. Ibid.
10. Ibid., 31.
11. See Günther Metken, "Behind the Mirror: Notes from the Portrait in the Twentieth Century," in *Identity and Alterity: Figures of the Body 1895–1995: La Biennale di Venezia, 46. Esposizione internazionale d'Arte* (Venice: La Biennale di Venezia Marsilo, 1995), 35.
12. See Hamid Naficy, "Veiled Visions/Powerful Presences: Women in Post Revolutionary Iranian Cinema," in *In the Eye of the Storm: Women in Post-Revolutionary Iran*, eds. Mahnaz Afkhami and Erika Friedl, with a forward by Robin Morgan (Syracuse: Syracuse University Press, 1994), 136.
13. Ibid., 136–37.
14. Ibid., 136.
15. Frantz Fanon's *A Dying Colonialism* (New York: Grove Press, 1965), Albert Memmi's *The Colonizer and the Colonized* (Boston: Beacon Press, 1965), W. E. B. DuBois's *The Souls of Black Folk* (New York: Dover, 1989), Ashis Nandy's *The Intimate Enemy: Loss and Recovery of Self under Colonialism* (Oxford: Oxford University Press, 1989), and Ngugi Wa Thiongo's *Decolonizing the Mind: The Politics of Language in African Literature* (New York: Heineman, 1986) are chief among a few classics that have started this reflection on the critical formation of Self under colonial conditions.
16. See William O. Beeman's *Language, Status, and Power in Iran* (Bloomington: Indiana University Press, 1986).
17. Compare Naficy 1994: 136 with Beeman 1986: 10–13.
18. For an exemplary study of the cinematic construction of the feminine body, see Camilla Griggers, "Phantom and Reel Projections: Lesbian and the (Serial) Killing-Machine," in *Posthuman Bodies*, eds. Judith Halberstam and Ira Livingston (Bloomington: Indiana University Press, 1995), 162–76.
19. Naficy 1994: 136.
20. See Mary Sheriff, "Fragonard's Erotic Mothers and the Politics of Reproduction," in *Eroticism and the Body Politic*, ed. Lynn Hunt (Baltimore: Johns Hopkins University Press, 1991), 14.
21. See Jean-Paul Sartre, *Being and Nothingness* (New York: Gramercy Books, 1956), 351.
22. Ibid.
23. Ibid.
24. See Lynn Hunt "The Many Bodies of Marie Antoinette: Political Pornography and the Problem of the Feminine in the French Revolution," in her edited volume *Eroticism and the Body Politic* (Baltimore: Johns Hopkins University Press, 199), 41–62.

25. Ibid., 57. Anne Deneys's conception of the "sign" and the "signifier" is flawed, but her point is well made.
26. This film is also known as *A Moment of Innocence*, a name that MK2, the French distributor of the film, has given to it, contrary to Makhmalbaf's own wishes.
27. See Caroline Walker Bynum, *The Resurrection of the Body in Western Christianity, 200–1336* (New York: Columbia University Press, 1995), 343.
28. See Hunt 1991: 126.
29. Ibid.
30. See Abu al-Hasan Ali ibn Uthman al-Jullabi al-Hujwiri al-Ghaznawi, *Kashf al-Mahjub*, ed. V. Zhokowski, with an introduction by Qasem Ansari (Tehran: Zaban va Farhang-e Iran, 1979), 341–404.
31. Qur'an 2:3.
32. Qur'an 11:49.
33. Qur'an 6:59.
34. See Jacques Le Goff, "Head or Heart? The Political Use of Body Metaphors in the Middle Ages," in *Fragments for a History of the Human Body*, ed. Michel Feher (New York: Zone Books, 1989), 23.
35. See Martin Jay, "Sartre, Merleau-Ponty, and the Search for a New Ontology of Sight," in *Modernity and the Hegemony of Vision*, ed. David Michael Levin (Berkeley: University of California Press, 1993), 176–77.
36. Qur'an 2:212.
37. Qur'an 3:14.
38. See Abu Ya'qub Sajistani 1979: 2.

CHAPTER 4

1. *The Financial Times* (Weekend, July 31/August 1, 1999).
2. Ralph Rugoff , "The Internationalist Aesthetic, From Santa Fe," *LA Weekly*, August 12, 1999, http://www.laweekly.com/content/printVersion/31194/.
3. There is an English translation of Shaykh Ahmad Ahsa'i's *Kitab Sharh al-Ziyarah* in Henry Corbin's *Spiritual Body and Celestial Earth: From Mazdean Iran to Shi'ite Iran* (Princeton: Princeton University Press, 1977), 180–221. The question of bodily resurrection is, of course, not limited to Islamic metaphysics and has a long tradition in other Abrahamic religions. For the most comprehensive study of the subject, see the magisterial work of Caroline Walker Bynum, *The Resurrection of the Body in Western Christianity, 200–1336* (New York: Columbia University Press, 1995). Ahsa'i's division of the human body into *jism* and *jasad* is remarkably similar to Edmund Husserl's distinction between *Leib* and *Körper*—although, for each of these two categories, Ahsa'i has two subcategories. See Edmund Husserl's "Material Things in Their Relation to the Aesthetic Body," in *The Body*, ed. Donn Welton (Malden, MA: Blackwell, 1999), 11–23.
4. Ahsa'i 1977: 183.
5. Ibid., 184.
6. Ibid., 185.
7. This is an abbreviated version of a more elaborate account of Ahsa'i's theory of the body. See Ahsa'i 1977: 176–89 for the full account.
8. Ibid., 184.
9. Ibid., 186.

10. Ibid.
11. Caroline Walker Bynum has thoroughly documented this in the case of medieval Christianity. See her *Fragmentation and Redemption: Essays on Gender and the Human Body in Medieval Religion* (New York: Zone Books, 1992), 183: "From the early Middle Ages down into modern times, pieces of dead holy people have been revered as the loci of the sacred."
12. Bynum has also documented the assumption of this affinity among medieval Christian mystics. See "The Body of Christ in the Later Middle Ages: A Reply to Leo Steinberg," in Bynum 1992: 79–117, especially the section "Genitality and Sexuality," 85–88.
13. Bynum has studied this relationship in the medieval Christian context in "The Female Body and Religious Practice in the Later Middle Ages," in Bynum 1992:181–238.

CHAPTER 5

1. The details of this match and the banning of Iranian women from watching it while the Irish women were allowed made it to the international news. See, for example, the November 5, 2001, report from http://www.sportsillustrated.cnn.com.
2. For historical references to Tahereh Qorrat al-Ayn and her extraordinary significance as a revolutionary activist, see Peter Smith, *The Babi and Baha'i Religions: From Messianic Shi'ism to a World Religion* (Cambridge: Cambridge University Press, 1987), 16–17; *inter alia*. See also Abbas Amanat, *Resurrection and Renewal: The Making of the Babi Movement in Iran, 1844–1850* (Ithaca: Cornell University Press, 1989), 303–12; *inter alia*; and Hamid Dabashi, *Shi'ism: A Religion of Protest* (Cambridge, MA: Harvard University Press, 2010): chapter 6.
3. For a collection of Parvin E'tesami's poetry, see her *A Nightingale's Lament: Selections from the Poems and Fables of Parvin E'tesami (1907–1941)*, trans. Heshmat Moayyad and A. Margaret Madelung (Lexington, KY: Mazda Publishers, 1985).
4. From Forough Farrokhzad's reflections on her own poetry in *Gozineh-ye Ash'ar* [Selected Poems] (Tehran: Morvarid Publishers, 1369/1990). A pioneering study of Iranian women's writing with exceptionally insightful readings of their poetry can be found in Farzaneh Milani's *Veils and Words: The Emerging Voices of Iranian Women Writers* (Syracuse: Syracuse University Press, 1992). Equally noteworthy is Farzaneh Milani's other essay on Forough Farrokhzad, "Paradise Regained: Farrokhzad's 'Garden Conquered,'" *Forough Farrokhzad: A Quarter of a Century Later*, ed. Michael Craig Hillmann (Austin: Literature East and West 24, 1988), 91–104.
5. Forough Farrokhzad, "Window," in *Iman Biyavarim beh Aghaz-e Fasl-e Sard* [Let's Believe in the Commencement of the Cold Season!] (Tehran: Morvarid Publishers, 1352/1973), 59–65. All translations of Forough Farrokhzad's poems are mine. For a more comprehensive essay on Forough Farrokhzad's poetry, see my essay "Forough Farrokhzad and Formative Forces of Iranian Culture," in *Forough Farrokhzad: A Quarter of a Century Later*, ed. Michael Craig Hillmann (Austin: Literature East and West 24, 1988):7–36.

6. See Jamal Omid, *Farhang-e Cinema-ye Iran* (Tehran: Negah Publishers, 1366/1987), vol. 1, 48–49. See also Mostafa Zamani-Niya, *Farhang-e Cinema-ye Iran* (Tehran: Adineh Publishers, 1363/1984), 126, who also identifies the director only as "Shahla."
7. Mas'ud Mehrabi, *Tarikh-e Cinema-ye Iran* (Tehran: Film Publishers, 1363/1984), 79.
8. Among the major filmmakers, Abbas Kiarostami is the only one who is now also a published poet. Among the major poets, Ahmad Shamlou wrote a few scripts. But with all due respect to both—one happily alive, the other sadly diseased—Kiarostami's poems are as good as Shamlou's scripts.
9. For a biography of Forough Farrokhzad and an introduction to her poetry, see Michael Hillmann, *A Lonely Woman: Forough Farrokhzad and Her Poetry* (New York: Three Continents Press, 1987).
10. See Mohsen Makhmalbaf, "Forough Was Our Sister," in *Zendegi Rang Ast: Gozideh-ye Neveshtar va Goftar, 1370–1375* [Life Is Color: Selected Essays and Speeches] (Tehran: Ney Publishers, 1376/1997), 77–95. For a more detailed study of Forough Farrokhzad's poetry and cinema, see Hamid Dabashi, *Masters and Masterpieces of Iranian Cinema* (Washington, DC: Mage Publishers, 2007): chapter 1.
11. Farrokhzad 1352/1973.
12. Ibid.
13. Forough Farrokhzad, "Window," in *Iman Biyavarim beh Aghaz-e Fasl-e Sard* [Let's Believe in the Commencement of the Cold Season!] (Tehran: Morvarid Publishers, 1352/1973), 59–65. All translations of Forough Farrokhzad's poems are mine. For a more comprehensive essay on Forough Farrokhzad's poetry, see my essay "Forough Farrokhzad and Formative Forces of Iranian Culture," in *Forough Farrokhzad: A Quarter of a Century Later*, ed. Michael Craig Hillmann (Austin: Literature East and West 24, 1988):7–36.
14. Forough Farrokhzad, "Window," in *Iman Biyavarim beh Aghaz-e Fasl-e Sard* [Let's Believe in the Commencement of the Cold Season!] (Tehran: Morvarid Publishers, 1352/1973), 59–65. All translations of Forough Farrokhzad's poems are mine. For a more comprehensive essay on Forough Farrokhzad's poetry, see my essay "Forough Farrokhzad and Formative Forces of Iranian Culture," in *Forough Farrokhzad: A Quarter of a Century Later*, ed. Michael Craig Hillmann (Austin: Literature East and West 24, 1988):7–36.
15. Ibid.
16. Forough Farrokhzad, "Swamp," in *Gozineh-ye Ash'ar* [Selected Poems] (Tehran: Morvarid Publishers, 1369/1990), 174–179.

CHAPTER 6

1. Amnesty International Index MDE 13/024/2000 (08/09/2000). For a pioneering study of torture in Iran, see Darius M. Rejali, *Torture and Modernity: Self, Society, and State in Modern Iran* (New York: Westview Press, 1994). Too tied to Foucault (for, of course, much of its insights, but also for its limitations), this book manages to connect the rise of modernity with disciplinary machination in the Iranian context. Foucault's *Discipline and Punish: The Birth of the Prison* (New York: Pantheon Books, 1977) needs serious remodulations when applied to the colonial context of modernity. Rejali is equally oblivious to

the metaphysical roots and the cultural conditionings of torture in an Islamic context. Nevertheless, his study is a critical contribution to our understanding of modernity in Iran.

2. Amnesty International Index MDE 13/028/2001 (10/08/2001).
3. For a general introduction in English to the historical roots and scholastic divisions in Islamic law, see N. J. Coulson's *A History of Islamic Law* (Edinburgh: Edinburgh University Press, 1964).
4. Amnesty International Index MDE 13/024/2001 (11/07/2001).
5. Given the atrocious record of the Islamic courts in violating the due process of law, there is no independent way of verifying these charges. With some 20 percent of the population in possession of 80 percent of the wealth, according to Iranian officials sympathetic to the reformist movement, rampant poverty is conducive to the massive influx of poor peasantry into urban centers and the turning of young women to prostitution.
6. Mulla Sadra Shirazi, *al-Waridat al-Qalbiyyah fi Ma'rifat al-Rububiyyah* [Heartfelt Revelations Concerning the Knowledge of the Divinity] (Tehran: The Iranian Academy of Philosophy, 1979), 79–80.
7. Shirazi 1979: 81.
8. Qur'an xxii:19–21.
9. Shirazi 1979: 80–81.
10. From Forough Farrokhzad's poem, "Only the Voice Will Remain," in *Gozineh-ye Ash'ar* [Selected Poems] (Tehran: Morvarid Publishers, 1369/1990), 229. All translations of Forough Farrokhzad's poetry are mine.
11. Farrokhzad, "Only the Voice Will Remain,"1369/1990: 230.
12. Mawlana Jalal al-Din Rumi, *Mathnavi*, ed. R. A. Nicholson (Tehran: Amir Kabir, 1363/1984), bk. 3, v. 3901–906. All translations from Rumi, both from the *Mathnavi* and his *ghazals*, are mine. Though Nicholson's monumental work on Rumi is greatly appreciated, his translations leave much to be desired.
13. Mawlana Jalal al-Din Rumi, *Koliyyat-e Shams ya Divan-e Kabir*, ed. Badi' al-Zaman Foruzanfar (Tehran: Amir Kabir, 1339/1960), vol. 5: 120 (Ghazal Number 2309).
14. Rumi 1363/1984: bk. 3, v. 1496.
15. For a more extensive treatment of this and other forms of realism in Iranian cinema, see my *Masters and Masterpieces of Iranian Cinema* (Washington, DC: Mage Publishers, 2007).
16. Rumi 1363/1984: vol. 4, vv. 3637–643.
17. Ibid., vv. 3634–645.
18. Ibid., vv. 3646–649.
19. Ibid., vv. 3650–656.
20. Ibid., vv. 3657–667.
21. In a major retrospective organized by the Film Society of Lincoln Center in New York City in September 2001, the date of *Requiem* is erroneously given as 1978. Naderi started shooting this film in late 1974 and finished it in early 1975, and it was immediately banned. This is not a pointless quibble. It is extremely important to keep in mind that this film was made three to four years before the events leading to the Islamic Revolution, when the massive oil revenue resulting from the Arab Oil Embargo of 1973, in which Shah did not participate, had given the monarch and his retinue absolute conviction that they were eternally in power. The hubris and arrogance of the Pahlavi monarchy at the time Naderi was shooting this film ought to be kept in mind in order

to understand the courage and imagination behind the film's quietly corrosive surface. I have the correct date of *Requiem* and all other related information about the film directly from Amir Naderi himself.

22. See Gianni Vattimo, *La Fine della Modernità* (Rome: Garzanti, 1985).
23. "Justice Department Covers Partially Nude Statues," *USA Today*, January 29, 2002, http://www.usatoday.com/news/nation/2002/01/29/statues.htm.

CHAPTER 7

1. *The New York Times*, September 14, 2001. Emphasis added. For a transcript see http://www.pbs.org/newshour/bb/terrorism/july-dec01/wide_war.html.
2. Max Weber, "Politics as a Vocation," in *From Max Weber: Essays in Sociology*, ed. Hans Gerth and C. Wright Mills (Oxford: Oxford University Press, 1946), 78.
3. See Max Weber, *From Max Weber: Essays in Sociology*, trans. and ed. Hans Gerth and C. Wright Mills (Oxford: Oxford University Press, 1946), 78.
4. Ibid.
5. Ibid.
6. Ibid.
7. As quoted in Ernst H. Kantorowicz, *The King's Two Bodies: A Study in Medieval Political Theology*, with a preface by William Chester Jordan (Princeton: Princeton University Press, 1957), 194.
8. Ibid.
9. See M. Goldsmith, *Hobbes's Science of Politics* (New York: Columbia University Press, 1966), 250–51.
10. Thomas Hobbes, *Leviathan*, eds. Richard E. Flathman and David Johnston, Norton Critical Edition (New York: W. W. Norton, 1997), 9.
11. See Michel Foucault, *Discipline and Punish: The Birth of the Prison* (New York: Pantheon Books, 1977), 3–6.
12. Ibid., 55.
13. Ibid., 136–37.
14. See Martin Heidegger, "The Question Concerning Technology," in his *The Question Concerning Technology and Other Essays*, trans. Williams Lovitt (New York: Harper Torchbooks, 1977), 3–35.
15. See Ferdinand Tönnies's *Community and Society/Gemeinschaft and Gesellschaft* (New Brunswick, NJ: Transaction Publishers, 1997) and compare his typology of *Gemeinschaft* with Emile Durkheim's notion of "organic solidarity" in Durkheim's *Division of Labor in Society* (New York: Free Press, 1997), which is equally applicable to such moments of revolutionary frenzy that can result in the suicidal sacrifice of one for all.
16. See Emile Durkheim's *Suicide: A Study in Sociology* (New York: Free Press, 1997). Durkheim's student, Maurice Halbwachs (1877–1945), did a splendid follow-up on Durkheim's study of suicide in which he objected to the category of "altruistic" suicide and offered the term *sacrifice* in such cases that the organic good of the whole is believed to be served best with the mechanical elimination of one. See Halbwachs, *Les Causes du Suicide* (Paris: Alcan, 1930).
17. For Levinas's reflections on and incorporation of Buber, Marcel, Rosenzweig, and a whole slew of others in his critique of the subject and immanence, see his *Outside the Subject*, trans. Michael B. Smith (Stanford: Stanford University

Press, 1987). For his own major philosophical statement, see *Totality and Infinity: An Essay on Exteriority*, trans. Alphonso Lingis (Pittsburgh: Duquesne University Press, 1961).

18. Levinas 1961: 194.
19. See Michael Tausig, *Defacement: Public Secrecy and the Labor of the Negative*, 52–53.
20. See Shlomo Malka's interview of Emmanuel Levinas and Alain Finkielkraut during the immediate aftermath of the Sabra and Shatila massacre in *The Levinas Reader*, ed. Seán Hand (Oxford: Blackwell, 1989), 289–97.
21. Read "The State of Caesar and the State of David," in Levinas 1989: 268–77.
22. From Mahmoud Darwish, *Memory for Forgetfulness: August, Beirut, 1982*, trans. Ibrahim Muhawi (Berkeley: University of California Press, 1995), 182.
23. Christopher Caldwell, "French Secularists Finding Foe in Islam," *International Herald Tribune*, December 22, 2003, 3.
24. In a conference on the possibility of cultural dialogue in Rabat, Morocco, December 10–13, 2003, Bernard Lewis publicly claimed credit for the phrase and the idea of "the clash of civilizations" long before Huntington did. He richly deserves the banality of the phrase and the terror of the idea.
25. Hussain Haqqani, "For Clumsy Secularism, Deadly Rewards," *International Herald Tribune*, December 22, 2003, 8.
26. For the text of Eric Harris's suicide note, see *Harper's*, February 2002, 14. Consider the last few phrases of this note, written more than two and a half years *before* September 11, 2001, just prior to the April 20, 1999, massacre: "[I]f by some weird as shit luck me and V [Klebold] survive and escape we will move to some island somewhere or maybe mexico, new zealand, or some exotic place where americans can't get us. if there isn't such a place, then we will hijack a hell of a lot of bombs and crash a plane into NYC with us inside firing away as we go down. Just something to cause more devistation." (All errors are in the original.)
27. As quoted on *BBC News, World Edition*, August 29, 2002. See "US Considered 'Suicide Jet Missions.'" at http://news.bbc.co.uk/2/hi/americas/2222205.stm.
28. A brilliant collection of essays on genetic engineering is brought together by Gregory Stock and John Campbell, *Engineering the Human Germline: An Explanation of the Science and Ethics of Altering the Genes We Pass to Our Children* (New York: Oxford University Press, 2000). Stock's more recent book, *Redesigning Humans: Our Inevitable Genetic Future* (New York: Houghton Mifflin, 2002), gives an excellent survey of what is in the offing for genetic engineering, a cool meditation on otherwise phantasmagoric possibilities.
29. For a cogent analysis of what cloning has now made possible, see the distinguished Princeton University geneticist Lee M. Silver's *Remaking Eden: Cloning and Beyond in a Brave New World* (New York: Avon Books, 1997).
30. See Stanley Fish, "Postmodern Warfare: The Ignorance of Our Warrior Intellectuals," *Harper's*, July 2002, 33–40. See also Stanley Fish, "Don't Blame Relativism" and a series of responses to it in *The Responsive Community: Rights and Responsibilities* 12, no. 3 ("Can Postmodernism Condemn Terrorism?," Summer 2002): 27–66. Both in Fish's defense of "postmodernism" and in shorter comments made for or against him by an array of prominent academic intellectuals, there is an astonishing ignorance of the most elementary facts about Islam and the contemporary Muslim world; however, even that is not the major catastrophe of this series of writings. In this collection of essays, not a single

writer—of the top guns of the US intelligentsia—ever takes the US foreign policies to task instead of sheepishly responding to their accusers. The US Army now has a Muslim chaplin. American intellectuals may hopefully soon follow suit and have a colonial interlocutor.

31. See Judith Halberstam and Ira Livingston, eds., *Posthuman Bodies* (Bloomington: Indiana University Press, 1995), vii.
32. See Jacques Derrida, *Aporias*, trans. Thomas Dutoit (Stanford: Stanford University Press, 1993).
33. Darwish 1995: 154.

Conclusion

1. See Catrina Stewart, "Veils Go Up in Flames as Yemeni Women Protest," *The Independent*, October 27, 2011, http://www.independent.co.uk/news/world/middle-east/veils-go-up-in-flames-as-yemeni-women-protest-2376410.html.
2. See Rebecca Solnit, "Letter to a Dead Man: Dear Mohammed Bouazizi," *Middle East Online*, October 19, 2011, http://www.middle-east-online.com/english/?id=48608.

Index